Diary of a Mindful Dad

Diary of a Mindful Dad

DOMINIC WATTS

Copyright © Tecolote Publishing, 2025

All rights reserved. No part of this book may be reproduced or used in any manner without written permission of the copyright owner except for the use of accredited quotations.

978-1-7384469-2-6 (Print)
978-1-7384469-3-3 (E-book)

First edition December 2025

Published by Tecolote Publishing

To Nadine,
for blessing my life

"Wisdom tells me I am nothing. Love tells me I am everything. Between the two, my life flows."

— Sri Nisargadatta Maharaj

Introduction

Have you ever noticed what it feels like to think? Does it feel like anything? Have you ever watched the way that thought comes into your experience? Have you seen how it twists and turns, darts around, dragging you in and then disappearing in a flash? Have you actually seen that happen?

Where does it come from? Does it just appear, or can you watch it arrive? Is it you? What is your relationship to it? It's *in the mind,* you say.

Where is that? What is it? Does it have a border, some boundary which separates it from other minds? Is it inside the brain? Science has never found a single thought, nor a mind.

Does a thought have weight? If not, how can it exist? Does it gain weight when it eats too much? Thought certainly has immense power; it can make us do all sorts of things. So where and what exactly *is it*? No, not the electrical impulse. We know where that is, and that's not a thought. I mean the *actual thought,* you know, the one you *experience.*

What about consciousness itself? Is that a thing? Does it belong to you, or is it you? Where does it go in deep sleep? If it is you, what is the source of it, or could it be the source of everything?

Finally, and most importantly, what is love? Does it exist? Is it a feeling, an action, a force? Can you reach out with your consciousness and connect with the heart of another? If you do,

Introduction

are there still two of you? Is it possible to find a love so all-encompassing that it obliterates everything else? Is that what life is really all about?

Do you find these questions exhausting and confusing? Interesting?

Welcome to my world.

My brother once said, with a chuckle, that he would love to be in my brain for a day. I said he should be careful what he wished for, and this book is proof of that. In fact, in this book, you will find yourself in the unfortunate position of being there for over two years. Don't worry, it's not too late to back out now.

My name is Dom and I live in Dubai with my wife, Nadine, and an undisclosable number of rescue animals. I studied Psychology and Philosophy at university and discovered the wonders of meditation when I was 15 years old. Since then, I have relentlessly pursued answers to these so-called 'big questions', and that journey has transformed me in every way I can think of. Matters of life, death, mind, soul, suffering and freedom are always ticking away somewhere in the background – or foreground – for me, and this has come as both a blessing and a curse.

Thankfully, I've zig-zagged my way into a job that relies on my passion for these questions. I explore the enigmatic adventures and tangles of human life with clients of all ages, always aiming to move beyond the limited, mind-made world and into the *magic and mystery of the now*.

On one fateful day, at a parenting conference, a group of mums asked my colleague, "Where are all the dads?"

She replied that I would be having a baby soon, and she would ask me to write a book about it. Where did that come from? I wasn't supposed to be having a baby soon, and we had never discussed the topic at all. Yet the seed of this book was planted that day.

However, I guess *Diary of a Mindful Dad* really starts in a packed restaurant in Nottingham, England, in 2010, when Nadine and I were out to dinner with our housemates, and the two of us had a bit of an argument. We don't argue very often, so this was all very exciting for our friends.

"I want to have a baby by the time I'm 30," she declared.

I let out a shocked laugh and replied, "Oh, do you now! No way – that's way too early." Suddenly, she realised I might have different ideas from her about our future and it became a little heated.

Fast-forward ten years, and there we are: both 30 and trying for a baby. Who would have thought it? She was right. My dad says she only pretends to let me have a say in things.

What on Earth were we talking about? How did we know when we would, or would not, want to do something so momentous? We assume so much control of our lives: control which, I suspect, is far more lacking than we would care to admit.

In a way, this book is about control; the kind of control which the mind thinks it has just before reality laughs in its face. But it's also about love, joy, stress, fear and all the other things which come with being a human. It turns out that females of the human species can actually grow a miniature human inside them and bring it out into the world. Did you know that?

We think we do, but 'knowledge' turns to dust in the face of the reality of such things. It's probably too much for us to grasp this stupendous fact before it becomes relevant to our lives, or to ever fully understand it at all. The process is unbelievably miraculous at every stage, and quite impossible to put into words. So I'm not going to do that. I'm not a biologist.

What I *am going to do* is invite you into my adventure, for a while. Most of my job centres around understanding the mental and emotional world of humans, and I've spent a lot of time working with children; surely I'd be a great dad, then? That's what many people said. As mindfulness is often touted as a panacea to cure all ills, especially stress, people also assumed that my experience in that realm would make the difficulties of parenting easier for me. Maybe. I didn't want to fall into either of these traps, though. In my experience, when someone thinks like that, life gives them a swift and sharp backhander just to put them in their place. I thought I would experience just as many challenges and ups and downs as every other parent, but I also hoped that all my 'inner' training would make a difference, and I was excited and interested to see how. Would I be able to be calm in the face of parenting storms? Would I need to be? Would I want to be? Would I be able to raise my children in a 'mindful' way? Is there even any such thing?

I hoped that the journey to come would provide surprising and illuminating answers to these questions and more, and it didn't disappoint. *But this book isn't about answers, because life isn't like school.* It doesn't come with a textbook.

In fact, I want this book to be as far from a textbook as your high-school biology textbook was from your first sexual experience: filled, as the latter was, with inner content – the *real stuff* – which is impossible to fully convey to another.

When I started writing this, I was yet to become a parent, so I knew it could easily end up being more of a comedy than anything else. As the title suggests, the book is in diary form, so you are receiving the raw mess of daily life, the real-time reflections of someone right in the thick of it, rather than perfectly curated words of 'advice'.

On this note, the title of the book is at least partly ironic. When we think of what it means to be 'mindful', we end up with a strange sort of hippie caricature. There are all sorts of misconceptions about mindfulness, and they can be quite difficult to untangle. For example, I'm not sure you can actually be a 'mindful person'; I'm not even sure that I'm a person at all! But maybe we can get to that later.

So what on Earth *is* mindfulness?

The modern mindfulness movement purports to answer some

of life's big questions, like should I be using my phone whilst having a poo? How much will those loose-fitting trousers actually calm me down? If I keep sitting quietly, in this position, will life leave me alone?

Yet it also seems to be full of contradictions. Does 'living in the moment' mean that thinking about the future is bad? Then how can I get to work? Can I be 'in the present' and 'in the mind' at the same time? How can meditation, which looks like going *nowhere* and doing *nothing*, take me *somewhere* and bring me *something*? Paradoxically, it can, but talking about what that means usually ends up in a bit of a mess.

We are sold this idea that, if we just learn to meditate, all our problems will go away and eventually we will find 'enlightenment', some ultimate happiness which ends the travails of life. We will be sitting just like Buddha, and have that enviable smile of his – maybe the belly too. This vision is simplistic beyond belief and actually very unhelpful. Sorry, but I'm not buying it, and buying this book certainly won't buy it for you. Instead, I'm hoping that it will give you something deeper and more *real*. That seems to be more like what we are really searching for, in a world so full of superficiality.

Mindfulness asks us to *be here now*. Yet this mandate is confusing because the entire world of mind – whatever that is – *is also here now*. Self-centred thought, rooted in desire and fear, causes huge trouble by distorting our perception, and it does this all the time. *Unfortunately, it's really hard to see this happening.* Thought appears and creates illusory realities for us to inhabit, as if someone else were placing little VR headsets on us, without our knowledge or our consent, over and over again. We get sucked right in and then the bubble suddenly pops, just as it does when we wake up from a dream. This strange phenomenon is so normal to us that we don't even *realise it is happening*. The result is that our normal way of living is *akin to a dream state*.

Rather than advising us to be calm and happy, then,

Introduction

mindfulness asks us to *pay attention to what's happening*, in both the inner and outer worlds. Yes, it does ask us to use our energy to attend to the external situation we find ourselves in. Yet beyond this, it also invites us to liberate ourselves purposefully from the many distortions and illusions which we project onto reality, and in so doing, to find our true essence, which is peaceful and whole. That doesn't sound the same as just sitting on a lovely cushion, does it? It is a very tall order, in fact, and rather different from how mindfulness is often presented or received. What we usually think of as mindfulness is only the *beginning* – a doorway to another world.

One big problem is that anything like mindfulness can easily become just a load of ideas, or 'principles', and that's when it stops being real and it stops being meaningful. We learn best from *experience*, and as we know from novels, films and mirror neurons, this includes the experiences of others as well. I guess that's partly why I decided to give you a front-row ticket to whatever was about to unfold.

On the topic of brain cells, please don't expect much more of that sort of talk. I considered including up-to-date science in this book on some of the topics covered, but I really don't want it to be about that. Science on mindfulness may have its uses but, for me, the most meaningful and transformative learning comes from the raw, visceral reality of facing what is in front of us. I have always found that theories and concepts just *get in the way of that*. So if you're looking for someone to give you a lovely, neat little parcel of labels which have been made for all the confusing things in the world, so you can feel like you have them under control, this book isn't for you. This book is about real life; it's an attempt to get to the *heart* of the matter, not the head.

My hope is that these tales can amuse and inform in equal measure, offering a window into what it was really like for me to embark on the beautifully chaotic adventure of parenthood, with years of mindfulness and meditation practice in my back pocket. I'm sure you'll see that what people call 'being mindful' is far more messy, and mysterious, than just sitting quietly, being happy and not having any thoughts.

The truth is, I had *absolutely no idea* what I was in for.

1

To Create a Human

"It's a dangerous business, Frodo, going out your door. You step onto the road, and if you don't keep your feet, there's no knowing where you might be swept off to."

— Bilbo Baggins, *The Lord of the Rings*

<u>Wednesday 23rd October</u>

When I was excited to finally start 'trying' to conceive a child, the last thing I expected to see was impotence. Yet there it was, staring me in the face: an unfamiliar and terrifying foe.

Weren't expecting that, were you?

Neither was I.

Well, it wasn't quite 'impotence', but it was in that ballpark. 'Performance issues', they say. Whatever you want to call it, it certainly didn't feel very potent. Apparently, this is quite common. According to a study reported by the *Independent*, which people in my situation would *love* to believe, a surprisingly high percentage of men take a nosedive of sorts during this time, and it makes sense.[1] The act of sex, which has for such a long time been one thing, is now completely transformed; it's no wonder the mind starts to get involved.

"Wait, we're supposed to be doing *what*? *This* is for *that*?!"

The study, conducted on 400 men without a history of impotence, showed that four in ten experienced it during 'timed sexual intercourse'. It seems this was a big factor for us. Nadine had bought all the latest tech in order to understand when we were most likely to conceive. It's very clever stuff, but it turns out that needing to have sex at a certain time isn't a very powerful aphrodisiac.

For me, the root of this issue couldn't have been clearer: there was 'trying'. Totally nonsensical really. If I had never had to try before (except obviously when I was a terrified teenager and at various points since), why would I now? It had come totally out of the blue. Yoda famously said, "Do or do not. There is no try," and I have no reason to doubt his tiny green nuggets of wisdom. But did he say anything about what to do when there *is try*? Maybe that bit was edited out.

The act of attempting to purposefully create a human life unsurprisingly brings with it such burdens. Thankfully, I could see beyond any doubt that this was only happening for the reason mentioned above. Yet this logical understanding alone didn't make the problem vanish. That would be too easy.

Nadine and I are very open with one another, and I don't tend to be too easily embarrassed. So I laughed. When I laughed, she laughed. We talked about it, instead of sweeping it under the rug and letting it fester and grow with fear. I explained why it was probably happening and we went on with our business. Yet on some level, of course, it played on my mind, and hers too. The mind started to wonder, creating all sorts of stories about 'how long this would go on for' and the like.

It's funny to consider that, at this stage, this had only happened once. The mind is so powerful in its ability to project things into the future that it can turn one event into a 'problem' with nothing more than a casual flick of its wand.

It happened again, almost certainly *because* it had happened the first time, but the second time was more than twice as annoying. It was already worse than boring by then. When you know why something annoying is happening, but you feel powerless to simply stop it in its tracks, it can get you down.

Couldn't I have tried to use lots of willpower to push this experience away and get rid of the 'problem'? That's just the kind of thing the mind *loves* to believe, isn't it? But isn't it also the *mind* which is causing the trouble in the first place? Why should we trust its idea about what to do next?

On the contrary, I have seen countless times that fighting our experience only fuels the fire. Take sport, for example, when the mind, poisoned by fear, often tries to take control over someone's physical movements, and things only go from bad to worse.

Really, it's the opposite which is required: *less control, not more.* Sometimes we just have to take our medicine…and medicine doesn't always taste like Calpol.

Instead of fighting, then, my energy was directed towards *witnessing, detachment, non-action.*

I watched the mind dance, watched it twist and turn with its lust (excuse the pun) to turn things into problems. Each time it told me a story about how annoying or terrible this was, or how it would go on forever, I continued to give energy to *watching this unfold.*

I had forgotten that this way of doing things was at all unusual until my friend Freddie laughed at me on the phone the other day because I had said that I 'watched the mind' do something. He pointed out that normally people would just say, 'I thought'. Although this might seem strange, it's called 'non-identification' with mind, and it's *very helpful* in situations like this.

We're so used to living with mind that we don't realise what it's doing, or that it's doing anything at all. We don't see that it's creating problems and *then* proposing solutions to them. That 'our' idea of what to do about something is actually just *the mind's* idea, and often it is a blunder. You know that feeling that it would be good to chase down the person who just overtook you dangerously? That kind of thing.

I also purposefully 'sat with' the feelings that the situation brought up – which means *feeling them fully,* instead of trying to change them, or pretending they aren't there – and waited for the storm to pass.

And it did, of course, as everything does. Something which might have been a bigger deal disappeared as if it had never been there in the first place.

It might sound simple written down like that, but that sort of 'inner work' is very counter-intuitive and takes a lot of energy. The mind doesn't want you to *really watch* it without reacting, and we don't usually *really feel* our feelings!

Nadine's role in this can't be overstated; her being understanding and not remotely judgemental (outwardly, at least!) was incredibly helpful. She just let me get on with it and shared my faith that it was just 'one of those things'. No doubt she was struggling with emotions and stories herself, but she didn't let them affect me and make things worse.

This episode was a dramatic, eventful and unexpected introduction to parenthood, and it made me particularly grateful for my past selves being so obsessed with meditation and self-awareness. The journey had begun!

Friday 25th October

Nadine is a primary teacher and something fascinating happened when she was at school today. Her colleague, the school counsellor, found her in the corridor and said she needed to speak to her. She told Nadine that she has *prophetic dreams*, and gave as an example a recent event in which she had dreamt that her close colleague's father was ill. She immediately told her colleague, who checked and confirmed she was right: he had been taken to the hospital the very same day. After relaying this extraordinary tale, she said to Nadine, "I dreamt you were pregnant, so if you don't want a baby, you need to use contraception!"

What are the odds that she would suddenly have this dream in the exact same month that we decide to give up contraception? I never ignore such things. The phenomenon of precognition (particularly through dreams) has received an increasingly serious level of scientific study in modern times: see, for example, the work of Dr Julia Mossbridge of the Institute of Noetic Sciences. I experienced a precognitive nightmare myself many years ago, in which I was desperately trying to call the police as I witnessed something horrific. I told Nadine about it in the morning, and in the afternoon, the incident – just as I had seen it, with many very unusual details – took place in London and became nationwide news. After sharing this story with a few people over the years, I have been surprised by how many of them believe they have experienced something similar.

There is an ancient and alternative way of understanding mind, consciousness and reality (one version of which is presented beautifully by Rupert Spira in *The Nature of Consciousness*, for example)[2] which sheds light on how this sort of thing might work, and entails the possibility of our 'individual minds' sometimes being able to reach out beyond their ordinarily narrow purview.

Naturally, then, I feel that her dream is significant. What a strange dream it was for her to have, especially considering that she does not work closely with Nadine and they rarely speak to each other.

Monday 16th March

"Period?"

"Mmhmm."

That's how a few months have gone by. A heavy cloud fills the house and the consciousness of us both.

"We failed," says the mind, as quickly as can be. Ever the delightful house guest.

Then it serves up its dessert: a slice of uncertainty about the cause of the 'failure', garnished with a drizzle of fear of infertility. Just beautiful.

Most of the time, when this happens, Nadine won't tell me. But the change in the atmosphere is difficult to miss, and so I ask. Then we chat about it. She conveys to me just how difficult this fear is for her to deal with.

How long will it take for us to conceive, if we can at all? Most of us, if we want children, take for granted that one day we will have them. Perhaps we aren't told enough stories about infertility because it's a taboo subject, just like impotence and sex itself.

I wasn't worried about any of this, to be honest. I'm very optimistic, and I had quite a matter-of-fact attitude towards these fears. I felt deep down that we would be lucky enough to have children one day. Yet it's easy to see how these fears build and build with each passing month; the mind making the most of its time-travelling powers again to show the future you want to see the least.

The mind also wants an answer, some certainty, so a quick Google search might alleviate some of the anxiety associated with getting pregnant. It does, a little, in this case. We find that it takes between six months and a year, on average, to conceive a child for the first time.

Nadine is usually extremely grounded and stable, and so I haven't often seen her too worried or concerned. Yet, during this period, I can see just how much having a child means to her. It's funny how a subconscious assumption about your future, which has always been silent and invisible, can suddenly be so powerful when it takes the stage.

A continual challenge for me, throughout this process, is trying to understand when it is OK to probe Nadine (no pun intended) and when it is best to give her time and space. My habit is to be open and talk about everything, but this isn't how everyone processes their emotions, and I've noticed recently that it isn't always appropriate or helpful.

This has been a powerful lesson for me and quite a difficult one to learn, especially considering the nature of my work on a day-to-day basis, which is supporting others through emotional tangles and dilemmas such as these.

In light of this, I'm noticing more and more when it might be better to *show* that I care instead of saying so. It's amazing how powerful a nice cup of tea or just a hug can be when words might turn to dust.

Diary of a Mindful Dad

Saturday 25th July

Yesterday, I finished doing a coaching session on Zoom and, as I left the room, I smelled something delightful: the house was filled with incense. I went into the living room and sat down to watch some TV. Before long, Nadine came down the stairs, and it felt like something was up. She wasn't being herself.

Suddenly, she couldn't hold it in any longer, and she squeezed her hands together and said, "We did it! I'm pregnant!"

Her face was a picture, and so must mine have been. We hugged and jumped for joy like we were in some sort of 6/10 rom-com, with incredible excitement and an enormous sense of relief. It has been a testing few months.

I had almost forgotten that we were 'trying', and that there was a possibility of this right now, so I was really taken by surprise. I was over the moon and I still am as I write this.

We had many conversations about who could know and when, and it became clear that I had a lot to learn about this whole process. I'm what fans of *Peep Show* call a 'sayer', so if it were up to me, loads of people would have known immediately. I get excited and love to share – it's just my medicine. Hence this book!

Nadine was careful to settle me down. She explained how often people have miscarriages, and that you are only 'supposed to' tell anyone after 10–12 weeks, when things are more certain. This was something I had no idea about, but I reluctantly agreed, and told my inner puppy: *Sit. Stay.*

We have decided to tell our mums, though, because they know we have been trying and mine, in particular, has been worrying a little about whether we would be able to conceive; I'm the youngest of four brothers, and none of us have had children yet.

Then we signed on for an online meditation session, which was pretty interesting to participate in, with our hearts and minds aflame and buzzing with excitement.

The mind loves to look for causes of things, and this was no different. We wondered if Nadine's changes to her routine had assisted with the conception. In the last month, she has been applying progesterone cream to her belly every day, as she read it can be an excellent way to help with conception. She has also been giving herself belly massages with oil and visualising her tummy growing. Might any of this have helped? Who knows? Does it matter? Not really.

After the session finished, we took some time to acclimatise to the extraordinary new reality we had finally found ourselves in.

Saturday 1st August – 5 weeks

The last week has been full to the brim with excitement and smiles, and we went for our first scan yesterday, at five weeks. In Dubai, the medical service is quite unbelievable. They give you scans every time you see the doctor, apparently, and it was incredible to see. The first thing the doctor did was confirm the pregnancy. Eventually, we could see the little sac on the monitor, and it was a really special moment. Nadine's face was a picture.

In stereotypical dad fashion (sorry, New Age), I had no idea what was going on. The object in question was so minuscule, even on the screen, and I have no knowledge of what a baby is right at the beginning. Nevertheless, I felt the joy of it all and nodded and smiled at all the right moments. Later on, Nadine explained it to me. Unsurprisingly, it's fascinating, and a quick Google search will show you that it looks like a little Plumbus from *Rick and Morty*. (If you don't know what that is, you should probably search for that first, and then take a long, hard look in the mirror. *Rick and Morty* is beyond excellent.)

At five weeks, the embryo is 2 mm long and already developing the baby's heart perfectly. The foundations for all major organs are already in place and it's quite ridiculous. I'm blown away by a lot of things in life, to the point where family members have compared me to Will Ferrell's 'Elf', so you can imagine that this is pretty jaw-dropping for me; I see it as truly miraculous.

Then we had the terribly serious sit-down conversation with the doctor. She said that some of Nadine's 'levels' were low and, of course, we immediately felt concerned. She prescribed something, and we left the consultation with a bitter taste in our mouths and hope in our hearts that everything would be OK.

As we approached the pharmacy, we looked at the prescription and read the words:

'*Threatened abortion and ectopic pregnancy*'.

What?! The doctor said everything was fine! Thankfully, Nadine knew what an ectopic pregnancy was (I still don't), and she knew she couldn't be having one because the baby was in the correct position. This made us assume it was just a routine procedure for the doctors to write this to give us a prescription for the progesterone medicine. Still, it seems pretty irresponsible to have it written there, and the words 'threatened abortion' have obviously been ringing in our ears ever since. Oh, fear – what joy you bring!

Saturday 8th August – 6 weeks

Today we had a call from the hospital:

"Ma'am, our results show that your HCG levels* are low, so you need to come in for additional testing."

Delightful. A wonderful car journey with anxiety taking up its own, quite considerable, space. We did the test and came home; of course, it creates a cloud over everything. Suddenly, reality is tainted with a new colour and it all just feels a bit itchy and not right. We will have to wait three days for the result. It feels as if we've been forced onto an escalator with two different possible exits at the top: one amazing and one absolutely awful.

---

* HCG is a key marker for how a pregnancy is progressing.

I guess that, over the years, my relationship with thoughts and emotions has become quite different from the norm because of all the meditation practice and inner work I've done. It occurs to me now, whilst writing this and reflecting on these times, that I really do find strong thoughts and feelings incredibly *interesting* when they arise. When something powerful and dramatic enters my inner world, like this fear about losing the baby, there is often some small gap, some space, which opens up and allows the 'inner object' to be received and attended to consciously. This idea is perfectly encapsulated by Rumi's provocative poem, 'The Guest House', which is one of my favourite poems ever:

The Guest House

This being human is a guest house.
Every morning a new arrival.
A joy, a depression, a meanness,
some momentary awareness comes
As an unexpected visitor.
Welcome and entertain them all!
Even if they're a crowd of sorrows,
who violently sweep your house
empty of its furniture,
still, treat each guest honourably.
He may be clearing you out
for some new delight.
The dark thought, the shame, the malice,
meet them at the door laughing and invite them in.
Be grateful for whoever comes,
because each has been sent
as a guide from beyond.[3]

Isn't that beautiful? I have found this stance incredibly transformative, and it is perhaps the cornerstone of mindfulness practice. Our instinct is to fight, flee or freeze in the face of difficulty, inner or outer. But this is different. It's an active, interested and *loving* standing still, an alertness which won't be moved, which eventually becomes an *embrace*. Learning to *be with* emotions in this way has changed everything for me.

Tuesday 11th August

The three-day wait is over and we received the phone call today. It was good news. The HCG levels had gone up enough to say that the pregnancy was progressing normally. Of course, we are massively relieved and celebrating this good news. But we aren't getting ahead of ourselves and assuming things will definitely be fine. Isn't it funny the games the mind plays?

Friday 14th August

Nadine has been experiencing a lot of 'spotting', which is when blood is leaking during pregnancy. We know it won't help, but can't resist still doing a quick 'Doctor Google' check – just to make sure we are *really* confused. The extent to which it was unhelpful is genuinely laughable, and the absurdity of that, in itself, has kept our spirits up. As usual, cursory research creates perfect contradictions, ensuring that the conclusion in our minds is both *definitely fine* and *definitely going to lose the baby*.

It's interesting to notice how the mind is almost constantly aware of the fear of miscarriage due to all of these factors. It's like an ongoing dance, and we have to be constantly vigilant to avoid falling into the standard thinking traps day after day. To speak about it like that makes it sound quite exhausting, but the alternative – falling into every trap and turning it into a huge drama – is sure to take more energy away and cause more trouble. I'm sometimes making a point of telling Nadine when I experience a little mind-drama, and laughing about it, to ensure that we are together on this and she knows it's hard for me as well. We have a scan booked for this weekend because of an adverse reaction to the progesterone Nadine was prescribed. Another scan!

Saturday 15th August – 7 weeks

The scan today was incredible. We heard the baby's heartbeat for the first time and it was totally surreal. There is a functioning human heart inside my wife's tummy. Madness!

This is the first moment when I have truly seen Nadine embrace the excitement of this journey, and that has filled me with a deep joy. Today, seeing and hearing the heartbeat, the ultimate sign of life, makes it feel right to be excited.

Saturday 22nd August – 8 weeks

Now, a week later – you guessed it: another scan. Believe it or not, at this point I've actually forgotten the reason for it. Oh yes, Nadine had further 'spotting' and it didn't seem right to her. Our friends in the UK can't believe how many scans we are having and think we are lucky. In a way, we are, because we get to see our baby every week! But it's also nerve-wracking each time, and probably makes us think about the negative possibilities more. As usual, just before we walked into the doctor's office, we looked at each other with the silent understanding that we would come out of this room in one of two very different realities.

The scan showed that everything was fine, and it was a lot easier to piece together what was going on this time. We could hear the heartbeat again and it was very strong.

Then, at the very last moment, cool as you like, the doctor said, "There's quite a lot of fluid here, I'm just going to give you a quick swab to test the fluid."

Suddenly, panic. Of course. *What the hell does that mean?*

Nadine asked, "What happens if this is a positive test?"

"Oh, you will lose the baby."

That was really how she said it. Casual as you like, as she was fiddling with her many gadgets.

The next few moments were intense, as you can imagine. A cloud of fear settled in the room and pulled up a chair.

After a pause worthy of the *X Factor* final, she finally declared, "No, it's OK."

Thank God for that! What a relief. Yet again, the free rollercoaster didn't disappoint.

Tuesday 25th August

As you can see, fear has been the theme of the first trimester up to this point, and it has turned up the heat lately. The uncertainty and anxiety make time pass more slowly. The weeks are really dragging now. We naturally wonder what we can do to protect the precious little bit of magic inside Nadine's tummy. Each night, we do a meditation together, with our hands placed upon it, visualising love and nourishing energy entering that magical realm. I feel (in this case, not always) that deep down this comes from fear and a desire to control, but at the same time, I'm aware of how amazing the mind can be and the effect such things might be able to have.

Something quite extraordinary has been happening to me during these meditations. Ordinarily, I can quite easily visualise this sort of thing; I've done it so many times and it's always a bit of an adventure. When you set your mind to it with clear intention, another layer of imagination takes over and the images seem to take on a life of their own.

I remember when my brother's cat was very sick at a young age, and we decided to do healing visualisations for him together. I even had my class of five-year-old children do a group visualisation for him one morning. When I was guiding this meditation,

I remember being stunned by the images which naturally arose through the imagination to support my intention.

The cat had kidney failure and really needed water in the body and to process the water effectively. Without any conscious control of the images, I saw how all the water in the world was related and connected, and the water in his body began to glow in my imagination. Each tiny bit of the water had its own significance, its own beauty, and I saw the cells of the body all opening up to a beautiful light which was present in all things, rather than shutting this light out. All of these things happened so quickly – in 'thought-time' – and it's a faculty I suspect we do not use enough. The cat recovered in the end, and the vet thought it was miraculous; they were definitely expecting him to die, and they don't know what happened. I have no idea if it was related to our visualisations or not, but it would be interesting if so, and I know this is an area many scientists have tried to probe experimentally in recent times. I highly recommend *Why Woo-Woo Works* by David Hamilton, for a great overview of such studies and more.[4]

Yet in my meditations each night for the baby, right from the beginning, when I have tried to imagine sending some love and nurturing energy, my imagination has suddenly taken a turn and shown me horrible things happening to the baby. Each time it is extremely uncomfortable, to put it mildly, and really gives me a jolt. It feels like a tap has been turned on and everything that comes through is awful! It has been so jarring and unpleasant that I have instinctively decided not to imagine anything anymore, just on the small chance that any negative energy from me could have an impact on the baby. Instead, I am just trying to feel the love I have for it, and for Nadine, and to keep this as my focus.

Naturally, this has been preying on my mind, though, as it's not happened to me before in such visualisations. What does it mean? Is it the negativity bias of the brain and a manifestation of subconscious fear in me? Or is it telling us something is wrong?

The mind wants to see it as a battle, one which I need to *fight*, to transform the negativity into positivity. I'm not buying it; again, it feels like that's coming from fear and control. Nevertheless, this pull is strong and nagging at me every now and then. I have faith that things will turn out as they are supposed to, and it's not necessary for me to do anything at all to contribute, except feed Nadine and get her tea. The body is an amazing thing and it knows what it's doing – certainly more than I do!

Friday 28th August – 9 weeks

Nadine has told me about the magical point when 'everything is almost certainly OK'. Percentage chances of miscarriage are being thrown around daily, and quite unhelpfully, I must admit. I can look online and immediately find out how likely it is, statistically, for my unborn child to die in the next week; amazing, right?

We know many people who have had miscarriages, including one of our good friends, who has just had two in as many years, at different times throughout the pregnancy. Someone else we know has had three in the last two years, and perhaps can never have a child. These stories are so horrible to hear and they really make us feel for those people. The most extraordinary story so far, though, has come from my landlord. Believe it or not, she had *ten miscarriages, and a stillbirth, but still managed to have six children!* I had a hard time getting my head around that.

All these stories made me realise that when I was younger – probably up until university – I'd never even heard of a miscarriage. Nobody talks about it. Yet this knowledge, when it comes, does what you would expect it to.

It tints and distorts everything once it comes into play. Of course, Nadine's body is changing dramatically, and she can always feel all sorts of different things going on internally; it's so easy for any of these changes to be seen as a problem.

Reading up on Google doesn't help. Every single person says

something different about what to expect and what each of the symptoms might mean. It seems that different pregnancies can be so varied in how they affect the body, and this has really surprised me.

Dealing with these fears is incredibly difficult for Nadine, and the role of the partner is very interesting in these times, as I have already touched on. Pregnancy is such a personal thing for a woman; Nadine's experience is totally unknown to me. I don't know how it feels to have a baby growing inside me, and I don't know what's happening with her hormones, or how they're affecting her thoughts and emotions. Yet I thrive on connection, and I like to feel emotionally in sync with the people around me (particularly my loved ones), so this new gulf between us, in terms of our experience, is tricky to navigate.

I'm trying my best to support and reassure Nadine, gently reminding her to look at the difficult thoughts and feelings when they arrive, to welcome them in and not run away. I try to do this in the moment when something difficult has actually arisen, so it doesn't become just another overwhelming idea. She probably finds such suggestions incredibly annoying, so I try not to do it unless it feels as if it will truly be helpful in that moment.

I make sure that I offer the other side of the coin when Nadine speaks about the negative possibilities of what could happen. This is sometimes helpful in taking fuel away from the fire. I'm also trying to just make space to listen. Again, cups of tea and hugs are proving very useful too.

We both know that it's uncertain whether this pregnancy will get to 'full-term', as I've now discovered it's called. Over the years, we've learned to sometimes laugh together at difficult things like this, and in the past couple of days we've managed to do that a few times. All anyone can do in this situation is take things day by day, and try to stay present and connected to life as it is *now*.

Tuesday 1st September – 10 weeks

There has been tremendous fear in this pregnancy, yes, but there is also great excitement. We want the baby so much and this is the main reason for the fears. We know it's still too early to tell anyone else about the pregnancy (12 weeks is supposed to be the key turning point), and this causes annoyances of its own. We are at ten weeks now and both feeling better and better about it all.

We took the step the other day of allowing ourselves to discuss baby names, and to decide if we will want to find out the gender of the baby, given the chance. We've decided that we do want to, mostly for the reason that it will be so helpful when it comes to buying clothes and decorating the nursery, and it will allow our interactions with the baby in the womb to feel more real and intimate if we can use their name.

The ten-week scan is coming up next week, and Nadine has told me that the 'percentages go right down' after that. It's funny how such talk becomes normal, how words can deceptively insulate us from what they are referring to. This is the percentage chance that we will lose the baby!

Saturday 5th September

Yesterday, we went out for breakfast with friends and had a nice time. However, just as we left, I saw Nadine rushing to the bathroom – she said she was spotting. Of course, I was worried. Every time she says that, it is worrying for us both, even though Dr Google says it's probably fine. This time she said it was worse than normal, though, so we went straight to the hospital. We weren't too far away.

We went to the emergency room, explained the situation and waited for a while. Soon, they ushered us into a downstairs room which had different equipment from the baby equipment we were used to; it didn't seem to be a room which was usually used for this sort of thing. The doctor said that she would try to have a look, but couldn't guarantee a clear view of everything with this equipment. "*Why are we using it then???*" we were thinking.

She then left inexplicably and we waited for her to return. This took an eternity. We were both fearing the worst by this point, as we had many times before. But this was different; it really felt like there was a problem. After a few long minutes, she reappeared, scanned Nadine's tummy and, as she had suspected, the image wasn't clear enough. She left the room again and I glanced over at her computer screen.

I believed that it showed there was no heartbeat and the doctor didn't want to tell us; she wanted to move us upstairs instead and let them do the horrible job. We discussed what we could see on the screen together, and Nadine was not convinced by my interpretation; she thought that we were seeing the previous patient's scan. This also made sense. We played around with the buttons on the machine for a while to see if we could access our scan, but we couldn't. Fear was up to 99.9% by now.

Still waiting.

Eventually, the doctor returned, and Nadine was put into a wheelchair and moved upstairs. She was really shaky now, and her voice was starting to quiver. It was horrible. I held her hand and reassured her, and myself, as best I could.

A new doctor came in and quickly got her gloves on and prepared herself for an internal scan. We watched the screen as the scanner moved around the embryo and the sac. We could see the baby, but it wasn't moving.

There was no heartbeat.

The doctor carried on checking, over and over, but Nadine and I both knew. The doctor said, "There is no heartbeat I can find. I'm sorry."

That was it. Finally.

All the waiting and fear were over. Here we were.

I felt the wave hit me as we phase-shifted into our new reality, and it was *devastating*.

Nadine burst into tears loudly and suddenly, shaking like a leaf. The doctor then said, very unhelpfully, "There is still a chance. Would you like me to do another scan?"

She knew there was no chance. She just wanted to bring a little positivity into the room, but it failed dramatically. It was obvious what had happened; we all knew.

The tears became worse and worse. There was an enormous feeling of dread and terror. My wife's beautiful face, always so serene and calm, was broken. She was shivering and her lips were trembling like I have never seen. She was going into a full-on panic attack.

At this point, I felt inwardly as I often do in powerfully emotional moments: completely still and silent.

Not numb. Not at all. I was definitely feeling extreme sadness and shock, but when the situation seems really dire, I always seem to naturally go into uber-quiet, present mode. It is hard to describe. I am actively witnessing what's happening, in the room and in my inner world, with full energy. The emotion was there, vital and full of power, but thankfully my mind remained relatively clear: whenever it projected a distortion of reality, some negative imagined future associated with this event, I was able to instinctively 'defuse' from it and return my energy to where it needed to be.

I was ready for this and I was not surprised. We had both feared this all along and now it had finally happened. In that moment, I needed to be with Nadine, and so by this time I was only focused on holding her hands, cuddling her and telling her everything was going to be OK.

Her panic attack was really frightening to witness, especially because it is so strange to see her feeling out of sorts at all. She was practically convulsing, crying so loudly and hyperventilating. The doctor was saying very strongly, "Miss! You need to calm down or you can hurt yourself. It's very important that you breathe slowly or you will hurt yourself!" This goes right to the top of the list of things not to say to someone who is having a panic attack. Unfortunately, the urgency and panic in her own tone of voice, coupled with this relatively poor choice of words, had the opposite of the desired effect.

It made me instinctively feel much more concerned and go into overdrive in terms of trying to calm her down. I was breathing deeply and making her go along with me, looking into her eyes and seeing the total hopeless fear which had overcome her. It was absolutely awful. She just couldn't control what was happening.

I have had a panic attack before, and so has Nadine, so I had a fair idea about what they feel like. If you haven't had one, you are lucky! This whole episode, in that fateful room, lasted for another ten minutes, and Nadine was by no means calming down.

Eventually, they took us downstairs with Nadine still in the midst of the storm. We were given a room and we closed the curtain. We were both together, and alone, so I was more able to help Nadine calm down by speaking more candidly.

I did my best. I kept reassuring her that everything would be OK and we just needed to be as calm as possible right now, through the 'waves', until the panic subsided. I gave her water and lots and lots of hugs. We cried together, and it was horrible… but it was also beautiful.

Maybe that sounds crazy, but it's true. Sadness can be very beautiful because it is *real*. Life is real and these are the things which happen in life. Sadness, when we really 'turn towards it' and allow ourselves to feel it in its full force, shows us what we value and reminds us that we are here, alive, now, and that we care. Caring about something so much, with my wife, felt truly intimate and, in a sense, transcendent. It is, after all. It's transcending the mundane, the treadmill of repetition and things which don't really matter, which life can so easily move along.

There is no use in trying to escape from these powerful events – it only makes things worse.

One thing which surprised me was just how long the panic attack lasted. The physiological panic was present for at least an hour, coming in wave upon wave. We spoke a lot about everything during this time.

I must say that our mums were absolute diamonds. They were so good on the phone at consoling Nadine and showing her that everything would be OK. We were able to have a real laugh with each other, somehow, because our mums were on top form. We didn't want to delay telling anyone about it because we knew how hard it would be. So I sent a quick message to my family group to get it over and done with. Of course, they were all devastated for us.

Nadine's mum has friends who have miscarried, and my mum had three miscarriages herself. This immediately makes the dark cloud recede a little, and brings hope that we will be able to have a baby one day.

One thing which was so difficult about this miscarriage was the fact that we had seen this baby's heartbeat and had 5,000 scans. We had truly bonded with this being and had been following its journey closely. During this time, I wasn't thankful for the wonderful little app which showed exactly what the baby looked like from week to week. That kind of thing is only wonderful if the baby survives.

I also wasn't thankful for the unpleasant and remarkable incident which followed. Nadine had to be wheeled down to a different room for 'The Radiologist' to come and do a scan to check up on her. She was extremely fragile, understandably. This doctor came into the room with a quiet "Hello" to me, then walked straight up to Nadine and closed the curtain on me. I didn't hear it, but apparently the only words she said to Nadine for the entirety of the check were, "Put your mask on properly."

Just that. Nothing else. Can you believe anyone could be so cold? We weren't expecting 5* hotel service, but this was a bit much. It really affected Nadine as well, which shows how these 'little things' can make such a difference. Maybe there's a time and a place for a 'clinical' attitude; this might be the place, but it was definitely not the time.

We had to stay in the hospital that night so Nadine's body could begin to process the miscarriage. It goes without saying how awful this is for her to experience. The worst part about this is the pressure from the doctors to have a D&C (dilation and curettage). This is a surgical procedure which removes the fetus and cleans out the uterus properly. Apparently, there is a possibility, if you try to miscarry naturally, that something will be left inside, and you cannot get pregnant again until you have a D&C to remove it. Many people, therefore, opt for the D&C straight away instead.

However, we are hippies and naturopaths at heart, and Nadine is not at all keen on the idea of being put under general anaesthetic, so she was dead against the D&C. There are also many risks associated with it, according to our best friend Dr Google. It was painful to see how pressured she felt to take this option, and how anxious she was about not being allowed to make her own decision. She definitely wanted to go down the natural route, and I assured her that I would help her stick to her guns with the medical team.

I went home to gather our things in preparation for spending the night in the hospital, and we eventually went to sleep, well and truly exhausted, our minds still trying to adjust to our new world.

Sunday 6th September

Yesterday morning, we returned home, and Nadine began the process of miscarrying naturally. She has researched a lot online and sourced a veritable feast of home remedies which help speed up this process and make it go as smoothly as possible.

Coming home was a very emotional experience, of course. The house seems a different colour, because the mind's colouring of life itself is so different. Now, there is sadness everywhere.

The mind looks all over for causes of this horrible eventuality. What did we do? What did we not do? I thought back to our meditations. Why were we so convinced that we had to give the baby extra energy? Why was I seeing all those horrible images when I tried to send it love? Was I right when I thought that I should have fought back against this negativity? God knows. Nobody knows the answers to any of these things.

What about the prophetic dream? Did Nadine's colleague ever say she actually *saw a baby*? No. The mind frantically searches for security and certainty, and it just needs to be returned to this moment with gentleness and openness. That's all. Then the reasons disappear. They don't matter anymore. They don't exist. All we are left with is what is here, now. Yes, some of that is sadness. But! When I look carefully, with an open heart, there is a tiny crack in it – a tiny space.

In that space, I see a new beginning.

2

A New Hope

"The wound is the place where the Light enters you."

— Rumi

<u>Thursday 10th September</u>

As you can imagine, the past couple of days have been filled not only with sadness, but also with the fear of never being able to have a child. This has been really challenging for both of us to deal with. It is definitely the saddest that I have ever seen Nadine. It has taken away so much of her usual light. Seeing her this way is heartbreaking, and it makes me desperately want to be able to give her this blessing. I am hopeful, and I still have faith that it will be possible for us.

We have spoken to many people since the miscarriage, and I am absolutely stunned by how common this is. Almost every single person I have mentioned it to has had one themselves, or knows someone very close who has. I must admit that this has been very reassuring for us, and I think it's problematic that, as a society, we are not more open with these things. I understand that, sadly, miscarriage is often perceived by many women as a source of shame.

Nadine does not feel that, but she isn't keen on the idea of other people feeling sorry for her because of it, and I can sympathise with this. Yet I'm convinced that the 'official numbers' for miscarriage cannot be accurate. Yes, my research was a small sample size, but the result was basically 100%!

Nadine has been very strong in dealing with the natural miscarriage, and she went to the doctor today and was given a perfect all-clear. This means that she didn't need the invasive procedure after all, so she had made the right decision. This has come as a huge relief and I'm proud of her for trusting her intuition.

A New Hope

<u>Thursday 17th September</u>

'Trying' is an annoying concept when it comes to getting pregnant, as I've already discussed. This time around, I want nothing to do with it. What will be will be and, if we are to be blessed with a child, it will happen when the time is right. I feel happy with this and so does Nadine. We planned a lovely hotel trip in the desert to mark the end of the miscarriage and the beginning of a new chapter, and we have just returned home. It was energising and delightful.

In our meditation group, we discussed the importance of leaving your ordinary space in order to refresh yourself. This is what I have experienced at the hotel. It's not often that we leave our zoo and stay elsewhere, and I've fallen into the trap of thinking that I'm not really bothered about doing things like that because I'm very content at home. However, I can see how important it is now. Walking through the desert dunes was extremely tranquil and contemplative, and there is something deeply refreshing about a total change of scenery.

Nadine was a little concerned during the trip for a couple of reasons. She had been putting on weight, and her period had not yet returned. After a miscarriage, you would expect to lose weight, not to gain it, and you would hope that the normal menstrual cycle would have resumed by this point. All of this is difficult because it may mean that the miscarriage didn't go as smoothly as we thought, and that there may still be an issue. However, we have had so much experience with anxiety in the last couple of months that we were able to welcome it in and enjoy our time away nonetheless.

A particularly random pregnancy quirk came up when we were in the pool; Nadine's nipples were suddenly so sore and cold that she had to get out. It was strange, because this is supposed to be a pregnancy symptom, but she assumes it's just some sort of hangover from the previous pregnancy.

I kept telling her she might be pregnant! She laughed this off, said, "No way!" and refused to consider doing a test. She said she doesn't want to allow herself to go down that road and get her hopes up right now, and we left it at that.

Tuesday 20th October

As you may have suspected, we had some news incoming. Nadine is already pregnant again! I could not believe it when she told me; I had actually forgotten it was even a possibility at this time. We are absolutely jubilant and really shocked. Now all of the symptoms she was experiencing whilst we were away at the hotel make total sense: she had become pregnant again immediately after the first miscarriage. Apparently, this is very common, and even more reason not to be too concerned after having one. It's also called a 'Rainbow Baby', if it goes to full term, to symbolise hope after a failed pregnancy.

The worries we have had about never having a child have totally vanished, for the moment. We know that another miscarriage is possible, but I just don't feel concerned about it and, at this stage, neither does Nadine. Because we just experienced one, the 'horror' of it is no longer some unknown ghoul casting its shadow over us; everything feels lighter because we've already been down that road.

Friday 30th October – 8 weeks

I received a call today during a lesson from Nadine. She was driving home from school in floods of tears. She was bleeding quite badly, exactly like she had in the first miscarriage. My heart sank beyond measure and I was truly stunned. Again? Really?

She was in a terrible, terrible state. What a horrible thing to happen. She had to flee her school and go home as quickly as possible, without telling anyone why she had gone. She was in

A New Hope

full panic mode. I tried my best to calm her down over the phone and to remind her that the most important thing now was to drive safely. I ended my lesson there and then and went home as fast as I could. We went straight to the hospital as soon as I got home. It was not a fun journey.

The wait was beyond agonising. The sinking feeling would not let up, and I tried my best to sit with it, allow it to do its thing and reassure Nadine as much as possible. With each passing moment, I could see the hope draining from her eyes.

The new doctor we saw on this visit was in a very good mood and was extremely polite and caring. This was nice. We explained the situation and Nadine prepared herself to be scanned.

"This is a hematoma. You are not having a miscarriage. See? It's on the outside? Nothing to worry about."

What???

We were in disbelief. The symptoms were exactly the same as in the first miscarriage, so we had both been totally convinced it was another one. I don't know how difficult that would have been to bear, but my imagination helpfully did its best to show me, as it seems to love to do.

Nadine was given some pills to clear up the hematoma and we were sent on our way. I remembered that we always leave the doctor's with questions unanswered and not understanding what's really going on, so this time I asked lots of questions. What should we expect in the next few days? What means this is getting better? What means it's getting worse? What needs to happen for us to come back to the hospital?

I was doing anything I could to get away from needing to use Dr Google at any point. She reassured us and said that it was 'old blood' and that it was already clearing itself up. This was extremely good to hear, because a hematoma can cause a miscarriage.

The rollercoaster continues! What a bloody relief.

Saturday 7th November – 9 weeks

We went to the doctor this week and had some funny exchanges. "Your cervix is verrrrrryyyy long!" she announced to Nadine. I wondered if this was a compliment, as it might have seemed to a man receiving similar feedback. (It wasn't.)

She also looked at us quizzically at one point during the conversation and suddenly asked, "Are you cousins?"

"No!" was our emphatic reply, and we swept that straight under the rug. Is that a normal thing to be asked? Who knows.

In the live scan, this time we could see the baby moving its fingers around, and that was a really wonderful, surreal moment. How can that be happening?

When we got home, I realised that something has definitely changed in Nadine over the last few days. It's very hard to put my finger on it or to describe it in words, but I will try! Some vital portion of her energy, her attention, is now turned inwards. She seems totally detached from the day-to-day nonsense of the world and is just floating around. It's really amazing to see, and it is making me smile repeatedly. When I reflect on it, it makes sense that a deep part of her energy must now be used to create another being. She only cares about outer things to the extent that she has to, and she's getting along just fine.

My cooking skills are really taking off now. The only thing Nadine ever wants is mashed potatoes or bread, and whatever a 'wheelhouse' is, this is starting to rupture the edges of mine. Is it a house for a wheel? Weird. Oh, maybe a house for loads of wheels? Is that still weird? Anyway, I'm just about managing. The kitchen really is not my forte.

Saturday 14th November – 10 weeks

Since the last entry, Nadine's mental state has changed significantly, and this week she has been suffering from quite strong anxiety. It is approximately the same point at which we lost the previous baby, and so this is understandable. I am trying my best to help, and I have found that the most effective thing I have done so far is tell her that sometimes I feel anxious about it too. Beyond this, I am doing the usual things. Cups of tea, hugs, reminding her that thoughts are only 'telling stories', however real and powerful they seem. We don't need to believe that those stories are true. Again, there is only space for me to say something like this every now and then without being really annoying. This has been hard for me to accept, again, as it was in the first pregnancy. My ego feels wounded because I cannot help her more, but I have no choice except to watch this all playing out in the mind, or as my colleague says, 'pulling up a chair for the ego'. It's funny, when you really watch this sort of thing without reacting and falling into the trap, then it does transform.

Nadine has now bought a 'Doppler' to help with the anxiety. It's a machine which you can strap to the tummy and use to hear the baby's heartbeat. There is debate about whether this alleviates or increases anxiety, though; you can check any time, so perhaps you might get into a neurotic habit of checking every five minutes. However, she believes it will help her, once or twice a day, just to know the baby is still alive in there.

I must say I have found it quite hard to adjust to Nadine being so anxious because it is so different from the norm. I went through a phase of severe depression and anxiety when at university, and so I know what these powerful storms are like: all-consuming and absolutely dreadful. Her mind is doing the standard time-travelling, spinning up stories of this being 'how she is now', projecting it way into the future as a solid and fixed part of her identity. This is such a devilish and sly little trick, but one of the most powerful in the mind's arsenal. I remember discussing this same theme with my brother's girlfriend, after she had suffered a terrible tragedy and, in the aftermath, had come to believe that she would be 'an anxious person' forever.

This all became particularly relevant at our next doctor's visit, when she asked Nadine if she had "always been anxious". No, Nadine replied – this was new to her. The doctor then asked if she wanted medication for it, and Nadine said no again.

She wanted to deal with this experience herself, and I was impressed with her fortitude; I also believed that it was a better course of action for her in this instance. This doesn't mean I'm demonising any use of medication for severe mental health episodes, but I do think they are thrown around far too much and can easily prevent us from facing things which need to be faced. In fact, this was a significant factor in Jon Kabat-Zinn's creation of the MBSR (Mindfulness-Based Stress Reduction) course in 1979,[5] which then went on to become MBCT (Mindfulness-Based Cognitive Therapy);[6] he saw the need for a holistic and natural alternative to medication for facing the many difficulties which can arise in our inner world. The data is clear; it works (see e.g. *McCartney et al. 2021*).[7] By practising meditation regularly, in combination with applying various principles of mindfulness to daily life, it is possible to transform one's relationship with mind and emotion to an enormous extent. Nadine knows about all this as well and is keen to use what she has learned to help her through this time.

Saturday 21st November – 11 weeks

At last, the time has come when I'm allowed off the leash to share our happy news! We have debated this back and forth, because of the last miscarriage, but this pregnancy truly feels completely different. Generally speaking, it has simply not been laced with fear in the same way as the first one, despite Nadine having some difficult waves of anxiety last week. Is this because our intuition was telling us something was off last time and not this time? Maybe, or it could have just been bog-standard fear and paranoia last time. Who knows?

A New Hope

After telling my immediate family and close friends, I called my 'Auntie Margaret' (great-aunt, actually, who I have only just discovered is not actually called Margaret at all).

She was elated, of course, and straight away just said, "Are you looking forward to meeting your daughter, then?"

"What do you mean?" I said. "What makes you say that?"

"I just know it," she replied. She went on to tell me an amazing story about when a close friend of hers came to her house and Margaret suddenly knew that she was pregnant with a baby girl. She asked her how far along she was, but her friend replied that she wasn't pregnant. Sure enough, after Margaret urged her to take a test, it turned out she was right – there was indeed a little girl brewing in there.

Clearly, something was in the air, because how about this for a synchronicity? I called Nadine to tell her what 'Margaret' had said, and she couldn't believe it:

"Well, you'll never guess what just happened to me."

"What?"

"The same teacher who had the weird dream before just found me in the corridor and asked if she could speak to me quickly, in private. She said she had had another dream; this time, I was in it with a *baby girl in my arms!*"

I kid you not. This was 15 minutes before my phone call with Margaret.

Naturally, I am totally convinced now that there is a little girl in there.

Saturday 28th November – 12 weeks

All this meant that I was unusually confident when we went to the doctor for the 12-week scan, and she saw, beyond a reasonable doubt, the baby's gender. Much to Nadine's standard dismay when I overshare with strangers, I relayed the above tales to the doctor, and told her I was certain the baby is a girl. Why shouldn't

I? Why do we have to keep our personal thoughts and feelings hidden all the time from 'strangers'? This doctor was really not that strange. She was amused by this, intrigued and probably very sceptical. Nevertheless, she wrote down the gender in secret on a piece of paper and put it into an envelope for us to open on Christmas Day. That was Nadine's idea. Let's see, eh!

Saturday 19th December – 15 weeks

Today, for the very first time, I went shopping for something nice for the little one yet to emerge from my wife. I wasn't expecting it to be, but it was a really emotional experience. I found one solitary, wonderful toy. A purple, yellow and pink cuddly toucan. It had something about it. I picked it up and knew it was the one, and it made me feel light and fuzzy inside, butterflies and all, and I actually started to well up a bit. It showed me the absolute innocence of babyhood and childhood, in a moment…I think it's the first time I've ever really felt like a dad.

Saturday 26th December – 16 weeks

Yesterday was Christmas Day, and the envelope containing the secret of the baby's gender was waiting underneath the tree for us in the morning. Nadine's mum is here visiting us for the holidays, and there has been a lot of talk between us all about what it would say. I stuck to my intuitive guns.
　Girl.
　Those two Jedi were right! (Yes, that is the plural.) I wonder, now, how the doctor was feeling about those stories, writing down that they were indeed correct.
　I'm excited that we're having a girl. I have three older brothers, and so the only female member of my immediate family is my mum. Any baby is a blessing, of course, and gender is irrelevant. But it makes the whole adventure more concrete now, and we

can start buying little clothes for her and planning her nursery. This gives Nadine a chance to unleash her creativity and start to spoil our little princess, and she is rubbing her metaphorical hands together with glee.

Saturday 9th January – 18 weeks

On the 18-week scan (yep, another one!), I felt the baby kick from the outside for the first time. There is a human being kicking me from inside my wife. I think I'm going to read that sentence again. That was very surreal indeed.

Saturday 23rd January – 20 weeks

Then came the 'big one': the 20-week scan, when you get to see the 4D picture moving around; it's the first time I've been able to get a real sense of what our baby will look like. She looks a bit squashed in there, to be honest, but she does have a face, which is always a plus in this world, I think. Makes a huge difference when it comes to job applications.

We found out that she's a little bit smaller than she 'should be', which I find a rather irresponsible way of phrasing it. That's how big she is! It's like when scientists say that galaxies aren't 'behaving as they should'; err…who's wrong here? The galaxies? Anyway, the mind loves chewing on that comment and showing all sorts of terrible possibilities which it brings into view. Watch, laugh, reset, repeat.

Suddenly, after the scan, Nadine was desperate for a coffee; more so than I've ever seen her. As soon as it had been purchased, boom: she planted the cups straight on her nipples to keep them warm. Right in view of everyone, relief etched on her face, not even a *thought* of actually drinking it. I laughed heartily. It's a pregnancy thing, apparently; periodic waves of freezing nipples. What a weird and wonderful thing to observe!

Diary of a Mindful Dad

Wednesday 27th January

With all this talk of a fetus growing, week by week, it's about time for a nice little bit of *data*, isn't it? Nothing makes you feel more like you're getting your money's worth from a book than a really solid, delicious bit of data. Because that's it, isn't it? Data is *solid*. Without data, without *facts and figures*, how can you know that what you're doing is serious and important? Without lovely straight lines and neat little boxes, how can you be sure all of that knowledge you're drinking in will be safe and secure? I've got you covered. Without further ado, I present to you:

THE TABLE

Week	Size Approximation	Development Highlights
4	Poppy seed (1–2 mm)	Embryo implants in uterus; early neural tube forming
6	Lentil (4–5 mm)	Heartbeat begins; basic facial features start forming
8	Kidney bean (1.6 cm)	Arms and legs develop; brain growth accelerates
10	Kumquat (3.1 cm)	Vital organs start functioning; fingernails form
12	Plum (5.4 cm)	Reflexes begin; vocal cords forming
16	Avocado (11.6 cm)	Facial expressions; limb movements more defined
20	Banana (25.6 cm)	Can hear sounds; develops sleep-wake cycles
28	Aubergine (37.6 cm)	Eyelids open; brain activity increases
36	Honeydew melon (47.4 cm)	Muscle tone improves; practising breathing
40	Small pumpkin (51.2 cm)	Full term, ready for birth

What's all this, then? A lentil with a heartbeat? Fingernails fit for a kumquat? The eyelids of an aubergine? If I may be so bold, I'd say that's the last thing an aubergine needs.

In all seriousness, of course, all of that information is *stupendous* and *mind-blowing*. How can it possibly be happening? What otherworldly intelligence is sculpting all of those pieces of my child at those infinitesimal scales? I once saw an accurate animation of DNA replicating itself, with its multifarious factory workers walking up and down assembly lines, checking and carrying things, within a larger structure which is spinning the DNA as fast as a jet engine, and scrupulously copying it all *backwards* (just to show off, I presume).[8] What choice do we have but to close the door on such marvels?

Don't worry. Remember I said I didn't want this to be like a textbook? Here's the good news: you don't have to store any of that information *anywhere*. Not the vegetable fetuses, and *certainly not* the DNA thing happening inside you within 50 million cells approximately 300 *quadrillion* times every *second* (apparently an underestimate).

There's no test at the end of this. Let's just *settle right down*. In fact, let's stick the middle finger up at the education system properly by *purposefully forgetting all of it as quickly as possible*, just like you did with everything you learned for – insert serious name for scary-sounding exam – straight after you closed the paper.

Done? Great. You get a gold star.

Friday 29th January – 21 weeks

Nadine has now entered what they call the 'nesting phase', and it is fascinating and beautiful to bear witness to. I must admit that I'm not experiencing it at all, really. Don't get me wrong, I'm really enjoying the process of preparing the house, but I don't feel the same as her about it. For her, it is a *deep need*. She is being pushed to do it from within. She cares so much about every part of the house now and is overjoyed to be planning the nursery. I'm even thinking she might stop leaving her handbag at the bottom of the stairs and her shoes in the middle of the hallway every day. We can all dream.

We have also started the HypnoBirthing course, which has been quite interesting. It seems, essentially, to be applying mindfulness and a positive attitude to the whole journey of birth. So far, it's definitely helping us both to feel psychologically prepared for the experience, in different ways. It's showing me how I can potentially be more than just a shell-shocked and irritating spare part, and it's giving Nadine the confidence to think that it *really can be OK*. Presumably, when you know the monumental scale of the task ahead of you, this is a pretty significant help!

Monday 15th February – 23 weeks

We humans are funny – we love to *moan*. I remember, when I was teaching, that after every staff meeting the group you were working with would come out with all sorts of moans and groans, regardless of what had been said. There is a stereotype about people from England: that we love to moan about the weather. It's true. It's bonding, somehow. By sharing our gripes, we connect – and not just the English, of course.

Jaron Lanier's incredible work on the various evils of social media shows that it's the so-called '*negative*' emotions that show up most dramatically in our facial expressions.[9] These are detected by the little camera on our phones, fed back to the giant evil robot (presumably hiding in an underground lair), which then uses mathematical tentacles called algorithms to feed us media (like we are little zombie hamsters) designed to make us feel like that *again*, because it makes us *engage*!

OK, he didn't say the bit about the robot, but I've read between the lines. I'm sure we can all agree that this is a true horror story – the ultimate vicious cycle.

I've noticed that this same propensity shows up in all its glory during pregnancy. For some reason, all anybody wants to tell us is how AWFUL everything is going to be when we have a child! I realise I may well be asking for it here, and looking back on this in six months and laughing at how much of a fool I was, but I can cope with that.

Yes, we know (on an intellectual level, at least) that having a child is going to be ridiculously hard in all sorts of ways. How could we not? It's all anybody ever says. Why does it need to be the dominant narrative?

Do we want other people to feel worried and frightened? I don't think so. All of this just seems to roll off the tongue so much more easily.

Like negative birth stories, for example. Why tell someone who is pregnant all about that? A friend's mum enjoyed spending about half an hour relaying some horrific tales, in *enormous* detail, and I think it is par for the course in these situations. Nadine also received a blow-by-blow account from a parent of someone she teaches at school, believe it or not, which went into huge detail about every negative aspect of the birth experience. I can understand the motivation to share your experience and how it really was, but it's a good example of not quite being as considerate of someone else's emotions as we could be. I hope I can remember not to do this to other people in the future.

We chose to have this baby, and we are so excited to meet her and for all the challenges she will bring. When I hear all of this negativity, it doesn't bring me one iota of panic or concern. Thankfully, Nadine is the same.

Monday 22nd February – 24 weeks

This evening, I met a friend at the pub and, in light of the previous entry, it was so refreshing. He was the first person who instantly spoke so positively about everything relating to childbirth and parenthood. The way he described the love a parent feels genuinely gave me a good old dose of goosebumps.

Have you ever wondered what they are? Just the *word 'goosebumps' being known* stops us from noticing, from questioning. The word is a *barrier*. "Yeah, the hairs all over my body just stand on end when people talk about ghosts and stuff, and sometimes when someone says something really important." Let's just close the door. Move on. Go back to work. Go back to sleep.

Wednesday 24th February

Today, Nadine and I finished buying everything for the little one and sent out the list of items which others can buy for us, if they would like to.

Then we had our first ever proper conversation about parenting, which touched on a deep and emotive topic: 'self-soothing'. We've both seen research here and there about this, but Nadine was insistent today that, at a very early age, crying is the baby's only way of communicating, and so there might be a lot of danger and trauma associated with ignoring these cries. I'm definitely sympathetic to that view, and the whole area is interesting to me.

I am all for resilience; it's obviously very important. One of the biggest issues in the modern age is instant gratification. I do not believe that giving an iPad to a child as soon as they are bored is good for them; I think it sets up psychological habits that work against resilience. What happens when they are an adult, living alone in difficult circumstances? Are you helping them to face this and come to terms with it, or to escape?

One of the cornerstones of mindfulness practice is sitting with difficult emotions and 'thought storms' with curiosity, and this is very tough. We have to *actually do this hundreds of times* before it comes close to being our instinctive habit. Yet to do so can be truly life-changing.

There are now a lot of books out there encouraging 'mindful

parenting', showing how a deeper quality of attention on the part of the parent can transform children's lives. Of course, it is true. Reactive parents – reactive children. We are always modelling what we see in society, and when we are young and growing up it stands to reason that this is amplified exponentially. It really is a miracle that Matilda ever made it out of the Wormwoods' house alive.

Are we interested in emotions? Our own or those of others? Or do we just want to cling to them if they are 'positive' and run from or squash them if they are not? We don't live in a world where a refined understanding of emotion is subconscious for us. This means that generation upon generation of human beings have been raised receiving bad advice on a very deep level. Our reactivity is hereditary, and it's not just from our parents. It's from our entire evolutionary history.

It's fantastic that such books are proving so popular. Nadine was interested to hear about how this works in my Holistic Tuition, as my attitude to emotion is probably the most important aspect of my job. I must consciously model curiosity about everything which comes up in the experience of a child – never closing the door to learning or adventure. This takes a hell of a lot of energy and engagement! I especially enjoy doing this with difficult and explosive emotions. The look on a child's face is absolutely priceless when I am genuinely excited by how terrible they feel. It causes a kind of glitch and meltdown in their mind.

What? This isn't supposed to be fun!

But this is a powerful message to send. As parents, human beings are sending these messages in every moment without necessarily realising it. It cannot be hidden, and this also means that one's attitude to these things cannot be contrived; you can't always be putting on a show.

Curiosity about emotions is not an *idea*. It is a genuine stance we can all take as we start adventuring through and investigating our inner world. When we live in that way, it cannot help but be transmitted to our children. When my child experiences pain, fear or sadness, I don't want her to run; I want her to experience those emotions in all their power and mystery, in a safe and nurturing environment. To do that, I need to be able to do it myself as well as I can. Then, hopefully, she won't have to learn how to do this on purpose like I've had to do!

Tuesday 2nd March – 25 weeks

Nadine and I had another discussion today about parenting, and it was my turn to try to put across something very important which I feel strongly about: silence. We don't have enough silence in our lives in this modern world.

I want to enjoy silence and stillness with my child. There is a lot of talk about the importance of speaking to your child about every single thing that happens in order to give them a broad vocabulary and help them master language. The research on this seems pretty clear; it works.[10] Language is hugely important. I definitely wouldn't be able to write this book if my mum hadn't read to me as much as she did when I was younger; what's more, it's unlikely that I would *want to*. I did English Literature A Level and adore reading, so this is by no means a dismissal of the power of language. Language is a sacred and special gift we humans have been given; a true blessing. It allows us to interact with one another, and reality itself, in a unique and powerful way, to create worlds in the imagination, and so much more.

Yet, at the same time, so much emphasis on words makes us forget to enjoy the simplicity of existence with a child. If we want children to have a decent attention span (which, relative to the world we are creating, is probably 16 seconds; one longer than a TikTok video) and to be able to amuse themselves without needing to be entertained for every single second of their lives, it seems like a good idea to model to them that it's OK to do nothing. I spoke to a new parent and dear friend of mine about this, and she said, months later, that she had actually been doing this and it had been extremely nice and, she thought, very good for her sweet little boy. Just enjoying silence together. There is a simple, beautiful, quiet and somehow talkative reality beyond and behind words.

Blaise Pascal famously said, "All of humanity's problems stem from man's inability to sit quietly in a room alone." I want my child to be able to do that. Not because they are forcing themselves to, or because someone else has forced them to, or because they are on a mindfulness course, but because it's OK to just do that sometimes. I feel that this will allow them to naturally develop a sensitivity and capacity for presence, which, aptly, cannot be put into words. Whether this is actually possible or not is another matter! This could well be another entry which I laugh heartily at in a few months' time.

Wednesday 10th March – 26 weeks

Every now and then, we are jolted from our dreamlike state and we experience true contact with the present. Sometimes the jolt is so strong, and what is seen touches us so profoundly, that it is unmistakable. Such moments are transcendent, and I don't believe that any effort can manufacture them. Occasionally, I become aware of how miraculous pregnancy is, and then it *can't be accessed anymore*. This is probably for the best. Sometimes we need to be shielded from how weird life is, otherwise we would freak out and probably stop playing our neat little roles in society.

I discovered earlier that Nadine has also been having some of these moments recently. She mentioned casually that she had been avoiding thinking about life because of how strange it all is. I was fascinated that she had never mentioned it before, and it highlighted to me again one of the big differences between us. I share so much of my inner world as and when it happens (can you imagine how annoying I must be to live with?) and she is very much the yin to my yang.

She said that she has been thinking regularly and involuntarily about how surreal it is that there is a human being growing inside her. There is *life* starting inside her. She is *creating life*. How can you, as a reader, access the reality behind those words? It's not possible, they are just words; what they are pointing to is a grand and unfathomable mystery.

She has noticed, like I have, that it's as if the brain suddenly accesses the reality of the situation and then, when it sees that it can't be understood, just sweeps it nicely and neatly under the carpet as quickly as possible. *Existential avoidance*, we could call it. I have a friend who cannot discuss time or space because she once became aware of how mind-bogglingly incomprehensible and paradoxical they are, and it made her feel physically sick and then afraid for quite a long time.

I wonder how often this sort of thing happens for children at a very young age? The comfort from parents has probably taken billions of children out of existential crises, both mini and severe, over human history. How much must a baby be freaking out psychologically when it first enters the world? It is completely impossible to imagine; no wonder there is so much crying. It's basically been a fish, so far, living in a wonderfully protected cocoon of magical, soothing water, nurtured by the life energies of a mother. Suddenly, it finds itself here, breathing the air, with all sorts of doctors everywhere with strange tools and two people it has never seen before (it has never seen *people before*) staring intensely into its eyes and making noises at it. This moment is far too mind-blowing to be imagined, and I can't believe that I'm going to see it first-hand in just a matter of weeks. I hope I can help that little soul adjust well to this mad world she's going to emerge into.

A New Hope

Sunday 28th March – 29 weeks

Am I ready to be a dad? As I took a little downtime today to reflect on the current situation, I began to experience an energetic squeeze as some difficult thought and feeling packages appeared. I tensed up a bit as I reflected on our uncertain financial situation: this is a big one for me. My job is totally uncertain, in a sense, because I have no salary and rely completely on hourly sessions with clients, any of whom could cancel at any time. This makes it potentially very easy for fear to take hold, as it did in this moment. I could feel the tension strongly in my body and terrible possibilities came into view. I tried my best to remain present, not fearing the fear or running away from it. I tried my best to allow it to flower and bloom over time. As I gave it the freedom to reveal itself organically, it gave birth to a healthier perspective after some time. I have faith in what I'm doing and in the loyalty of my clients. This is my natural orientation towards my work, and I wonder how often I am going to have to pivot back to that in the months and years to come.

My mind then turned to the stage of our lives that we had reached. I've always expected a lot from myself, and these expectations came home to roost during that moment. I haven't done many of the significant things I have wanted to do in my life, and I started to lament 'lost' time. Was my life over? Becoming a parent is such a milestone that it's almost like the end of one life and the start of another. Have I lived enough? How about going out with friends and having fun? Is all of that over? Am I finally a 'grown-up'? Surely not!

I spoke to Nadine about it and, as usual, she was all wisdom and a healthy perspective. She reminded me that everything in the past is done, and it was all meant to be – we are both total fatalists! Her comments helped me to shift my attitude into one of *honouring the past* and appreciating it, rather than focusing on what it was lacking. I gave a lot of time to letting this simmer and digest, to participating in the emotions fully as they arose. It ended up being quite a beautiful experience, and brought me into alignment with the reality of the situation.

I can see now, properly, that what is done is done, and it is OK for that stage of my life to be over. I can appreciate that this adventure is a monumental change, but that I am done with what came before, to a large extent, anyway – much more than before. This is surely a lesson which needs to be learned over and over, in a spiral, and which never really ends.

I wonder how important this shift is? If I had not given myself time to really reflect on and consider this, would this all eat away at me after the baby is born? Could it lead to resentment of my life? Is this happening for people all over the world? Presumably, yes. I think this sort of thing happens frequently for us all. These difficult energies do not exist just to scare us or annoy us, but to teach us, so we can integrate them as lessons and grow in understanding.

Nadine has her own fears to deal with at this time. Is the bump big enough? Why is it so much smaller than other people's at the same stage of pregnancy? How often does she need to kick-count? Why did the kicks just go away? A friend of ours just had Braxton Hicks 'practice contractions' and thought she was going into very early labour; that was a very scary experience for her.

I think that learning to see fear without fear, and to really feel it and let it unfold, would be incredibly powerful medicine for any pregnant mothers-to-be during these times, as well as fathers-to-be reflecting on this momentous stage of their lives.

Sunday 4th April – 30 weeks

Nadine is 30 weeks pregnant now, and things are becoming much more real. My friends who also have babies on the way are a few weeks further along than us and the fear is ramping up. Car seats are being secured, nappies purchased, and final couples' outings enjoyed.

We have been painting and preparing the nursery this week, and it's been a beautiful experience. The new arrival, relatively abstract for the father at this point, actually has a physical place to inhabit. It's an odd experience, but very lovely. You can start to feel their presence in your imagination: sleeping in the cot, sitting on the carpet and warming the cockles of the heart.

I wanted to prepare the nursery mindfully, with the caring and loving attention which transforms and sanctifies experience. I succeeded at times, except when, for example, Nadine 'politely requested' that I go over all of the most difficult parts of the ceiling again, standing on a bar stool. I must confess I wasn't really up for that. For now, at least, I appear to have got away with it, though I'm not sure Mr Miyagi would approve of this attitude.

Painting is a good example of an activity which makes it easy to be mindful. The feeling of pushing and pulling the roller of paint on the wall is very satisfying, and so the mind naturally rests upon it and makes contact with the present. This is what people mean when they say that an activity is 'therapeutic'; they mean that it naturally invites mindfulness. Performing such an activity for a long period may bring the mind into the present in a strong sense, potentially leaving one peaceful and content. However, this depends a lot on attitude.

Have you ever seen Karl Pilkington in *An Idiot Abroad*? It's a pretty good example of this. He goes to visit a sanctuary of monks, and he is trained in some of their ways. When asked to do a boring and repetitive task, he is totally unable to access this state of mind, because he can't intellectually get to grips with how it could possibly be enjoyable. His mind conjures judgements for the entire duration of the task, and he buys into their validity one by one – Miyagi would eat him for breakfast.

One thing this shows is that, when it comes down to it, mindfulness really is a *how* rather than a *what*, and the experiences of

Diary of a Mindful Dad

our lives can be transformed by a different attitude or orientation towards them.

However, this can all go a step too far when it is taken to imply that everything *should* or *must* be experienced like this. Then we end up living in a battle with the vicissitudes of life, believing that we should be able to enjoy and make everything profound and beautiful. I've visited those lands and, if I were you, I would stay away. Sometimes, life is just messy, and I suspect not falling for this particular misconception of 'mindful living' is going to help me in the months ahead.

One of my cats has just stopped me from writing by saying hello repeatedly and demanding a cuddle; it's amazing I ever manage to get anything done.

A New Hope

As you can see, when her son joined her, the laptop became fully inaccessible; I think it's a cat's favourite game. I had probably better get used to such unexpected disturbances! As usual, my companions are teaching me a lesson. There's probably a universe in which this bothered me, I shooed her away, and I missed a nice moment. In this universe, though, she started to groom him as only a mummy cat knows how, and I saw the simplicity of a parent's love. A rather fitting interruption for this book, I guess. How much are we missing by thinking it's just an annoying distraction from the rampant, speeding train of life, which gives us so little time to stop?

Sunday 11th April – 31 weeks

And then you find out about SIDS. What the hell is SIDS? Oh, as if having a baby wasn't scary enough already, SIDS turns out to mean that they can randomly just die. Yep. Just like that.

'Sudden Infant Death Syndrome'. What?! The risk of this drops significantly after the first three months, and then again after six months, so that's a relief. You only need to be concerned about your baby spontaneously dying for six months. I can imagine that people can get stuck worrying about this quite a lot. What fun!

Sunday 9th May – 35 weeks

Meditation is often tragically misunderstood, and I suppose that should come as no surprise. It's an otherworldly relic, reaching us from ancient times and cultures so vastly different from our own: a call to stillness, to transcendence, now shoehorned into this frenetic, modern world.

My friend Johnny asked me one day in the car, "Dom, do you meditate every single day?"

"Pretty much," I replied.

"What, you just sit there in your house, on your own, in silence?"

"Yes, mate."

Sounds weird, doesn't it? I guess it *is* weird – if you are only considering the *outer*. Yes, my *body* is sitting on a chair, but there's far more than that going on.

Meditation is the most beautiful, extraordinary thing; it feels like the antidote to all that is unnatural and disharmonious in our world. If you can *learn to do it* (and because of our totally dissonant society, it sadly does seem to need to be *learned*), it can change everything. When the weary mind sinks into the silent, healing space of the heart, it feels like your entire inner world undergoes a refreshment and transformation which is nothing short of miraculous. And that's just the beginning. Here are some helpful and important words from Sri Shantanand Saraswati, the guru who founded the London School of Meditation, on the mystery of meditation:

> *"The whole of our mind has for so long been associated with the outer world that it has quite forgotten the existence, let alone the language of the inner world. The moving mind looks for happiness in getting and experiencing things. These do not suffice, for when the mind has one thing it immediately rushes after another. The still mind finds happiness in everything. The kingdom within or the heaven within is the reservoir of peace and bliss. Dive in with devotion and swim around gently in that blissful heaven that is within you.*
>
> *When we go into meditation we reach a spiritual world where quietness prevails like that of a deep, undisturbed ocean. There is no movement – no waves, no currents – everything is absolutely stationary. This is the meditational world...*
>
> *It is not necessary to remain in this state for a long period. Most of the time spent during meditation is in preparation to lead one to this state. The stillness itself is the real experience of meditation. In a diamond mine, thousands of tons of stone are cut 300 feet below the ground... Thousands of people are engaged in picking over these*

small stones and looking at them. All this process goes on and ultimately they may find about 100 grams of diamonds.

This also happens in meditation – so you will have to give half an hour simply to get just a few moments of contact with the Self, and it is worthwhile because you do get a diamond – the real force, the most valuable precious material of anybody's life."[11]

I have found every word of this, in my experience, to be absolutely true. One of my favourite things about this quotation is that it shows people they don't need to sit and have an empty mind for half an hour (even though that can happen). Isn't that a relief? This misconception is the chief reason why most people give up meditation quite quickly, and I'm so thankful I didn't. As we get better at accessing this deeper energy over time, we also learn to access it during daily life, and I suspect that is going to prove invaluable to me in the adventures to come!

Saturday 15th May – 36 weeks

Every week, I sit down on a Saturday to sort out our finances. As I sat down this morning to do this, I noticed that I was carrying tension physically, in my upper back and neck; it was a somewhat shaky and restless heat, accompanied by pressure. I was shocked to feel it, and I could see that it was directly connected to our financial situation and trying to 'manage it'. The physical/energetic marker was so incredibly useful because it prompted me to *notice my feelings about what I was doing*. It prompted me to stop, to investigate, and to refresh my perspective.

I never used to be aware of these things physically, though, until one fateful day, when the mother of one of my homeschool clients invited me for a spontaneous therapy session. She uses 'Identity Therapy', which involves some of the same principles as 'Family Constellations', a more well-known therapeutic approach to healing family trauma.

She invited me to think of something I wanted help with, and to write a sentence associated with it, word by word, on different pieces of paper. Then I walked around the room and stood on these pieces of paper, one by one. When I stood on the first one, she asked me what I felt. "Nothing" was the answer to start with, but gradually associations built up about the word 'I' on the paper, and I started to feel emotions associated with how I perceive myself.

This was when things got strange. She was standing next to me, with her eyes closed, and began to tell me what I was feeling. Invariably, from paper to paper, before I said a word, she was right on the money, putting into words *exactly* what I felt in that moment. It was surreal. This continued for the duration of the session. In this therapy system, this is called 'resonance', and *we can all remember how to do it* (I say 'remember' because it is *old*, not *new*). However, this in itself is not what made such a lasting impression on me, because I already know that this is possible, however mysterious and interesting it may be.

Though we have been led to believe that we are 'individuals' – with a personal mind separate from everyone else's – this does not seem to strictly be the case. Rather, our 'personal mind' seems to exist within a larger web, a shared field of consciousness which we all inhabit. We are receiving information from this field all the time *as well*; however, due to our misunderstanding of the nature of mind, and how occupied we are with our personal story, we interpret everything invisible which we sense as *ours*. We say 'I think' and 'I feel', but how do we know it's ours? I know that sounds strange, but if we look closely, it is more true to say that our inner content *just appears* in our experience.

What was so mind-blowing to me, in this session, was that I started to feel 'physical' sensations very strongly associated with each piece of paper. When I stood facing the word 'family', lots of thoughts and emotions immediately came to the surface simply due to association. However, I was experiencing extremely strong sensations in the body. Throughout the adventure, I felt pushes, pulls, pressures and weights on my back, shoulders and torso. These were extraordinarily strong sensations which felt massive and heavy and so incredibly real, and they shifted very noticeably in relation to the different things I was thinking about and discussing. They were energetic structures which were part of my body, located just outside what we can see of it. I could perceive, directly and systematically, through my experience, the relationship between the energetic emotional world and the physical. I had perceived this kind of thing at times before, whilst practising Qi Gong, for example – but never as clearly as this. What is so remarkable is that all of this can be there, so vital and so powerful, *without us being aware of it.*

This is quite unbelievable when I consider how strong the sensations were during this exercise. How can we veil all this from ourselves? One thing which prevents us from feeling these blockages and sensations is the fact that we intellectualise and story everything so much. Normally, we are interested in the content of the situation (meaning-wise), and that is where our attention goes; every other level is therefore overlooked and ignored. The mind really is a master of deception and trickery.

The session went on for over an hour and I experienced an extraordinary amount of energetic release. Ever since that session, when the door of what is called the 'energetic body' was opened so strongly, I can feel these sensations in normal life much more readily when things happen.

When I felt this tension, as I sat and looked at the finances, perceiving the sensations was interesting to me and not a problem. I sat with the tension and the sensations, observed them, and felt them properly. In allowing them to reveal themselves in this way, we can begin to process such things consciously and allow them to unfold, transform and eventually be released. I am reminded again of how incredibly complex and intelligent the human body is, and all of the mysteries it contains. I wonder if our daughter is developing these energetic systems as we speak, to allow her to store and process the events in her life? To me, that is a tantalising thought.

Thursday 27th May – 38 weeks

One day, my good friend sent me a message out of the blue:

"Something interesting happened today. I stopped believing my thoughts."

What a wonderful thing to say.

Why do we always believe them? Do you even realise that you believe them? Thought comes so fast and feels like it's just 'us', so most of us don't realise this is going on.

Today, I had a hard day and thought: *I really need to sit down now; I can't do anything else*. Then, when Nadine immediately needed me to help her, I was triggered *because I had believed this thought*. That slimy little bugger!

Luckily, I was aware of my mind as it did this, so I caught it before it turned into an action, and helped her. It turned out that the thought was completely wrong; I *could do something else* if I needed to.

This has important implications when it comes to stress. If we believe we are 'having a hard day', for example, it distorts the events which follow, endowing them with a more problematic and irritating sheen. Both examples point to the need for an ability to reset and refresh, which doesn't actually take long in terms of time, but is difficult to get yourself to *actually do*. Sometimes I call it a 'weather check', in which you clearly survey your energy, see and feel what is operating (including which thinking traps you might have fallen into), and, in doing so, bring yourself back to a neutral or natural state. I wonder how hard it will be to avoid falling into all of these thinking traps with a baby around?

A New Hope

Tuesday 1st June

Nadine and I have developed a nice routine, which we have been doing for the majority of both pregnancies. Every night before bed we meditate together, and I have the chance to have my hands on the baby during our meditation. The whole thing feels *totally different* from the first pregnancy, when all of the negativity and fear was arising in my imagination.

Sometimes we listen to music and sometimes we do it in silence. It has become a really beautiful thing by this stage, which we both look forward to, and we rarely miss it. I have seen many times, throughout my life, the difference meditation makes to the atmosphere of a room. Something changes which can be felt or seen in its effects on the people or animals. One of our cats used to come and find me every morning, just as I started meditating, and sit on my lap and stay there for the duration.

In my opinion, it is impossible for this meditation routine not to have positive effects on our baby. It makes such a significant change to Nadine and me that it is only logical to assume that something is being transmitted to her wonderful cocoon. We are bathing in a beautiful energy field together, all three of us. The baby always reacts as soon as the music starts or as soon as we begin the meditation; I'm convinced that she can sense the change. My opinion is that it is connecting the three of us deeply and allowing her to share in and benefit from the peace that it brings. I would highly recommend creating some sort of routine like this for any prospective parents.

Saturday 5th June – 39 weeks

Towards the end of pregnancy women are advised to start 'kick-counting' once per day. There are supposed to be at least ten in an hour, and if there aren't, you need to get in touch with the doctor or go to the hospital. This presents a very difficult mental and emotional challenge. Nadine has been doing a great job since the 20-week scan of trusting in the process and letting her body do its thing, but this makes things a bit different. It brings an opportunity for anxiety every day, and for responding to it well.

Nadine said she hasn't counted very often so far; our little one moves around so much that she leaves no doubt about her wellbeing. She has only consciously counted the kicks if she has noticed a big change, and this has happened three times.

Do you go to the hospital or not? Once, out of the three times, Nadine decided to go and check it out. Typically, as soon as she got on the table, the baby went into ninja mode in there, whirling around like the best of them. Still, it put her mind at rest, and I can understand the perspective of 'better safe than sorry'. But I can also imagine that this might make someone go to the hospital every single day, and our doctor confirmed that this does happen. On the other two occasions that Nadine was worried about a decrease in movement, we waited it out for a couple of hours, and the little menace always started back up and got back into her 'normal rhythm'. The bottom line seems obvious: if you are extremely worried, sure, go to the hospital! But if you're extremely worried ten times a day, best to slow down, investigate and unravel that anxiety instead, then make your decision after that.

Thursday 10th June – 40 weeks

Due date! Uh oh! Nadine said it feels funny that, after all these months of waiting, it's like an alarm has gone off and the baby is expected to have come out! This is silly, obviously, as the due date is just an approximation.

We're going for a scan this morning to see what's going on, as there is no sign of any change, which is fine. The only thing which is slightly concerning for Nadine is that, in Dubai, 'induction' is mandatory ten days after the due date. This is essentially where the doctors do various things to force the baby to come out. Our HypnoBirthing course warned us about the dangers of induction, but we don't have a choice here. The objections to it seem to make sense; the baby comes when they are ready, so leave them in until they are! Yet our doctor has made many arguments in its favour to us, and I can see that it is a blessing of modern medicine that we can do such things when it is necessary. For example, if the placenta is not feeding the baby properly, and we can get her out and potentially save her life, of course that is beyond desirable.

Nadine's attitude to labour, generally, has astounded me: she's just not frightened of it at all. How? She told me that she has tried to consider why, but she can't put her finger on it. The only thing which has come to my mind is worrying for her about the induction; I wondered if knowing she would be induced would make her more fearful, as it's supposed to be much more painful than ordinary labour, and she has expressed negativity about it since we have done the HypnoBirthing course. I have thought about different things I can do to help her see it more positively; for example, framing the medicinal interventions in a more wonderful and magical, rather than cold and clinical way. From one perspective, this really is the case. Why not see it like that?

However, she said today that if she has to be induced, then so be it. She trusts our doctor, has listened to her logic and has accepted that it may be the way it goes. So she has confronted a potential source of stress and fear and nipped it in the bud, amazing me again.

I know from friends, though, that this attitude is not always possible, and if you are a prospective mum or dad, I hope that some of the things I've already said about facing fear can be helpful to you during these difficult days and weeks before the birth. Remember Rumi. Remember the Guest House:

Diary of a Mindful Dad

"Meet them at the door, laughing, and invite them in."
If fear is there, let it come. Feel it. Don't run away.

Sunday 13th June – 40 weeks 3 days

Bilbo Baggins once wisely said, "No, thank you! We don't want any more visitors, well-wishers or distant relations!"

I feel his pain, because we've been bombarded by a barrage of messages from people asking if the baby has been born yet! I definitely shouldn't have told anyone the due date; people have come out of the woodwork who haven't spoken to us in months! I find it funny, and it's nice, in a way, that so many people are excited to hear about the birth of our daughter. There is definitely something sweet about it. But I can also see why some people find it annoying; it can put unnecessary pressure on the lovely lady waiting to give birth, when she just needs to be resting and trying to enjoy the last stages of this momentous journey.

Tuesday 15th June – 40 weeks 5 days

OK, two days later and it's getting a bit ridiculous. We have to explain at least five times a day that she hasn't been born. Nadine, in particular, is becoming very irritated about it. She is trying everything (see below) to coax the little cherub out before induction is necessary, and the messages from people are really not helpful. I don't understand why people don't wait until they hear from you. Of course, when she is born, we will send people pictures! If you are a prospective parent, I would recommend the following:

⋄ Don't tell people the due date! Then they won't be waiting for that day.
⋄ When it comes to the due date, consider turning off the phone or sending a blanket message out to anyone who might be interested, to let them know that you will update them.

A New Hope

I just received a phone call on WhatsApp from a distant relative, five minutes after writing the above. No joke. I wonder what they wanted?

We are going 'mall-walking' every day, doing at least 6,000 steps to encourage the baby to 'engage the head' so we don't need to induce. The weather here in the summer means, sadly, that there's nowhere else to go for a walk! Already trying to force her to do something she doesn't want to do isn't sitting well with me at all, to be honest, but there we are. Nadine is being an absolute trouper, steaming around the mall like there's no tomorrow – ignoring the beguiling jewellery, thank God.

Since as early as week 34, she has been absolutely on it with the old wives' tales, doing anything in her power to encourage our daughter out into the world. She has tried:

- Sex (the most popular recommendation!)
- Pineapple
- Dates
- Primrose oil
- Clary sage oil
- Scrubbing the floor
- Bouncing on the medicine ball
- Circling on the medicine ball
- Squats
- Never sitting on the sofa

These last ones have been the most demanding. My poor wife hasn't relaxed on the sofa for a few weeks. She is constantly on the 'bloody ball' (as she calls it), circling and spiralling with reluctance and resignation. It's taken a lot of determination and perseverance, and we are hoping that at least something she has been doing will help her to go into labour before the dreaded (but not so much anymore) induction date.

In our scan today, Nadine had a cervical sweep, as she is 1cm dilated. A little bit of progress and success, from her point of view. There is movement! A lady in the mall was convinced that the baby will be here in three days, and our family have all chosen their dates in a sweepstake, each person putting in £10 so the winner will receive £150. This is a good bit of fun, which I would recommend to someone else going through this for the first time, if you end up telling people the due date.

We have also just taken the last 'bump picture' so we can have a collage of its progress over the nine months. It's surreal to see how much it has changed over time, and another thing I would recommend.

I don't know why any of us ever wanted to come out of the womb, to be honest; it must be so nice in there. I'm not surprised she hasn't come out just yet. It's 45°C!

Friday 18th June – 40 weeks 8 days

You might think that my mindfulness training would be really useful for helping Nadine with her stress levels through the birth process, but it's not as simple as that. The major difficulty that birth partners feel during labour is the feeling of powerlessness. As your beloved is in serious pain, you can basically do nothing about it. I'm going to really struggle with this, and my history with meditation and the like is quite possibly going to make that worse, not better. I'm going to *feel like I can help,* maybe more than most, and if this doesn't prove to be the case, then it will probably be harder for me to take than it would for many others.

We have just had a slightly emotional disagreement about this topic, and we are both in the aftermath of it right now. I woke up this morning ready to make notes on everything I can do to help, based on our HypnoBirthing course. One of the key ideas is the 'traffic light system'. As Nadine goes through a 'surge' (contraction), her stress levels will elevate to 'amber', and my role is to bring her back down to 'green' before the next one. This 'reset' helps to prevent the stress from accumulating and getting to the 'red' stage. I am very familiar with this sort of thing, having taught it in mindfulness sessions in the past. I could immediately see how powerful it would be, and I felt confident that I could use it to help.

Nadine came over to refresh her memory of the HypnoBirthing course as well, and she could see the notes I was writing. Some forum comments were fresh in her mind, and she justifiably felt the need to remind me not to overwhelm her with instructions during labour.

Instinctively, this upset and frustrated me. The course makes clear that birth partners can be genuinely helpful, and I believe I have the skill set to be. But, of course, that creates the perfect storm.

Nadine was right to remind me of this. Everyone is different, and what I think is helpful might not resonate with her in the moment. I can easily imagine how saying too much could backfire, no matter how good my intentions are.

I'm sure you can see how this ended up being a difficult interaction. Whilst I understand her perspective, I do trust myself to read the situation well and to be a positive influence during the birth process, rather than just a 'spare part'. When Nadine made her point (which she probably felt uneasy about doing because she knew how I might react), I felt like she didn't trust me to do this, and it hurt. I want her to feel like she can rely on me during this time. I tried to explain the kind of help I had in mind, and she explained what she thought might be unhelpful. We got there in the end, but the taste left afterwards wasn't nice at all.

I know, from previous disagreements, that I need to give Nadine some space afterwards, but I always feel like I need to close the circle before that point and ensure that we both know it is OK. It's an annoying habit, from her perspective, I'm sure – but I think it helps in the end. I tried to show her that I understood where she was coming from and apologised for upsetting her. I felt really guilty about the whole thing, of course. *She doesn't need to be flooded with frustration and stress right now*, the mind tells me. I know!

But it was also unavoidable; clearly, this conversation was coming, and it was perfectly difficult. Sometimes conflicting thoughts and feelings have to be exchanged. Should I not have reacted as I did? I'm not sure. Maybe it was just my ego that was hurt by her reminder, my pride in my ability to help, and I didn't actually need to make my point at all. But we're all human, and I won't beat myself up about that.

I know that, soon, it will be completely fine and we will both have understood where the other was coming from. I've taken on board what she meant, and I'll be extra-careful not to 'over-coach' her. My friend said that, during his wife's labour, it was a bit like playing golf with someone who's having a shocker: there's just nothing you can say to make it better; it's best to stay quiet. I can see what he means. We can't solve things for others, no matter how hard we try – especially not labour – and that's tough, because the mind is always looking for solutions. I'm not looking forward to feeling powerless, but I'll do my best to do the right things at the right time, and I know it'll be OK in the end.

Saturday 19th June – 40 weeks 9 days

The best thing about an argument is the slow dance back into harmony afterwards. For us, it always starts with a seemingly innocuous comment about something or other, just to push open the door a little and to start to reconnect. I am always amazed at how we can suddenly shut each other out, closing the door to our energy field. I can feel this strongly when the two of us argue; I'm suddenly not allowed in anymore. Then, as we start to interact again, this changes, bit by bit, until everything is normal again. That happened to us yesterday afternoon and now all is well.

Nadine had a few mild contractions last night, so it looks like things might be getting real…

Sunday 20th June – 40 weeks 10 days

It has just become Father's Day in the UK (20 minutes past midnight) and I am writing this from the hospital in Dubai; Nadine is lying on the bed, having the baby's heart rate monitored, because we have been booked in for an induction to begin today, as it is ten days past the due date.

Just like her mother often does, the little one is waiting until the last minute to make an appearance. Over the last two days, though, Nadine finally seems to have gone into what is called the 'early labour' stage, meaning that the Braxton Hicks contractions have evolved into early labour contractions, which are more frequent. We are hopeful that she won't need to go through the whole process of induction, as the body seems to be starting to do it naturally, just at the last possible moment.

It has been an amazing day. Leaving the house for the last time, knowing you will return with a baby, is very strange. Knowing you have an actual date in the diary, at last, when you know (give or take one day) that your child will arrive, has changed things completely from the usual uncertainty.

"I can't believe this is it. We've been leading up to it for all this time, and *it's finally here*," Nadine just said to me. It is surreal.

The surges (a different word for 'contractions', recommended by HypnoBirthing) are becoming more powerful, and Nadine has been visibly uncomfortable with them for the first time in the last hour. We have decided to call them waves now, instead of surges, because I suggested it and Nadine said that's how it feels. Water seems peaceful, and so do waves, although of course they can be extraordinarily strong.

Diary of a Mindful Dad

It is incredible to think about how this whole process unfolds. For Nadine, the labour process started months ago, gradually building over time in frequency and now in power. Of course, this is going to ramp up massively in the next 24 hours, but it is a great example of the formidable intelligence of the body, which is so easy for us all to take for granted.

So the doctor just came in and gave Nadine the 'pessary', which is designed to dilate the cervix, and then she left us. About 15 minutes later, during an episode of *Peaky Blinders*, Nadine really needed the loo, but she wasn't sure if she was allowed to go or not, because the heart monitoring needed to continue for ten more minutes. Yet the problem was that she *really* needed the loo (a number one).

As I walked past the bed, I noticed that Nadine was weeing herself, and she realised at the same time. It was shocking, but also very amusing in the moment: "Can't you just stop weeing yourself?"

"I don't know! I don't think so?"

It was all very strange and jovial.

But it kept going. I quickly went to get the nurse to ask her what she should do. Then she confirmed what Nadine had already begun to suspect.

"Madam, your waters have broken."

No wonder she couldn't stop weeing! It wasn't wee at all.

That was it. We knew that the pessary had done its job and that the real process of labour was beginning. One can never know how long it will take, but the baby is almost always born within 48 hours of the waters breaking. We were so excited!

This is a few hours later, and I just asked Nadine what it feels like. She said, "Imagine someone holding your intestines and squeezing them really hard. Like, if you grab your cheek right now, imagine squeezing it really hard…but on the inside."

I said, "Sounds really nice!"

She laughed and replied, "Yeah, it's lovely!"

We are both so excited and giddy. Nadine is smiling all the time and I find that amazing. It's clear that the 'waves' are becoming much more intense at this point, and I am encouraging her to breathe. She said she needs to save the good tools for as long as she can, but on the very next one I saw her breathing deeply. Things are speeding up now and so I won't be writing any more.

After the last entry, the waves became more intense and frequent, and we kept wondering when we were supposed to go down into the labour room. We are in a hospital in Dubai which is well known for having the most amazing room for a water birth. We chose the hospital specifically because of the magic of this room and the amazing reviews it has had. Naturally, we wanted to go in there as soon as possible. The on-call doctor's reply was "As soon as it becomes painful, madam."

Hilarious. It has been painful for Nadine for a couple of hours! Within half an hour, we assumed that it was painful enough to justify what the doctor meant, and we asked to move.

The waves were very regular by this point; approximately three in ten minutes, which signifies active labour. All of our bags were transported to the labour room, and we walked through the magical doorway.

Everything was very dark, quiet and peaceful. The walls were a deep purple, and there was a laser cosmos shining green stars all around the room. It was such a lovely setting. I had so many things in the hospital bag to set up: the camera (just to get a few nice pictures for us to remember it all by), a Bluetooth speaker, mobile phones, drinks, snacks, a TENS machine (to ease pain during waves), a bowl (for pouring warm water over Nadine's back during waves), massage oils, among other things which I've forgotten. But there was no time for any of it!

Waves were arriving like clockwork, every three minutes, but I was so busy helping Nadine to be calm between them, and to move from one place to another, that it was hard to find time to organise anything. My antics perfectly matched the Benny Hill theme tune which somehow ended up playing during the very first contraction – it really set the tone. Eventually, I had to leave her to herself for one contraction here and there to prepare everything. Then, it was time to put into practice everything we had been learning on the HypnoBirthing course. Nadine had four different places for her waves: standing up and leaning over a table; standing underneath the shower, using the shower head to spray warm water over her tummy and back; on all fours, leaning on the large exercise ball; and leaning over the hospital bed. For the next seven hours, this was our life. Going from contraction to contraction, from one place to another, almost totally in the dark, every three minutes. We were hyper-alert for every single second and it was extraordinary. It felt like we were in a black hole, totally beyond time itself; whenever we discovered the real time in the 'outside world', many hours had vanished without a trace.

We were using a pregnancy sound bath on the speakers, which Nadine said was very helpful. It wasn't annoying her with lyrics, and she said she didn't feel like listening to piano music or anything like that. She just wanted some relaxing, healing background sound. Of course, she didn't actually say that. She yelled, "*No! Not that!*" as I put on the wrong music. Eventually, I worked it out and managed to elicit a loud and reluctant grunt of approval from her that the sound bath was OK.

It was incredibly intense. During every 'wave', I was doing everything I could to help and support as we had discussed. I was coaching her with her breathing by loudly counting as she breathed: four seconds in and eight seconds out. Even this was difficult, because I had to adjust the speed of my counting so that it slowed her down when she was going way too fast, but not so slowly that her breathing was out of sync with it, so she felt she was doing it wrong. As you can see, I was having a really tough time (this is a joke).

I felt most helpful and supportive when I ended up strongly breathing with Nadine for the full counts. This allowed me to synchronise with her energy, and I began to feel much more a part of the process. I could tell from Nadine's behaviour that this change was helpful for her as well. If I could do it all again, I would do only this right from the beginning, alternating with sometimes counting for her instead.

This whole period of time and the power of the process were incredible. I could somehow feel when the waves were coming *in my own body* (resonance?) and we were both prepared, every time, for the whole first seven hours. She was doing such an amazing job at 'coming back down to green' after each one. As we thought it would, this idea allowed her to forget the past, to a certain extent, and bring all her energy to the next wave.

I was always holding onto her, at the top of her hips, and pushing inwards; then, as things became more intense, she told me to push hard on the middle of her lower back instead. I was always with her, for almost every wave, and I could feel that it was psychologically supportive for her. It must be so hard for someone to do this alone.

After seven hours, the doctor came in to check Nadine's progress. She was 3cm dilated before we came down to this room, and we were assuming perhaps an increase of 2–3cm, which would mean perhaps not too many hours left. She hadn't used any pain relief by this point, including gas and air.

The doctor shattered everything: "Still 3cm, ma'am."
What?
Are you joking?

Our energy was destroyed. Seven hours of this madness. For what? Literally nothing. It's called 'inefficient contractions' or 'failure to progress'; terms both of which make women feel really great about themselves during this time, I imagine.

The cervix was still not dilating because the head was still not engaged. If the head had been engaged before labour, we would likely have been almost at the pushing stage by this point.

I had the words of the doctor at the 12-week scan, which had made us laugh so much, ringing in my ears: "Your cervix is verrrrry long!!!" We didn't realise how significant that was going to prove to be.

We didn't know what to do and, at this point, to make it worse, the waves had become way more painful. Everything had transformed. The atmosphere in the room had gone from serene and relatively calm to frenetic, intense and anxious.

I tried to get as much information out of the doctor as possible at this point. She said it could take another 12 hours without any progress, meaning total labour could be up to 24 hours.

Decisions had to be made and I was not prepared for them. After the HypnoBirthing course, we had written our birth preferences, asking the doctors and nurses not to offer the epidural and other pain relief because Nadine wanted to try to have an 'unmedicated birth'. If this is what you want, it must be explicitly requested, because otherwise many people opt for pain relief during the most difficult time (the 'transition'), and afterwards regret having done so, believing that if it had *not been offered to them*, they might have been able to continue without it.

But our situation right now was far more real than anything my paltry knowledge had equipped me for, and I had no idea what to do. At some point, I was going to have to speak properly to Nadine to ask her what she wanted, but the new waves were ridiculously bad. Her pain level had clearly doubled, and each episode was much longer, leaving less time in between. The doctors and nurses all wanted to recommend an epidural, but knew they weren't allowed to because of our stated preferences. The main doctor had a very difficult conversation with me because it was clear that she thought, based on our preferences, that we thought we knew it all. But this couldn't have been further from the truth! We only copied those preferences from someone else doing a course that we trusted.

I urged her to give me as much information as possible about where we were, what she would advise and why. Eventually, within the next 15 minutes, I was able to speak to Nadine and make a call. The pain was ludicrous by this point, and I could see that Nadine was finding it very hard to cope. The waves had been lasting a full five minutes and now she felt like they were not even stopping at all; it was just one big mess of pain.

This totally disrupted our rhythm of breathing and my support for her. My faith in the process was shaken, and so I was a lot less helpful to Nadine at this time, completely preoccupied by what we should do.*

We eventually worked it out, and I got Nadine's consent to go for the epidural. It was horrific to see how difficult it was for her at this point.

Unfortunately, the time from giving the go-ahead for the epidural, to when it was administered, was excruciatingly long – probably an hour. This was the most difficult hour by far, and the pain was close to unbearable for Nadine. It is impossible to describe in words how this time felt for me, let alone for her. We were moved to another room, and the nurse kept

---

* Obviously, we should have been ready for a situation like this. Nadine agrees. She says that she wishes she had known about how differently labour can go depending on one's body, and that there are many cases when it is definitely better to opt for pain relief.

trying to talk to Nadine during the waves, which was incredibly unhelpful.*

At this point, one of the most annoying things happened. The doctor came to administer the epidural and, whilst Nadine was shouting in enormous pain, he calmly stood there with his clipboard and said, "OK, sir, there are a few risks you need to know about before we administer the epidural and you agree."

You're telling me this now?? I couldn't believe it. It was so obvious that there was no way I was going to refuse it, and I didn't understand why this conversation had not happened earlier, when we had checked into the hospital to give birth.

I have forgotten the side effects he mentioned, but they were horrific; I'm pretty sure they included paralysis and death. I was relatively delirious as he was talking about this, and obviously just said, "Yes, let's do it." Throughout all this time, Nadine was having less than 30-second breaks between five-minute contractions.

About 15 minutes later, the needle went in. Nadine actually cried with relief. The ordeal was over – for now. The pain was completely gone. We couldn't believe it, and took a little time just to process it all. We laughed a lot about how wrong the HypnoBirthing course had been for us, in many respects. I guess that's why I just subconsciously went back to using the word 'contractions'?

For the next few hours, we set ourselves up as if we were in a hotel room. The laptop came out and we refreshed ourselves with some comfort food. Nadine was totally fine. It is magical, the power of medicine in such cases. She was hooked up to a machine which allowed us to see that the contractions were still

---

* Looking back, I wish I had had the strength to simply be firm and ask her not to speak to us during those times. The problem was that she had been great for most of the time and so I didn't want to be rude. Curse my English sensibilities!

going on, but she could barely feel anything at all. She said she could feel a slight tightening, but that was it.

We both took this chance to get some sleep, and we napped for about two hours. I had a shower and got some takeaway food. The contrast between this luxury hotel bliss and the manic panic of the time before the epidural was stark. This time allowed Nadine to fully 'get back to green' so that she could be ready for the pushing stage. I didn't realise this, but you can't have total pain relief during the pushing stage, because it makes it too difficult to actually get the baby out.

During this more than welcome interlude, I spent some time making the delivery room feel special, like the room we were in before. After we had woken up from our naps and I had finished my shower, I set up our 'laser cosmos' light display and put the relaxing music on. I had a little meditation. Everything felt different.

We could see the baby's heartbeat being monitored and the contractions being drawn onto a piece of paper, still causing no pain at all. One thing which surprised me about all of this was that the heartbeat remained so steady during each contraction, even the most painful ones before the epidural. How could she just be chilling in there, oblivious to what was going on?!

Then things started to ramp up a bit when Nadine noticed a change. Once she was 8cm dilated, our nurse turned down the epidural slightly and told us that we were approaching the pushing stage. Then she went to get the doctor who had been looking after us throughout the pregnancy process. About five minutes later, she came in with lots of nurses, and they set up all sorts of clever and sharp equipment on various tables. Clearly, it was showtime.

As they discussed what was going to happen, Nadine and I had to choose a hat for the little one to wear once she was born.

This was a beautiful moment and elicited a truly golden smile from Nadine.

The doctor gave Nadine very clear instructions on how to push effectively, and asked me to stand right up by Nadine's head, so I moved away from the 'business end' and took her hand in mine.

Then, it began.

With every push, the doctor was giving Nadine lots of encouragement, which was helping. I was trying my best to join in when it seemed that she needed it, and the notorious hand-squeezing was in full swing. It looked absolutely excruciating and equally exhausting. After each push, Nadine was so tired that it was a huge effort for her just to catch her breath to be ready to try again. It really seemed as though there was no energy left and that giving up was a real possibility. The doctor started to speak with more urgency then, strongly affirming to Nadine that a few more pushes would be enough.

Eventually, I heard her saying that they could see the head and that Nadine had to keep going. The exhaustion had ramped up a level by then, and I could see in her eyes that she wasn't sure if she could.

This was when everything turned. Suddenly, the baby's heart rate dropped significantly during a push, and I could see that the doctor was concerned because she kept looking over at the numbers more frequently. It was bloody terrifying.

She then said to Nadine, with great force, that she had to keep going and get her out in the next few pushes.

"*Baby's heart rate is dropping,*" she warned, so Nadine had to try as hard as she possibly could and "*get angry*". I was urging her on as much as I possibly could. It truly was a matter of life and death, and it bloody felt like it. Adrenaline was at 1,000,000 percent and I was just a semi-innocent bystander.

Then things went from bad to worse, as the doctor came right up to me and gave me some very quick and quiet instructions in my ear:

"When the baby comes out, you cut the cord and then go straight to the doctor with her and I will stay with your wife."

Wtf?!

This knocked me for six. I had no idea what the hell was going on, but I knew something was wrong. During every push, the heart rate was dropping so much and I had no idea why, or how bad it was. All I could see was a huge number suddenly turning into a minuscule one on the screen, over and over again, and then staying low. I kept encouraging Nadine with all that I had, and trying to give her as much energy as possible.

"She has to come in the next two or three pushes," the doctor kept saying, and Nadine could do it.

By this time, I was just about processing the sights and sounds of the myriad objects which were interfering with Nadine. The doctor had tried to take the baby out using one and then had to resort to another, the 'suction cup', so it was clear that nothing was going smoothly, and it was touch and go.

The next push came. By this point, everything was frantic beyond belief. I could see from the behaviour of the doctor and the nurses that they were all concerned, and well and truly at their battle stations. I didn't have time to feel as sick as I feel now, writing this and looking back on it.

Then, it happened. A truly ALMIGHTY push with ALMIGHTY screaming, and *there she was*. The doctor pulled our baby out of Nadine, and I saw her head for the first time.

This was supposed to be perhaps the most 'profound' moment of my life: I've never felt worse.

She looked completely purple and her eyes were fully closed. She looked as lifeless as I can imagine a baby could look. My fears were shown to be justified when the doctor cut the umbilical cord herself, in as much of a hurry as anyone could possibly be, instead of letting me do it *as she had said just minutes before,* and gave her to the nurses who rushed her over to the treatment table in the corner of the room. I was over there in a flash to see what was happening and if everything was OK.

There I was, standing over her as she lay on that table, totally motionless. There were four nurses crowded around the table, and I was trying to squeeze myself in, frantically asking:

"Is she OK? What's going on? Is this normal?"

"No, sir. It's not normal," one of the nurses replied.

I cannot explain how I felt in that moment.

They were covering her with tubes and putting them in her mouth and up her nose, and it was impossibly traumatic to witness.

"We are waiting for her first cry, sir," one of them said.

Those moments lasted a lifetime. She was in such distress, but moving now and clearly alive, struggling to breathe.

Then it came. *A small, miraculous cry.* Because of what they had said, I knew that this was the beginning of the end of the nightmare and the best moment of the whole saga so far. I was so relieved and tears filled my eyes. I turned to Nadine and told her she was OK and found myself saying, *"She's so beautiful. She's so beautiful."*

Nadine was so reassured by the look in my eyes and what I had said that she burst into tears as well, with a huge smile lighting up her face.

But I didn't feel like it was over because our little baby was in so much distress and everything had gone so badly. The nurses were still doing a million things to her, and she did not look at all comfortable breathing.

I kept asking them if she could go and see her mum, and they kept saying, "No, not yet." There was clearly still something wrong. Nadine was so panicked and kept shouting at me to ask what was going on. I still felt absolutely terrified and was so concerned about her.

Eventually, the nurses reluctantly and quickly put the hat on her and agreed to let her go to Nadine, 'just for a minute'. We had read so much about the 'golden hour' (just after birth) and how important it is, for both baby *and* mother, that she can be put on the breast immediately. The nurse brought her over to Nadine, and I was astonished to see her *instinctively* breastfeed. The intelligence of it all completely blew my mind. How the hell does the baby know?!

Then they told Nadine that they had to take the baby away, after just 20 seconds of breastfeeding. They had only given her as a token gesture, so both of them could have that experience for a moment, but she was clearly still in danger. It was a truly heartbreaking moment because she was crying *so loudly* from the moment she was taken away. Nadine was visibly devastated and delirious with worry.

I was told I had to go with them to the intensive care unit (or NICU) immediately, and I did. I kept asking them what on Earth was going on, and now I was able to get some clearer answers. She just needed to be in the NICU on oxygen until she could breathe properly on her own. They were reassuring me that she would be OK and seemed sincere now and more confident. It allayed my fears a little, but not completely. I was in full-on life-or-death mode still, and would be for a while.

I sat there, watching her in that little bed in the NICU, and it was indescribable; the love I had for her was pure concern at that point. The most concern I have ever and possibly will ever feel for any being. I felt completely powerless, but fully present and ready to give her everything.

I placed my hand on her chest and gazed at her, talking to her, consoling her and trying to send her love and reassurance. Staring straight into my eyes, she took my finger in her mouth and immediately began suckling on it, and it melted and broke my heart all at the same time. It was so meaningful to interact with her for the first time, but most of all I just knew that she needed her mother. That was what she needed.

I closed my eyes, praying for her and trying to send her all the love in the world and the strength to breathe properly.

We both began to calm down a little after some time. When I felt I was able to, I quickly left her and ran back to the other room to reassure Nadine. To my dismay, I saw that she had been left on her own! She was so worried. I told her what had happened and that everything was fine, and showed her a picture of our little daughter:

Elfie. Short for Delphine. Born on Father's Day.

We cried together, and she made sure I ran back to Elfie, after a minute or so, to be with her. I set up a Zoom call on Nadine's phone immediately, so that she could video-call us in the NICU, and it was a sorely needed use of technology.

The nurses told me that she was doing well and her breathing was improving. The nightmare was over, thank God! After an hour and a half, she was released from the NICU, and I walked her down the hall in her trolley and presented her to Nadine, capturing the moment on video. It was so magical when she took her in her arms for the first time and began to feed her, gazing down at her dear little face in total amazement. I was unfathomably relieved, so proud of them both, and took an extraordinarily deep breath.

I knew that the ordeal was over, and I was witnessing one of the most profound moments of our lives.

3

The First Six Months

"The little space within the heart is as great as the vast universe."

— Chandogya Upanishad

<u>6 hours later</u>

"God. Having a baby is terrifying!"

This is a direct quote from Nadine, about six hours in. It sums it up well.

We feel very strongly that we should not be left alone with this thing. How can we be??? Is that really how it works? I don't even know what it is! I certainly can't hold it, feed it or do anything else it needs. Why would society leave it with us? It seems horrendously irresponsible. I am also struggling to process the fact that the hospital we are in is just on the side of a main road; nobody driving past has any idea about the madness occurring in this otherworldly realm, where other realms genuinely meet this worldly realm. Thank God for my excellent wife. I am attempting to embrace and be amused by my feelings of inadequacy and insecurity as a dad. *Shit. I'm a dad!*

It's naptime now and my two girls, cuddled up together, look so beautiful. It's an idyllic image and everything feels right. She has had her first sneeze and hiccups, and all of it has been seriously cute. Naturally, at first I thought the hiccups were her not being able to breathe and that she was dying, so that was fun. Understandable, I guess, especially after the start we had.

She has had lots of 'skin-to-skin time' with us both, and she has mainly just been crying because she wants the boob – I don't blame her. It instinctively hurt my feelings that she just wants to be with Mum, but that's an easy one to observe and dismiss. I was warned about this! I suspect it's the first of many such times.

Monday 21st June

As I started to go to sleep last night, my own trauma about the birth came to the surface of my mind. This had happened numerous times throughout the day, and I had been paying attention to it, but when I was in bed, I had a good chance to confront it in more depth. I observed that, as a memory of the ordeal rose up, the mind saw the image and revolted immediately, closing its eye like a vice. When it did so, everything tensed up and the image-making process was distorted, interrupted and then stopped. All of this happens in a split millisecond, and so it probably normally occurs beyond the threshold of consciousness. As the mind's eye closes, shutting the door on the traumatic experience, the 'poison' is buried and its potential fruit lost, as it burrows down into the subconscious.

Years of inner work have shown me how important it is to keep that door open, though, so I consciously went in the opposite direction instead. As I observed the mind, I encouraged the images to continue instead, and allowed my system to feel all that was there to be felt *with full force*. There were so many layers to the experience! It was very difficult, but also very powerful and poignant, to allow the mind, in the end, to return to the present and feel that now everything was OK. Both of my girls were safe and sound. I wonder, does this trauma create a strong bond between parents and children? It certainly feels like it. I can see now why people share their 'negative birth stories'… because it's just *so insane!* How can you not? I also appreciate the amusing irony of me moaning about this phenomenon in the *same book* as sharing our story *in full!* Oops.

This morning, the nurse was visibly shocked at the fact that Elfie was close to getting herself out of her tiny cot, and expressed that this sort of strength was very unusual. I observed some pride rise up within me in response to this early sign of her 'progress', and so did Nadine, and then we both laughed hard at this. How ridiculous.

Then the bad thing happened. The nurse was helping us with various things and Elfie started choking. She couldn't breathe, and Nadine and I went into full life-or-death mode again. That's probably normal. What's not normal, I assume, is the nurse bloody doing it as well. Good lord, that really got to us. She was trying to burp her to stop the madness, and it just wasn't working. Then she sped out of the room when Elfie's face was turning purple, and started calling down the corridor in a panicked voice for help. She had sent us a clear message: PANIC!

This went on for God knows how long (about a million years, if I had to guess) and then eventually she managed to stop it. WOW! That was some serious anxiety for the body and mind. A great workout and a bit more trauma to process later – lovely stuff.

Later, a different nurse came in and told us everything we needed to know to care for the baby during these first few days. I cannot describe how comforting this breath of fresh air was; she seemed like an angel delivering a holy message. She could see how incompetent I felt (and definitely was) and she helped me to burp Elfie properly and hold her, after laughing at the fact that I couldn't do anything at all. Nadine also enjoyed that. I can't believe that before this conversation, I didn't even know how to *hold a baby*. Why have I listened to an audiobook about bloody baby-proofing the home when they are two years old, yet have no idea about how to hold one? Why does Nadine do it all perfectly? How the hell does she know? I'm just trying to push through the tidal waves of my incompetence with a relatively positive attitude.

'Swaddling' is a good example of this – have you ever heard of it? Basically, you wrap the baby up like an adorable little Christmas present in a gigantic, ridiculously comfortable cloth prison so they can't do anything at all. Perhaps surprisingly, achieving this is no mean feat, though; the cloth is *enormous*! Even armed with the multitude of amusing diagrams in the book of babies chuckling at their parents whilst they try to incapacitate them, I still failed repeatedly, each time met with the unmistakable feeling of silent mockery emanating from my unparcelable parcel.

We tried the '5 S's' in combination – a recipe devised by Harvey Karp in *Baby Bliss*[12] – to get her to sleep: shh, side position, swaddle, sway and suck. But she just wanted the amazing boobs again – who can blame her?

Six hours ago it completely switched from – *Oh my god! What even is she? Is she going to make it?* – to her now being a standard part of life as we know it. This is so odd, and I'm surprised that I noticed this shift. At almost exactly 24 hours old, every perspective from before is lost and you suddenly *know her*!

Tuesday 22nd June

Can I discuss this birth trauma with friends? Can men be emotional with one another? I hope so. I'm continuing to allow the ordeal to play through, and it's orbiting my centre of consciousness a bit less frequently now. Maybe every hour or so it peeks its head back in to say hello, and I'm a little more welcoming each time.

Today we had several appointments to attend, and it was a bit nerve-wracking inwardly in every room we entered. *Does this thing we've created have a properly working body?* They checked Elfie's ears, which were fine, but then they did a heart scan, which revealed that she has a 'heart murmur'. What the hell is that? It sounds terrible, just not the kind of thing I want anyone's heart to be doing. I'd rather it was just magically, silently going about its business – not murmuring. They said it's no cause for alarm at this stage, as it usually goes away quite quickly. Ohhhh, I see, it's just another dose of fear. Got it.

Of course, we were concerned about it, and Dr Google helped us to allay our fears. Hahaha. Good one.

Lastly, she had to do a test for jaundice, something I have never heard of. It's really weird to wheel her around the hospital in the pram as if the whole thing is somehow *normal*. A few hours after this, we were given permission to go home, which was also surreal and *totally mad*. I took a picture of her in her seat, and she did a 'force push' right out of *Star Wars* at the perfect moment, already dreaming of bending the rules of this realm, two days in.

That's my girl.

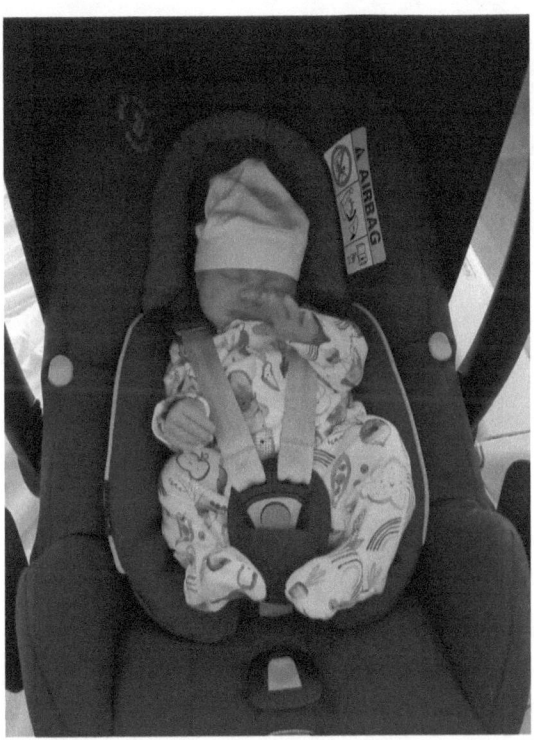

Our friends were in the house to greet us, and they had prepared a truly beautiful welcome. There were balloons, ribbons and enormous smiles aplenty. I popped Elfie on the floor in her carrier, just for a minute, and the cats came to investigate her. The very first time she saw any animal except a human being was her big, lovable new feline brother, Aragorn. He sniffed her for a very long while.

Wednesday 23rd June

We have suddenly realised, waking up in the house in the morning to quite a few unsettling coughs and sneezes, that it's possible she might be *allergic to cats*.

Shit.

Shit, shit, shit.

What if she is? Fear loves that, doesn't it, 'what if?' I've never really considered it before; I'm such an optimist that I've just assumed that the world would never be so cruel.

Knock, knock, says fear.

But what if?

Oh my God. *What if?* It would cause unspeakable problems. We would have to rehome all of our pets (who are our family), and there are a lot of them. That would be devastating and really doesn't bear thinking about. What would we even do right now, for the next few weeks, if the doctor told us she can't stay at the house until the pets are gone? I have absolutely no clue! Should we even tell the doctor the truth? It has really shaken Nadine up as well.

Nadine would have to look after Elfie alone whilst I somehow rehomed all the animals. It all fills me with a powerful sense of dread.

No. It won't be like that. Have faith. I remind myself. *It's just a test. A poke, a prod.*

But every time I look at her, she is coughing. Again, again, and again. Sneezing again, again and again. *Google! Help! How often should a newborn cough? How often should a newborn sneeze?*

Totally useless, as always. How can Google not answer something like that? It can tell me exactly how many results there are, up into the hundreds of millions, but it can't give me a decent answer in just one of them? Are there loads of amazing websites hiding on page 34,787 which none of us ever click on? It's so frustrating and seems to be just one more manifestation of a cosmic law:

New parents NEED TO WORRY. A LOT.

There are no shortcuts.

It's constant, the coughing and spluttering, and it sounds and looks exactly like the kind of coughing and spluttering beings might do if there were too much cat hair in their immediate environment.

So we drove to the hospital to get the jaundice results and discuss them with the doctor, and tried to decide whether or not to tell the truth about how many pets we have at home.

We were tempted to lie, but we decided against it. Thankfully, the doctor said it "shouldn't be an issue" and didn't ask us how many we had! He didn't answer with any clarity how much they should cough and splutter, and he didn't know what was causing it, and so we were still left wondering, worrying. As you can see, it was not a very insightful appointment, but sometimes just having the man in a white coat chuckling nonchalantly at your situation and emotional state goes a long way.

The next appointment revealed that the jaundice results had come back and they weren't great; in fact, they meant that she needed to stay in the hospital for another 72 hours in some sort of weird incubator, under a weird light, wearing weird glasses. We were naturally upset about this and, of course, very worried as well. We had made quite specific plans (fools!) for this time, and our friends who had been looking after our pets at home would now have to come back to the house for another few days.

The disruption of this in itself is unsettling, but of course the worst bit is worrying about her health. What even is jaundice, and how bad is it? We eventually managed to track down the doctor, and she said to us, off the record, that it is definitely not a problem at all, and she would stake her job on the fact that she will be completely fine.

Wow. That's word for word *exactly* what you *always* want the doctor to say! I wish they did that more often! I thought it was quite brave of her, but clearly this issue must happen in newborns all the time.

Whilst Nadine has been in hospital with Elfie, I've taken action. 'Throw money at it' was my decision. I organised a full steam clean of the entire house and bought two expensive air purifiers, one for the bedroom and one for the living room. We have three days to sort this out and try again, but the waves of anxiety were still there, reminding me of the horrible possibility of a serious cat allergy.

Reset, refresh, breathe.

I went home to supervise the steam clean, leaving Nadine and Delphine at the hospital. Nadine was in full control and the two of them were getting on like a house on fire.

I had a nice shower at home, which helped me to reset, but the cat-astrophising (get it?) and storying were still going on with a fair amount of intensity.

Then, when I arrived back at the hospital, something wonderful happened. A monumental epiphany:

I am not in control of her health.

This insight hit me like a ton of bricks.

That may sound strange, and untrue at first glance. Yes, we need to feed her, help her to sleep the right amount, and so on. Some things are in our control, and they *are* our responsibility. If she is allergic to cats, it will be our responsibility to respond to that. But, ultimately, whether or not her body can *actually do the things it is supposed to do* is not up to me. The anxiety I was experiencing wasn't just about the cats or the jaundice. It was about *her. Her life.*

I surrendered totally.

But not on purpose; it just happened. In that moment, I could see what I had been doing, why the anxiety had continued in the way that it had.

I was fighting.

I was trying to fight the *reality* of whatever her health situation was. I was trying to *control her health.*

I could see, in an instant, that whether or not she was going to 'be OK' – today, tomorrow or at any point in the future – was, to a huge extent, out of my control. Most importantly, I had perceived, in that moment, exactly where that line was.

This insight blasted the anxiety into smithereens and transformed all the energy up several octaves. Suddenly, as always after a shift in perspective, everything was different. I was no longer living within the illusion of control, and I was able to feel my natural faith in whatever the future might hold. This stance was the natural result of the insight and totally different from contrived 'positive thinking'.

I was reminded, again, that surrender – *real surrender* – is not intellectual, and it is not something which can be brought about on purpose. Surrendering to fear means really feeling it and somehow perceiving the *totality of it*; if we can really do this, we are *out of it*. We can't see *all* of something *unless* we're out of it. But thought can never see the whole. Thought sees in straight lies, not circles. That's the best typo I've ever done, probably, so I'm keeping it in. Straight lies, straight lines, same difference. They *are lies*. What can bring about this total seeing is very mysterious, and I like the word 'grace' having something to do with it.

What I've described above is sometimes referred to as 'acceptance', and it's so powerful because it's not what we normally do. It goes against our instinct, which is to fight, to control, to change. That's what I was trying to do with her health. But we *don't realise that we are doing this*; it all takes place in our blind spot, beyond the threshold of consciousness, as you can see in this example for me today.

I spoke to my mum about this, because she worries about me and my brothers a lot, and had already been anxious about Elfie before she was even born. To be fair to her, she had four children, and my birth, in particular, was incredibly traumatic for us both. She had a full-blown NDE – near-death experience – before 'dragging herself back to Earth', and I almost died and didn't see her for the first ten days of my life because I was in another hospital in an incubator. Definitely no 'golden hour' for me! I guess, then, her fear is very much understandable. Yet she had definitely fallen into this most formidable trap, which I felt so fortunate to have (at least partially, for now) stepped out of. She said that perhaps this insight is exactly what she needed, and that if she had been granted it many years ago, she might have experienced far less anxiety in her life.

You might think that lots of what I did makes sense; for example, maybe I needed to get the house cleaned, and that is perfectly reasonable. But a huge chunk of the *anxiety* came from my distorted understanding of what I could control in the situation.

How often are we doing this? Fighting what can't be fought? Trying to control the uncontrollable? It is just so hard to catch the mind in the act when it plays these powerful tricks.

Now that the birth is done, we can see the HypnoBirthing course in a new light. One of Nadine's conclusions is this: "The affirmations simply aren't true!"

Ah, that's a bit of an issue. Thoughts such as 'I can have an amazing birth' turned out to simply not be true for Nadine. The problem is that Nadine's pelvic shape was *always* going to make birth extremely difficult for her – more difficult than normal, that is!

The nurse told me that only a few decades ago, both Nadine and Delphine would have died during the ordeal – Nadine from two separate events, so twice! So it's simply not right to make everyone believe they can have an amazing birth, and this has irked Nadine quite a lot. She did such a good job at convincing herself and now feels like she was lied to.

BUT! And it's a big but. We cannot, and must not, underestimate the power that this positivity had on the journey leading up to the birth. Nadine was not worried *at all*! She was excited! Even the day before the induction, when we were mall-walking and one of our friends came with us, she was astonished at Nadine's attitude; all smiles and not a care in the world. Her affirmations had given her an incredibly positive attitude – the placebo effect at its finest. Isn't this worth something? I think, in our case, it was worth quite a lot. Nadine was always going to have a difficult birth because of her body shape, but the HypnoBirthing took away any potential anxiety before, which is for *months*. She fell for it hook, line and sinker, and so did I, but I'm glad we did!

Thursday 24th June

The first few days with Elfie, and barely any sleep, have been managed by adrenaline. Of course, it has been an absolute whirlwind. Sleep is so strange; we've had such a small amount that it has ended up almost not seeming to matter. Everything just blurs

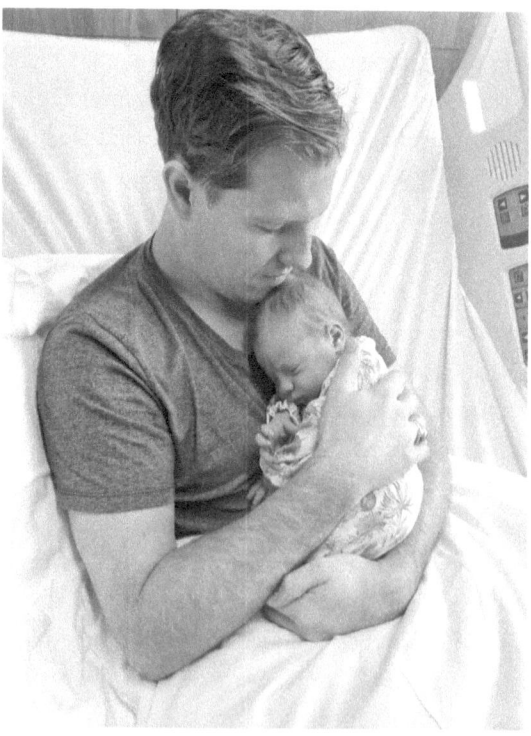

into one, and you're trying just to keep everyone alive and ticking over. Learning on the job. Get her fed, try to stop her crying, and help to keep her asleep for as long as she wants or needs. Then, and only then, consider attending to your own needs.

One high point is the fact that the best thing ever in the world is your baby cuddling into you and sleeping on your chest. I just had one of these precious cuddles, for about an hour, and it made me feel a love the likes of which I have never felt before.

The jaundice treatment has finished now and it was very odd. She was in an incubator in the room with us with these seriously cool sunglasses on, which made her look just like a cute little Darth Vader. The light was so bright in there and she handled it like a pro. We thought she was going to be crying endlessly, desperate to get out, but it was just like she was sunbathing the whole time. Maybe she will be well suited to the Dubai weather! Now that's done, we're allowed to go home this evening. Properly, this time!

Friday 25th June

Have you ever shat yourself? I have a vague, partially repressed memory of maybe doing so once, and it being regrettable in the utmost. Can you imagine doing that every single day? Not only that, what about pissing yourself? Imagine shitting and pissing inside your clothes every…single…day. You won't imagine it, will you? You don't want to. *Exactly*.

Is that really the best we can do for these babies? It surprises me that nobody has come up with anything better. I asked Nadine this morning (mostly in jest, but not completely) if we can just sit Elfie on the toilet a few times throughout the day and hope she does a poo, before realising how foolish this was. But is there nothing better?

Luckily for Elfie, today she was able to swap the discomfort and indignation of pooing herself for the majestic excitement of shooting her product in the direction of her primary caregiver, Nadine.

It was a filthy fountain, a glorious gunshot which flew out of the changing table and all over the floor. Nadine just laughed a lot; what more could she do? I was lucky to escape this time, but I know she has her eye on me and I could be in the firing line at any moment. I have to have my wits about me.

Saturday 26th June

It's been so delightful to be at home with Elfie, and we're trying to embrace the chaotic, unknown elements of the adventure as well as all the cuteness. I'm doing my best to support Nadine, and constantly marvelling at how naturally motherhood comes to her. They are inseparable, and it already feels as if Elfie has *always* been with us. I'm taking the lead with most things at home, naturally, and doing my best with my share of the parenting.

Sunday 27th June

This book is a testament to the fact that I am no stranger to oversharing. In the past, this has sometimes got me into trouble. But it has also allowed me to ensure that I share things which *should be shared* and which others perhaps might not. For example, Nadine told me this morning, when I woke up, that I had slept right through the night. I was shocked by this, as we had two alarms and I was supposed to be helping her with one of the night-time feeds and nappy changes.

I felt guilty because I could see that Nadine was more tired than I was, and it didn't seem fair. After I came out of the shower, I told her that I felt guilty about leaving her to do everything for the whole night, and asked her what we should do about it. I asked her if she was bothered by it, and she said she honestly wasn't. But after more discussion, we agreed that I should do the second night-time feed (approx. 5:30) with a bottle of milk she has expressed.

Maybe if I hadn't noticed my guilt and brought it out into the open, we wouldn't have had such a productive discussion; maybe instead it would have festered and turned into resentment on Nadine's part, causing more explosive trouble down the line. This is why I always try to acknowledge my emotions and share them with her, so she knows where I'm at. Yes, this can be annoying at times, but I think it has saved us heaps of arguments over time.

Monday 28th June

One week in, and Harvey Karp's get-your-baby-to-sleep hack – the 5 S's – has been invaluable many times. This morning, his magic came to the rescue yet again, when Elfie was lying on my chest for a cuddle and began to wail loudly. I gave her the dummy (S #1), but it didn't work. I spoke to her and tried to entertain her for a little, but no dice. This lasted probably three minutes or so (or 20 seconds which *felt like* three minutes), but she had only had a feed quite recently, so I wanted to try to calm her down myself without resorting straight away to another feed.

OK, the other S's – let's go. I somehow managed to swaddle her, surprising both of us no end. Then I went to the rocking chair, started swaying and then shushed loudly in her ear (louder than the crying, as he specified) and she stopped. Then she went straight to sleep with the dummy in her mouth, just like that. I woke her up a little later to bottle-feed her, and she wolfed it straight down. Thank you, Mr Karp!

Tuesday 29th June

Just a minute ago, Nadine enjoyed the sight of my head slowly drooping towards my chest before suddenly jerking back up in shock. Then again, and again, and again. I can see why, to the untrained eye, this may not look like meditation.

Does this sound familiar?

If you've tried meditation on your own and don't love it, chances are you've experienced something a bit like this. Or, if not this, then perhaps the good-old-fashioned 'watching my mind think about a million things and nothing else happens'. Not very satisfying, is it? So what is everyone on about?

Really, all of this is just preparation for meditation. Before we can taste the miraculous wonders it has to offer, we have to go through a few of these weird layers. It's not normal, in our society, to stay awake with your eyes closed, so we should expect a few roadblocks.

For me, I always have a good little head-bobbing session when I've had an extended period without meditating properly. When I combine this time off with less than six hours of sleep, it's usually almost inevitable.

Meditation is so powerful, though, that even after one of these 'fails' of a session, we can still find some of the deeper energy.

After one or two of these, I'll be right back into it, and my mind will remember how to weave its way through the dancing clouds of thought and dream to find that still centre of deep and profound rest, which so easily and naturally purifies the mind and heart. When my routine is in place, this happens quickly and dependably and dramatically improves every aspect of my life.

Wednesday 30th June

Elfie just wants to be on Nadine's breast at all times at the moment, and I'm wondering if it is driving her nuts or if she is enjoying it. It must be this sort of thing which can dramatically affect the wellbeing of new mothers, so I want to make sure I check in on her regularly to see if she is handling it OK. We've just managed to get Elfie off to sleep at last, so now Nadine can finally have the shower she has been craving for a long while.

I know there's not much I can do to ease her burden here, but I can at least try to make sure I keep the house clean and tidy, and offer her food and drink when she is nursing. I've also been making conscious efforts to remind and encourage her to have her own time as soon as the opportunities present themselves, assuring her that I can look after Elfie, even if she wakes up and cries a lot. I hope that level of support is helpful, and I can understand how it could be so draining and difficult for someone to do this all on their own.

Thursday 1st July

One of the difficult things for me about writing this book is the fact that most of the things I do because of my meditation and mindfulness practice are subconscious; I don't know I'm doing them. Yet, as I write, I am noticing them more and more. For example, last night we changed Elfie's nappy. Everything was going swimmingly (excuse the pun).

We had done our routine perfectly, and she was so sleepy as she started her last feed of the day. Then, obviously, she did another poo *immediately*. Nadine and I looked at each other and laughed out loud. It was actually a wonderful moment. I realised then how nice it was to see the event in that way, and how differently we could have responded, and then I remembered that we have consciously learned to do that together over the last few years.

Having so many pets to look after means that we have dealt with a lot of stress since moving to Dubai; sometimes the situation has been absurd in terms of difficulty. I don't know when it happened, but I started doing a fake laugh really loudly when something very annoying happened, and Nadine started doing it back. It totally changed the vibration of the situation and we haven't looked back. Now that I think about it, this idea has spread into other areas. For example, emptying the cat-litter trays is a shit job (don't excuse that pun, enjoy it). Throughout both pregnancies, I have had to do it every time, and it takes ages. So I started talking about it as though it were an absolute treat and my favourite part of the day. We frequently have exchanges such as:

"Oh my God, do you know what I forgot?"

"What?"

"I get to do the cat-litter trays later."

"You are so lucky. I wish I could."

Ridiculous? Yep. Cringeworthy? Very. Helpful? Definitely.

This all points to an energy of enjoyment and getting on with it, which we've used to turn so many difficult situations into a laugh. Neither of us wants to be stressed and grumpy about things. When things are hard, we often take the piss out of each other as well and, when Nadine does this to me, it's so annoying, but it destroys the grump very quickly. She will see that I've gone into a grumpy mood and say with an infuriating level of satisfaction and enjoyment, "*Oooo…Is someone having a gruuuump??*"

In that moment, grumpiness just wants to be justified so that it can be fuelled and continue, but the whole thing is so disarming and funny that I have no choice but to drop it eventually, after the grump tries very hard to keep me frowning. Sometimes I have to hide my face because I don't want her to notice in that moment that I'm laughing, because I'm supposed to be pissed off. Grumpiness wants to be taken seriously, so undermining it completely *really works*, but often you need someone else to do it for you!

Diary of a Mindful Dad

Thursday 8th July

I had a terrible night's sleep last night. All I can remember is yelling and wailing the whole night (Elfie, not me, I think).

But that's the thing about memory – it can be deceptive. It turns out I slept 'like a baby' for about seven hours (if only that's how babies actually slept!). I only have this perception of last night because *my memories are all from when I was awake*. Yes, every time I woke up, it was because of the baby crying, but apparently I swiftly went back to sleep whilst Nadine did her motherly duties. Sleep is oh so confusing.

The First Six Months

Friday 9th July

I've had such a beautiful morning with my daughter, the nicest bonding time we have had so far in her tiny little life. The difficulties of caring for her, like changing nappies and stopping her crying, seemed to be perfectly balanced this morning with the joy of interacting with her. Each time I had to expend energy to make her OK, it was as if she was somehow giving me a little burst of love back. I hope this lasts!

About half an hour ago, I was holding Elfie and rocking her whilst Nadine got herself ready for bed, when I noticed that she was rushing. Every movement was fervent and a little frantic because she knew that Elfie wanted to be fed. It's so easy to get caught up in this, and we both have hundreds of times, but this time I noticed. I got Nadine's attention and encouraged her to slow down and enjoy her night-time routine. She knew I was right and noticed herself. I assured her that I was looking after the baby whilst she got ready, and it didn't matter how long she took. She was really pleased by this and visibly relaxed her body and mind.

I want to remember to do this as often as possible, because it's such an important reminder for both of us. It's far too easy to rush in this world!

Saturday 10th July

Postpartum depression (PPD) refers to the depression which can afflict new mothers after giving birth. It can be extremely debilitating, and just knowing it exists is a prominent factor in my desire to support Nadine as much as possible. My father's aunt was institutionalised in a psychiatric hospital because her PPD was so extreme, and people did not understand what was happening in those days in the way we do now. Of course, so much of the reason for this difficult phenomenon relates to the tumultuous changes in a woman's body during pregnancy, birth and the aftermath.

However, I read two surprising BBC articles recently which exposed and explored the extent to which men can be psychologically affected by the whole process, though this is (somewhat justifiably) not usually discussed. One explored the hormonal shifts which men also experience after the birth of a child,[13] and the other discussed male postnatal depression specifically.[14] Is it that surprising? There are so many consequences of becoming a parent which are equally difficult for both parties.

New parents both face immense psychological challenges in dealing with their new lives; *who we are* seems to shift. We must let go of our previous identity and move into a new phase. It is difficult to overstate the significance of this; it is a *death*, and it must be honoured and navigated with respect and care for oneself and one's partner. Your life is suddenly not about *you* anymore; in a world like ours, so full of self-aggrandisement, how significant is that?! Add to this the extreme stress of raising a baby, and throw quite a bit of sleep deprivation in there as well – how could anyone not have a hard time?

I've been trying to pay attention to Nadine as much as possible and to look after her as well as I can, and I hope this will help reduce her chances of developing PPD during this time.

Firstly, I want her to know that I'm here to help her as much as possible. It's lucky for us that I'm taking quite a long time off work, relatively speaking. This should be helpful for her in many different ways. This shows her that she doesn't have to carry this burden alone, and this can hopefully bring a foundation of psychological security.

I'm also doing my best to ensure that Nadine won't have to return to work for as long as possible, and I am reminding her of this when things are hard. This is the job she has at the moment, and I don't want her to have to worry about anything else, if we can help it.

I think that truly feeling supported and loved is the most powerful possible remedy for something like PPD. Paraphrasing the cliché, *love* is the greatest healer; *time* comes in a close second. Of course, the huge hormonal changes mean that there will be inevitable and unpredictable storms, but this sort of love and care becomes a safe harbour that we can always return to. I think that it must be consciously voiced regularly, though, to ensure that it plays an explicit role during difficult times like this, and this is what I have been attempting to do. Nadine agrees that this is all vital for both of us to feel safe and secure, and therefore free to face the many difficulties this adventure brings.

Sunday 11th July

This morning, I noticed that Nadine was unhappy about some stretch marks which appeared during the last week of pregnancy, and it made me feel unhappy too that it was bothering her. We talked about it, and ended up on the topics of self-love and self-care. We agreed to spend more time massaging and giving thanks for Nadine's body and the miracle it has been a part of. How much of an impact could this have?

The philosopher P D Ouspensky, during one of his experiments using psychoactive substances under controlled conditions, perceived that:

> "(My body) all became alive, became thinking and conscious. I could speak to any part of my body as if it was a separate being, and could learn from it what attracted it, what it liked, what it disliked, what it was afraid of, what it lived by, what were its interests and needs."[15]

If this is possible, it is truly revealing and helps us to understand the mind–body connection, which is becoming more widely investigated and understood in recent years. I applied Ouspensky's insight to a long-term shoulder injury I was suffering from, with a visualisation meditation, and was able to transform pain I had been suffering from for two years, and I have experienced many more examples of this since.

Could this just be the placebo effect? Of course! Does it matter? Not really, if it works either way, but I don't see any reason to dismiss the possibility that energy really can be purposefully sent, received and make an actual difference.

If that is possible, could Nadine giving conscious and purposeful thanks and love to her body make a difference in this case too? It may not *remove* the stretch marks, or even change the physical aspect at all (though I must admit to being open to that possibility), but bringing conscious love into the equation might transform the *inner landscape* of it, which is likely more powerful than any physical change.

Monday 12th July

A couple of years ago, I was one of the teachers taking kids on a school trip camping for a couple of nights. The World Cup was on, and the previous night I'd been drinking with friends and watching England win the quarter finals on penalties. Naturally, I was a bit hungover.

It was my responsibility to look after the children on one coach, and the truth is I was feeling pretty sick. Then I discovered to my dismay that the bus had no sick bags (it's one of the things you need to check for as a teacher). I called the Head of Year and she said the only option was to just hope nobody was sick. *Great*, I thought. *It might be me!*

An hour into the journey, disaster struck. The children yelled and yelped excitedly and dramatically, in that way children only do when something terrible is happening, *but not to them*:

"He's been sick!!! He's been sick!!!"

Their wails rang out and reverberated around the ill-fated coach. Thankfully, their cries weren't directed at me, but my heart sank nonetheless. *Typical. The bus without the sick bags gets the chunderer.* I wandered over to the child in question, like a dead man walking, and was greeted by an incredibly memorable quote, accompanied by a guilty and terribly ashamed facial expression:

"It's OK, sir – *I drank it already.*"

I was almost sick on the spot upon hearing this, but thankfully I held firm and didn't need to drink any myself.

I was reminded of this tale by Elfie's 'reflux' (milk being brought up from the stomach), which is happening during and after almost every feed at the moment. If we keep the dummy in her mouth, then when she brings some of the feed back up, she imitates the wonderful child on the bus. Great little tip there!

Tuesday 13th July

I can understand now how people experience tremendous difficulty in their relationships whilst taking care of a young baby, but we have been very lucky in this respect so far; the truth is that we have barely had a cross word. Reflecting on it, I think this might be partly because of how we have come to support one another during our time together.

For example, we have developed an understanding that we both do what we can to make our lives harmonious and that, if our difficulties are unevenly split, this is not fair. It seems quite simple, but I have seen many relationships where this crucial foundation is not quite there and it can easily start to breed resentment.

I wouldn't feel right if I believed that Nadine has a harder and less enjoyable life than I do, if there was something I could do about it, and I know she feels the same. This shared understanding has helped both of us numerous times every day of this parenting journey so far. During the night, Nadine has to work harder than I do, because she is breastfeeding, so I feel like I'm 'getting away with it' a bit; however, because of this, I'm trying my best to make up for that when I can.

I had a dream last night that I was standing on the edge of a cliff and I could see something falling down and out of sight. As I focused in on it, I eventually discerned what it was: our sex life.

Only kidding – it wasn't a dream. Definitely, definitely real.

Nadine doesn't feel at all sexual at this time, unsurprisingly. Her body is still recovering from the ordeal of childbirth, and she is almost constantly breastfeeding. Obviously, I won't expect any such antics until everything has calmed down significantly.

Wednesday 14th July

I'm cracking up as I write this because Nadine has just been pranked by the universe in the most hilarious and predictable way, and I'm making sure we have a laugh about it.

The house has been neglected to such an extent that we hired a cleaner for the day to come and bring some well-needed order.

About an hour into her shift, I was in the shower when I heard Elfie crying quite strongly. This happens relatively often (at least once per day), and it takes Nadine some time to get her to feed properly. This was the worst I had heard so far, though, and it was going on for ages. It's always very triggering to hear her crying like that, but I knew Nadine would get her to calm down eventually. Then, suddenly, I heard the cleaner talking to Nadine.

What's happening? Why is she in the bedroom now? I thought. Nadine doesn't need any help, and she certainly doesn't want to be speaking to anyone except me whilst she is away in her bedroom, trying to breastfeed and calm a screaming baby; it's hardly the easiest situation.

The First Six Months

This was a recipe for disaster, and I chuckled to myself in the shower when I could hear them talking; I was desperate to hear what was being said. I hoped she was forcefully giving Nadine advice, because that was the funniest possibility. I know that sounds mean, but I knew that Nadine would see the funny side quickly afterwards, as she always does.

My dreams all came true. It turns out this is what had happened:

She came into the room whilst Nadine had both breasts out and was trying to calm and feed. Trigger 1.

Then she came right up next to the bed and brandished her phone, trying to force Nadine to watch a video which would stop the baby crying. Trigger 2.

Then she tried to demand that Nadine give the baby to *her* so that *she* could take over! Trigger 3.

Then she stayed right there, watching and waiting for the crying to stop, for at least five minutes. Trigger 4.

Nadine managed to stay relatively calm, but she admits to being so wound up that she couldn't even look the kind-hearted lady in the eyes. She just needed to be left alone, but the exact opposite was happening.

I was so amused by the whole story and asked Nadine if she was capable of "transmuting this into love and forgiveness; after all, she was only trying to help on account of her maternal instincts".

"Not right now!" she justifiably responded. She knew I was winding her up, despite this being obviously true!

We can all get on each other's nerves, even with good intentions, and we have encountered this lesson more than usual since having a baby. I remember when we first came back from the hospital, the same thing happened. Elfie was crying in my arms for the first time since she had been in our house, and I received a bombardment of frantic advice, both on how to calm her and on how to remain calm myself, from our two dear friends. I didn't need it! I wanted to be present and attentive myself and find my own way; the advice came so quickly that I hadn't even had a chance to try to calm her or get to grips with the situation. It was really frustrating, and I needed to make an effort to remember that they were only trying to help.

The sound of a baby crying is incredibly alarming and emotive – I get it. But these examples are telling and point to something deeper which ought to be attended to by us all. Do we really know the impact we are having on others?

I remember a little experiment I did when I was about 18 years old, after imbibing some of the teachings of George Gurdjieff. The premise was this:

You don't know how others perceive you. If you think you do, you are deluding yourself. Take some time to observe how people react to you.

So I did. I went to the pub on a Friday night, which had become a routine with the same group of friends. This time, though, I paid close attention to how people seemed to feel about me and react to the way I behaved – the energy I gave out. It was strangely jarring and extremely eye-opening. Simply paying conscious attention allowed me to bypass my distorted assumptions and see what was really there, and then I felt the dissonance between my delusion and the reality. I don't know exactly what I saw, and it doesn't really matter; it wasn't *negative per se*; *just different*. This demonstrated to me the power that the mind has to show us what we *want to see*, instead of what is *actually there*, which is one of the keys to 'waking up'!

We need to be aware of our own actions and the way they are affecting others, but this is hard. It takes conscious effort and an understanding of how our natural inclinations can sometimes cause harm or conflict. The desire to advise or help is so natural for all of us, and is surely a benevolent impulse. We see a problem and we believe we can solve it. So we jump right in before considering the situation beyond that point.

I had better go. The cleaner is about to come downstairs; maybe she will ask Nadine if she has checked her nappy yet. I love it! Poor Nadine, being married to me.

The First Six Months

<u>Thursday 15th July</u>

Elfie has just made her first ever seemingly volitional sound – a 'coo'. Suddenly, that thing we have spent so much time with has given us something back, *on purpose*, and made a *conscious effort* to connect with us. It was an incredible moment, and it felt somehow as if I were meeting her for the very first time; who she *really* is, not just her body with all its various functions.

Just to paint a quick picture, a day in her life at the moment looks a bit like this:

- Wake up
- Drink boob
- Nappy change, sleep in arms
- Stir, stretch, coo, cuddle and other cute things
- Get carried around
- More boob
- Survey the world, decide it's not worth it, go back to sleep
- Photograph taken relentlessly
- More nappy changes, each more perilous than the last
- More sleep
- More boob
- Bath time
- Bed
- Repeat

<u>Friday 16th July</u>

This morning Nadine woke me up to ask me to change the nappy. It doesn't matter how reasonable this is, when you are fast asleep it doesn't sound like the most fun. My sleeping self was devastated. Nevertheless, I got straight up and did my duty; it was a fairly standard procedure in the end.

Turns out, no – it wasn't standard at all.

"Dom?"

I opened my eyes again.

"Are you going to do it?"

What the hell did she mean? I had literally just done it.

No, I hadn't. I had gone immediately back to sleep and *dreamt of changing a nappy*.

Dear oh dear. How did it come to this? I absorbed the awful realisation that I had not done the deed in the realm where it counted most, and reluctantly dragged myself to do it, AGAIN.

My day went from bad to worse when the universe decided to prank me with a hilarious thought:

God, she's been so good the past week that I have nothing to put in this book!

Pretty obvious what happened next, but I'm not sure I deserved it.

Of course, after this thought, Elfie decided to turn it up a notch and have the worst day she has had in her little life so far. Everything that could have gone wrong, it seemed, did. She was constantly unsettled and crying, and every moment of peace we thought we would have was taken away from us, immediately, for some unforeseen reason. As usual, the mind wonders if this is just 'what she is like now', and we try to reset and refresh.

Saturday 17th July

Welcome to the beginning of 'Leap 1'.*

This message comes to you from my prison cell: the rocking chair. I am staring longingly out of the window at the clear, cloudless sky and the lush, green trees in the garden, totally unable to move. So near, yet so far. The curtains are only open a crack, for fear that I may awaken the sleeping beast.

---

* A 'leap' is the term given to significant periods of development for babies, which can dramatically alter their mood and behaviour.

The First Six Months

Yes, Princess Jasmine has become Genghis Khan. The only way for Nadine to get a decent sleep is if I do a shift from 6 o'clock in the morning, sitting here on guard whilst Elfie sleeps on her chest. SIDS (Sudden Infant Death Syndrome) is apparently a very real threat at this stage, so sleeping with your baby on your chest in bed, something which seemed fine to our forebears, is now off the table.

This means I have to remain in my cell, checking every few minutes that Elfie's nose and mouth are not buried into a cushion or duvet or part of Nadine's body. But this is the good part; I can sit here reading and writing and entertaining myself. It's the rest of the day which is the issue.

We are well and truly at her mercy. There is no telling when we will get our orders, or how loudly and shockingly they will be given to us.

Smiles have been replaced by screams and the 'babymoon' is *over*.

So this is what all the fuss was about.

Psychological fatigue is an important and interesting phenomenon which has taken centre stage for us new parents, especially during a so-called 'leap'. The phrase 'it's just one thing after another' kind of sums it up. We can have a 'stressful day', even though the day is made up of individual events which are unrelated.

Our mental and emotional reserves are used up dealing with difficult challenges, and then we are less able to handle something which comes along later.

Yet memory and thought play such important roles in this process, and it is certainly possible to take some of the power back.

Think about it like this: it's not 'one thing after another'.

It's *just…one…thing*.

Grouping together all the things which have annoyed you that day is incredibly counterproductive when it comes to facing what is here now, which is just one thing.

That's all you have to deal with, as well as you can: *one event*.

Is this a language trick? Yes and no. If you have ten things in the space of an hour, all unrelated, all stressful, yes you can say it has been a stressful hour and be talking sense.

But at the same time, it is the *mind* which groups the events together, relating them in time and allowing this grouping to add an *extra layer of stress*, the 'second arrow' of Buddhism. It is so easy to underestimate how much of an impact this has on our lives.

Have you ever had a 'bad year'? What about an 'awful holiday/birthday/other supposed-to-be-relaxing event or period' where 'everything just went wrong'? Of course, because this is one of the many games the mind plays. During each of those examples, there were aspects which could have been enjoyed and seen in a positive light and focused on to bring the scales back into balance, but we would rather enjoy the drama – gluttons for punishment and sympathy that we are.

Understanding that each challenge, each moment, is unique and *here now* helps us to focus and give it all of our attention.

The key is being watchful of the mind, and noticing when it pulls out this dramatic card, eager to box something up and seal it with that tape labelled 'bad'. Once you catch this, you can return your attention totally to the present and you will be amazed at how things shift.

Then you see that paying attention to and buying into the *story* of how much of a stressful time you are having, or how hard it all is, actually saps and drains lots of precious energy. You are feeding it! Of course you lose energy. So when this story is seen and discarded, you get all of that wasted energy back. Try it out! It works. I must have done this at least 50 times in the month that Elfie has been alive, and this is the beauty of it. With time, this sort of attitude becomes your subconscious habit, taking away a lot of unnecessary stress.

So when your baby does *another poo, straight after the nappy change, remember*:

The First Six Months

It's Just…*One*…Poo.
You can handle it.

Sunday 18th July

We almost completely forgot about our anniversary today. It just feels completely irrelevant because the little one has totally taken over, but we laughed at it this evening. We made an effort to have a nice dinner together, to reflect on the adventure so far and to make our time as romantic and lovely as possible. There were all sorts of disturbances from Elfie which kept interrupting us, but that's just the way it is!

Unfortunately, one of the unavoidable topics of conversation was the hospital saga which we are currently in the throes of. It has been manic, mad and horrible:

- ◇ Firstly, we panicked and went to the doctor about Elfie having reflux and fussy breastfeeding (this means crying all the time).
- ◇ The doctor prescribed us Nexium, but she didn't know why she was screaming during feeds. She also gave us a different position for reflux, said coughing was fine.
- ◇ When we got home, we researched Nexium in depth. It had been prescribed to us like the most casual medicine ever, like paracetamol. Yet we discovered online that there are some dangers associated with it which are apparently underestimated in their importance.[16] Where does that leave us? How are we supposed to know?
- ◇ Two days later she did one green poo. We looked it up and this isn't necessarily a bad sign. However, after this the poos got progressively worse.
- ◇ On Thursday, conjunctivitis appeared in both of her eyes (which looks horrendous and means she can barely open

- them) and her poos were at their worst (which means including blood).
- ◇ We messaged the doctor and she said to see her tomorrow, but we were too worried about her eyes, and the two things in combination made it anxiety-inducing. In true new-parent fashion, we feared there was something really wrong and made the decision to go to the emergency room because of the eyes. The doctor basically laughed us out of it and said, with a smirk, "First baby?!" Clearly, it didn't seem like a big deal, but she didn't really listen to any of our explanations. I trusted that it would be fine, but we still both felt enormous concern for Elfie and anxiety about it.
- ◇ The next day – back to the hospital because there was blood and mucus in her very green poo, and her eyes were still bright red. She seemed like an absolute mess! Now we realise they peaked together, so it made us think it was part of the same problem, but the doctors never considered they were related.
- ◇ I have become suspicious that giving her Nexium has caused the digestive problems, because of what I read online about it. The doctor was adamant that it wasn't, but we suspected that she was just covering herself. She probably thought we were incredibly annoying.
- ◇ Next came the weight 'disaster'. With everything that is going on, the last thing we needed was a new problem. Yet here it was. During the routine weight check at the appointment to discuss the other issues, we saw that she had lost over 100g in a week. That is not good at all. If they aren't gaining weight, it's seen as a concern; so to lose all that weight, not be feeding properly, have all these issues with her poos *and* conjunctivitis still in both eyes really filled us with existential terror.

The First Six Months

- ◇ The doctor was really confused; she could see no reason for such dramatic weight loss. We were very worried all day. Had to go back with a stool sample (£120) four hours later and book an ophthalmologist appointment. Then we went home and changed our mind (to save the money) and tried to ride it out. I can't believe this was yesterday! We were so stressed and preoccupied that we forgot to cancel our appointment and they tried to charge us for it.
- ◇ Next, another bloody poo and the antibiotics not working for her eyes. Substances might not be 'the answer', but whisky sure did seem to help a little here – we had a nice glass together and reset the clock.
- ◇ We went back for another appointment today (we have no insurance, so each of these costs at least the equivalent of £100). Her weight was *completely different*. It had been the ultimate cosmic prank: the *scales had been wrong!* Ahhhhh, science. Its infallibility cloak appears almost impenetrable; we never suspect something like that might be going on. The scales were 100g or so out, meaning her weight had actually been fine the whole time! Incredible feeling of relief and appreciation for a good prank on us by the universe.

<u>Tuesday 20th July</u>

This morning, I experienced a lot of stress and noticed something which I habitually do to make these times easier. I completely stopped and looked at what was bothering me. It turns out that the things in the moment which were bothering me were bothering me because *I didn't want them to be happening*.

I wanted to be on the way to work, instead of at home, *because I was late*. As soon as I noticed this, the *insight acted*. I naturally realised that I *would be* late for work and felt the acceptance of this reality. Suddenly, there was no need to rush, and no more stress, and I could feel the stressed energetic field coming back to balance, moment by moment.

Not facing reality causes suffering.

When we fall asleep, the bedroom disappears from our experience; in just the same way, when we are 'hooked' by a mental story, our 'inner' energy, or attention, is pulled away from what is present in our immediate physical reality. A story in the mind can consume us completely, blinding us to the rest of the present moment and, in doing so, robbing us of a vital sense of perspective.

Yet applying *intense* and *sustained* awareness to what the mind is doing bursts this bubble and helps you 'come to your senses' – quite literally. I wonder who coined that excellent phrase?

Thursday 22nd July

I've already seen the power of 'traditional Western', 'allopathic' or 'mechanistic' medicine on this journey, in how it helped both of my girls survive the ordeal of birth. That makes me incredibly grateful for the almost miraculous power of this form of medicine to save lives and deal with the most dangerous and life-threatening situations. However, everything has its shadow side, and this is no exception.

For every life saved, it seems there are unnecessary medications prescribed to treat conditions which could be treated in less aggressive and reckless ways. Unfortunately, every time one of these medications is dispensed, it's lining someone's pockets. According to the CDC, nearly 50% of Americans used at least one prescription drug in a recent 30-day period, and over 13% used five or more.[17]

This same cycle also holds the therapeutic industry in its grip, and this is illuminated fiercely in the book *Doctoring the Mind: Why Psychiatric Treatments Fail* by Richard Bentall.[18]

Too often, we are happy to treat the symptoms of something

without caring about its cause. In the psychological field, this leads to us mindlessly taking antidepressants just to make ourselves feel better, without turning to face the situation fully. This becomes a vicious cycle, which prevents us from seeing the dissonance in our lives, both individually and collectively. We just won't sit in the mess long enough to *see how much of a mess it is* and, through this avoidance, we tragically perpetuate it. We would rather have a Band-Aid, because it *allows us to carry on.* Yet as Krishnamurti famously said, "It is no measure of health to be well-adjusted to a profoundly sick society."[19]

This is not to say that antidepressants and other therapeutic drugs should not be used, but that they are overused, and this is to our detriment. Life is difficult, messy, sad and sometimes tragic, and facing all of this is our challenge as human beings.

I've heard it said that, in some ways, meditation is like preparing for the worst day of your life, and this seems right to me. When enormous events crash into my world, uninvited, I need to be present, not only to *deal with them*, but also to *live them*. Otherwise, what's the point?

Millions of people have been failed by the prevailing medical paradigm – dosed up to the eyeballs with pills that 'stop' all sorts of conditions, but also, accidentally, wreak havoc on other parts of the body, mind and beyond. Countless seemingly miraculous recoveries – through diet, lifestyle, and alternative, integrative medical approaches – point to something missing in our traditional view of health, and urge us to rethink not only what it means to be healthy, but what it means to be human.[20]

The past week has reminded me of where I stand on this medical question, and it has prompted me to be a bit more discerning and brave in future when it comes to Elfie's health. I want to be open not only to alternative medical approaches, but also to trusting her body to develop and heal as it's meant to – just as I've always done with mine. Still, I don't want to throw the baby out with the bathwater by recklessly dismissing all allopathic care, especially when it might be the most valid and powerful option in a given situation.

Whilst we're on the subject, does the medical industry have any ties to the sugar industry? We were given a little bottle of liquid which is apparently very important for the health of Elfie's little growing body: vitamin D drops. According to the scientific establishment and the pharmaceutical machine (totally separate entities in every way, of course), every baby is deficient in vitamin D if they are breastfeeding only. But don't worry: there's a solution for that which you can buy! We have been giving Elfie these drops for about three weeks, but we started to notice a pattern:

She bloody loves them.

So we nicknamed the drops 'the iPad' in honour of their beguiling power. Eventually, it started to really bother me, though, so I decided to have a drop myself.

Oh. My. God.

It was, and this is no exaggeration, the sweetest thing I have ever tasted in my life. Absurdly, apocalyptically sweet.

What is going on? I have quite a bad relationship with sugar, and it's one thing I really don't want to pass on to my child, so what the hell is this? Does it really have nothing to do with some parties' vested interests in getting people addicted to sugary foods? I'm sure that, in the world we live in, this topic is going to bother me repeatedly as time goes on when it comes to Elfie's health.

Friday 23rd July

So if you look up what we have been experiencing again today, it is affectionately called 'fussing whilst feeding'. These words are a hilarious understatement. It's more like having a fire alarm installed inside your brain, and I'm not even the one trying to feed her.

Due to these ongoing difficulties, Nadine decided to try out bottle feeding every now and then, with expressed milk. It seems to have majorly backfired. Now that Elfie has had a taste of the smoothness and predictability of a bottle, she is determined not to go back to the breast. What a diva!

I am totally in awe of how Nadine has handled this. She cries relentlessly, for sometimes ten minutes at a time (Elfie, not Nadine), refusing to suckle properly. All the while, Nadine just sits calmly and patiently, putting her back over and over again. It is really something to behold and she says she is determined, locked in and just ignoring the crying completely.

That was when it hit me: this is their first battle. *The Battle of the Bottle.*

It took me a few years to realise quite how stubborn my Arian wife is when pushed into a corner, but now I am under no illusions: Elfie has no chance with this one. There is only going to be one winner…for now.

It's very different for me, though. I can't do anything to soothe the crying during these times and I do find it extremely agitating. I've noticed myself reacting inwardly each time she cries and I've been watching it quite closely. Earlier on today, I really stopped and spent some time attending to it, so that I could unravel it a little. These were the questions which crossed my mind:

- Am I trying to escape from it?
- Have I accepted that it is happening and out of my control?
- Am I trying to change it when I can't?
- Do I want it to stop?

It was clear that these issues were all part of the tangled tapestry of my reaction to the crying, so I 'leant into it' consciously instead, welcoming and accepting the event exactly as it was. It made a big difference, and I could feel the energy transform to a certain extent. The cry was interpreted differently by my system. This is not just a 'trick' to make pain or emotional disturbance go away, because that's just another escape. Rather, it's an attempt to be present and connect with the emotional waves; to turn towards them, rather than away.

I wanted to escape the crying. I watched it. It changed. How many times must I have done this kind of thing? Whatever the answer is, it has transformed my life. Ironically, escaping gets us nowhere.

Wednesday 28th July

People said that having a zoo would prepare us for this adventure. They were right.

Looking after lots of animals in one house can be extremely stressful. It takes an enormous amount of time and money, and restricts your life a great deal. For example, Nadine and I have found it hard to go on holidays because it's so tough for anyone to look after our pets properly. This restriction is similar in kind to what happens to someone when a baby enters the mix. Keeping the animals happy together and preventing fights, especially when introducing a new one, is a significant cause of stress for owners of pets. So, over time, we have adjusted to a life full of little concessions of time, energy and money.

The only reason any of the zoo antics began is that so many cats needed rescuing at a local fish market, which was due to be destroyed and relocated. Overnight, 145 cats were going to have no home and nothing to eat, so we agreed to help some rescuers move them. This was a totally mad period in which, at times, we ended up being lumbered with loads of cats in cages in our bathroom overnight!

When we first moved to Dubai, we flew our two pet rabbits over in cargo, which proves that we were already fully animal-mad. The upside was that the crew found the bunnies so adorable, they bumped us up to Business Class for our life-changing voyage. But the fish-market saga was when the zoo really began to materialise.

Anyway, inevitably a couple of the buggers from the fish market ended up signing a long-term contract with us and are still here now. It all spiralled from there and a few others joined the crew.

Well, take all of this, plus the Dubai summer, when none of the animals can go outside, and chuck a newborn in. It is a right laugh. It takes a village to raise a child, they say. Damn right. Where's the village when you need one? As we are expats, we don't even have any family support out here, and I hereby confirm that it is really hard to do this without the 'village'; even a hamlet would do, at this point.

We didn't properly realise how difficult our house is to look after until we asked our friends to do so for us this year, whilst we went to the hospital to have the baby. When making them a video to show the night-time routine, I started to notice that the video…wasn't…ending. There kept being another part of the routine, another small action which is subconscious for us and which made it more and more difficult for them to replicate. Take this, for example: one of the cats always strays far from the house and used to get into a lot of fights. For this and a couple of other reasons, we bought a GPS tracker, so that we can find out where she is and go and get her if necessary. After getting all of the beasts in for a night-time feed, we have to take her tracker off and put it on charge. Easy, right? Yes, but there are a lot of little things like that.

Just bear in mind that all of this zoo upkeep is always going on in the background, now largely unnoticed and not really mentioned at all in this book!

Throwing the baby into the mix has obviously kicked things up a very large notch indeed. I think I'm now starting to see the crux of what people mean when they say things like, "You're not ready. You have no idea what's coming."

It's the sheer relentlessness of it all, and how all-encompassing it is. But I saw today that it's also because of the 'little things'. There were so many small stressors which happened today that, by the end, it was making us both laugh, and I decided to take five minutes to try to remember as many of them as I could, so that I could put them in a list in this book, as an example of what a 'hard day' with a newborn *actually* looks like.

I always used to be a little confused about why nobody could properly explain to me why the process was so stressful. I never got a good answer on this. One of my friends always just used to say, "Just you wait, mate!" So, here goes:

- Wake up
- Shower etc
- Husband feeds zoo
- Husband feeds wife
- Wife feeds baby
- Husband tidies house
- Go to hospital
- Weight down, digestion weird – no idea why – have to go to another hospital straight away on the other side of the city
- Baby needs to be fed – when can we feed her in this hospital and where?
- Go to a private room inside the hospital to feed
- Interrupted for appointment. Annoyed baby. Loudness again. Keep calm and carry on
- Doctor's appointment – conclusion: allergy – no idea which. Eliminate foods and then reintroduce them. If no change within a few weeks, pay for loads more tests
- Arrive home at exactly 2 o'clock – time of first client on Zoom
- Husband works four hours on Zoom
- Wife lets AC maintenance men come in to fix two leaking AC units soaking the bathroom floors (with baby strapped to chest)
- Wife has enormous epic battle of wills with crying and screaming baby and eventually wins

- AC men leave dirt and mess all over the floors
- Husband mops and tidies floors
- Cook dinner
- Leave hot dinner on kitchen worktop and drive baby around the community to hope she sleeps
- Fail
- Heat cold dinner up and eat whilst rocking baby in a chair on sofa
- Tidy upstairs
- Wash clothes
- Write this
- Put baby to bed
- Meditate
- Go to sleep

Now, here's the thing. Most of these are what you might see as the 'major' events of the day, the most memorable things. There are *a lot of them*.

BUT!

In between such events, on a *normal day*, you can *sit down*. You can *switch off*. You can *go to the toilet* with almost absolute certainty that the ablutions will be completed without interruption. But you have no such assurances when a baby is on your case.

Today, I purposefully noticed the little things.

At least seven things happened in the space of one and a half hours which were annoying and inconvenient and a little bit stressful, but manageable enough that we would normally ignore them and move on. But not today. Today, I paid attention, and each time I tried to stop and note them down (obviously adding a wholly unnecessary layer of stress to it all):

- I went downstairs with a load of washing in my hands when Nadine suddenly shouted to me that I needed to sterilise her bottle pump asap. As she is almost always incapacitated at the moment by feeding, a lot of these requests come my way when I'm in the middle of doing something else, and then they need to be remembered and acted upon. This regular interruption of ordinary tasks increases subconscious stress a lot.

- ◇ A cat opened the fridge and masterfully swiped a can of tuna out onto the floor, allowing the others to come and feast for honour and glory.
- ◇ A different cat opened Nadine's knicker drawer and decided to chuck all of the knickers out onto the floor.
- ◇ I searched everywhere three times for the 'Hakka' which collects milk, and eventually found it somewhere I had already looked. (Note: If this wasn't a mistake of perception on my part, it may mean that there are beings in another dimension – aka poltergeists – *purposefully making my day more annoying,* in addition to all the rest of this madness. That would really be taking the piss.)
- ◇ Nadine was finally able to stand up and walk around, came into the kitchen and couldn't pick up a banana (because holding baby), so I had to pick up the banana for her and hand it to her. She couldn't stand in the kitchen because two ants were there and she would have an allergic reaction if they bit her. A hungry rabbit nudged her ankles twice with his nose to tell her he wanted food. Fail. She left the kitchen.
- ◇ Dummy fell out of baby's mouth and had to be picked up and swapped with another one in the steriliser, and the clean one put in her mouth approximately 25 times over the day – no exaggeration.
- ◇ Baby appeared to be choking and not able to breathe for a while and needed to be tapped on the back for a time. Just pranking us again. Horrific wave of anxiety.

My mum says, referring to the added madness of the zoo, "You know other people don't live like this, don't you?!"

The First Six Months

Is it extra stress to write this book? Overall, no, I don't think so.* During the day, I try to make a quick note of things to write about properly when there is time and, when I do sit down to write, I enjoy it. Is it helping my ability to process everything that's going on? Yes and no. It's nice to look back and give time to things I wouldn't normally consider – to bring unconscious habits into consciousness – but being extra-aware of everything that's going on, so I can remember it and reflect on it, is unnatural to me and somehow affects the ordinary flow of life.

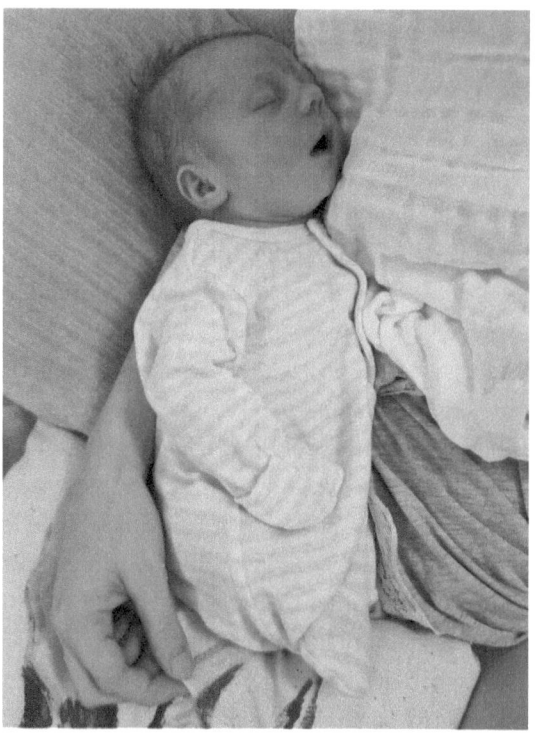

---

* Who am I kidding?

Diary of a Mindful Dad

<u>Sunday 1st August</u>

When your baby suddenly smiles at you, it's like being hit with a bolt of lightning. So powerful. So immediate. So whole. Elfie blessed me with a beaming smile this morning, just after we woke up, and the gift was total love and presence.

Now that was a smile! There are no two ways about it. It felt, in that moment, like the first *real smile* I had ever seen. With adults, on the other hand, often there are 'two ways about it'. Yes, we smile. Yes, we laugh, and we often do so fully. But generally, we are fragmented. We have so many tangles, knots, unanswered questions and unresolved dilemmas in our inner world that we are neither here nor there, neither then nor now.

My colleague and I have joked about babies being 'spiritual hoovers' and bringing them into a therapy or meditation room, after the adults have left, just to clean the place up: replacing the distorted, fragmented energy with wholeness and presence.

Can we live fully, like a baby, all the time? I have a picture in the living room which says:

"Enjoy Every Moment"

We're so used to empty words in this world, I doubt even the people who made that picture thought those words might actually help someone *do* it. But every time I look at it, it really does remind me to stop, look around and appreciate the present exactly as it is. It is especially powerful when something supposedly 'bad' or difficult is going on; it provides perspective. Such reminders, in the midst of life, can be invaluable.

But why are we so desperately in need of them? Are we grateful?

On the whole, I think not. Greed is the opposite of gratitude, and ours is an exceptionally greedy society. Worshipping the hollow god of so-called 'progress' keeps us perpetually moving and therefore never standing still; never *stopping* and having a moment to look around.

Yet if we reflect on the root of this word 'progress' – to 'go forwards' – doesn't that just mean *continuing in the same direction as before*? Isn't that what forwards means? It's nothing to do with anything actually improving! Then, if you look for the root of 'improve', you find that it means 'profiting'! Oh dear. I really should stop looking these things up.

Sometimes, such critical views are themselves criticised for ignoring the value of *genuine* improvement in civilisation (for instance, the success of modern medicine) and advocating some sort of just sitting around and doing nothing. But this misses the point.

Imagine a weighing scale with 'progress' on one side and 'peace' on the other. How much do they weigh in your life? How about the life of society, the education system? If you keep asking these questions, you see that the scales are tilted towards progress to the extent that they have fallen over and broken into pieces; the broken scales symbolising that even the question of that balance has been lost. That's probably partly why you're reading this book right now.

Questioning the altar of progress allows us to regain this perspective and begin to see a glimpse of the peace which we have sacrificed. It is this perspective which can make a *single* moment magical, which can make a moment shine.

To be grateful, we need to see that we have been given a gift. Life is this gift. The most extraordinary and eternally incomprehensible gift of all.

When we suddenly see how unbearably precious and precarious life is, our perspective is transformed, even if just for a moment, before we get back to 'the important business of living'. We cannot bear such truth for long.

When we consider our death, or the death of others we know, it feels impossible to comprehend it. Our response is to run away or squash it down, wasting a golden opportunity and another mighty gift.

The way we deal with death, as a society, is to pretend it isn't there. Through the modern, scientific lens, it's so incomprehensible and painful to think about that it seems we have no other choice. Yet what would happen if we were always aware that our time is finite? That we are mortal? That death is coming for every single one of us?

In many schools of Buddhism, regular contemplation of mortality – *maranasati* – is seen as essential for right living, encouraging presence, compassion and clarity. At the end of Gurdjieff's enigmatic *Beelzebub's Tales to His Grandson*, Beelzebub even goes so far as to suggest that such a constant awareness of mortality is, in fact, *the only thing which can save our species*.[21]

Yes, this might be almost impossible to bear at first, but eventually it would give rise to true perspective and therefore right action. We wouldn't need to be under the influence of any substances to tell our friends that we love them and how much they mean to us. The brother of my deceased dear friend told me at his funeral, with fiery passion in his eyes, "Tell your brothers you love them *every...single...day*."

Once, when I was about 23, I was thinking about a bad argument I had had with my father the previous night. It was extremely dramatic and seemed as if it would change our relationship irreparably.

I really wanted to resolve it and I didn't know how. Suddenly, a black car went by. Then another. Then another. Then I saw a hearse and, in the back, a coffin with flowers spelling the word 'DAD'.

It hit me like a ton of bricks. The resolution to our problems was so simple: Death. I decided, there and then, that whatever I had cared so much about (him not respecting my different perspective as much as I wanted him to) was so insignificant compared to the unconditional love I had for him, that it vanished.

That was it. I suddenly did not care about it anymore, and I just wanted to love him as much as I possibly could instead.

Amazingly, believe it or not (you probably won't!), it was on that exact day that our relationship transformed in 'real life' as well. Two hours later. As soon as I stopped feeding this narrative, the way he treated me changed, *in exactly the specific way I had been reflecting on.* Just like that.

This doesn't mean this is some sort of 'technique' to transform relationships. No way. Nor did it mean this would last forever and everything would always be perfect between us. It was a beautiful and mysterious synchronicity which blessed my life and shifted *something*. Some may see nothing but a fortuitous coincidence there, where others see the unknowable hand of fate.

So what is 'real life'? I put 'real life' in inverted commas above because I think the emotional event I experienced was just as real as, if not more real than, any other part of the story. Controversial, I know. The energy I was bringing to the situation was not one of love; it was one of *wanting something from him. Something different from what was there.*

It was as if my choosing love instead allowed the whole *invisible* situation to transform, and this transformation changed his actions. I have seen countless examples of this in my work too, when a client radically shifts their perspective and it 'magically' transforms the external situation (including the actions of others) as well – immediately. Though this may sound a little strange to most people, if we compare it to how we normally think of relationships, I don't think it is at all.

It only sounds strange if we dismiss the emotional elements of our lives as unreal and irrelevant footnotes, rather than realising that they are *really there*, full of power and impacting events. Ideas are so powerful that they can create – and destroy – entire civilisations, and our mental and emotional life gives rise to our actions. So are these examples really so hard to believe? The invisible world matters. What we attend to, and the *way we attend*, matters.

So when you look into your baby's eyes, and you see, just for a second, how incredibly miraculous they are, *treasure that moment. It is a gift.*

Monday 2nd August

After two really hard weeks of lots and lots of crying and not much decent sleeping, we are settling into more of a routine, and day by day taking steps to help Elfie sleep on her own during the day. Up until this point, one of us has always been incapacitated by needing to hold her or having her sleeping on our chest.

The baby sling has helped a lot as an intermediary in this process, but it is still a bit difficult for the person wearing it to do anything normally (I'm currently typing this with one hand with her in the sling). It was invaluable for helping her to sleep during the day, though, and for that it has been worth its weight in gold. I don't know how we would have survived without it.

We have started to do our normal bedtime routine for her *downstairs as well* for her other naps (swaddle, relaxing music, feed and put to bed) and it's working 50% of the time. This means we can both do our own thing sometimes during the day. It's amazing to think that we haven't had that opportunity for a few whole weeks. I wish, looking back, that we had started these tactics earlier – as soon as possible.

Nadine is also far more proactive now with pumping breast milk when Elfie is asleep, because apparently we need to 'fatten her up' after her slow weight gain due to the allergy. It's also really useful to give her an extra-big feed before bed so she sleeps for longer. Lots of people do this with formula, apparently, because it's 'so hard to digest' that it takes up lots of their energy, also resulting in more sleep. But it being so hard to digest is a major red flag for me, and makes me want to stay as far away from it as possible.

Unfortunately, pumping out the extra milk two or three times a day means Nadine has so little time to herself – almost none.

She is currently over the moon about having five minutes to do some yoga.

Tuesday 3rd August

John Koenig's ingenious brainchild *The Dictionary of Obscure Sorrows* names and defines aspects of the human experience which have been eschewed by the quotidian vernacular (sorry, I'm getting all excited about words). I'm bringing this up because Elfie loves 'midding' and, come to think of it, so do I. According to Koenig, midding is:

> "Feeling the tranquil pleasure of being near a gathering but not in it; hovering outside a party while others enjoy inside; resting your head in the backseat of a car listening to your friends chatting, feeling blissfully invisible yet still fully included, safe in the knowledge that everyone is together and okay, with all the thrill of being there without the burden of having to be."[22]

Beautiful, right? Whilst she is asleep in the sling, as she was just now, she wants you to be moving around and chatting; I can just imagine how idyllic that is for her, *feeling like being in the womb*, but out just enough to be part of the day. We could all do with a good bit of midding every now and then.

Wednesday 4th August

I have noticed so much selfishness and entitlement in our narratives about how 'difficult' parenting is, including mine in this book. Part of the reason for this book is to explore how difficult the parenting challenge is, because everybody says it is, but people all over the world, and in all time periods, have had so much more difficulty than this and had to just get on with it. This doesn't mean these people didn't complain about it, but I would be surprised if they did so as much as we do. It speaks to our expectations in modern society that life should be perfectly easy and orderly; clearly, there is something very wrong with that outlook. I used to work with a fantastic group of Zimbabwean people in a restaurant in England, and the head chef Mabel told me she used to walk 10km with a baby on her back, knitting and balancing a huge container of water on her head. Now, compared to this, I am more useless than a slug. I'm making a mental note to remember this if I'm ever moaning, though I know I probably won't! Can you remind me? Probably not.

Thursday 5th August

There has been a lot of catastrophising in this house in the last couple of days about Elfie's health, and we have to be very alert and pivot back to balance, presence and rationality time and time again. This back-and-forth has reminded me of an interesting episode I had relating to a phobia of flying, which I want to relay here, because it is a profound example of the power of watching the mind.

On the way back from our honeymoon, Nadine and I were flying over the Atlantic Ocean in the dead of night. I've never been overly scared of flying, but turbulence has unnerved me many times. On this particular occasion, it all went up about 100 notches. There was *huge* turbulence. Looking out of the window, all I could see was a vast, black ocean in all directions. Oh dear. What if?

Unfortunately, at this point, a lady sitting about three rows behind me started to have a full-blown panic attack. I mean *screaming. Loudly.*

Imagine the energy field of all the humans around her interacting with hers. After a short while, it hit me by osmosis and the 'What if?' became **'WHAT IF?!?!?!'**

I had the worst thought ever: *What if she's right...and everyone else is wrong?*

Oh dear. To believe that, even for a second, was extremely frightening. It went through my body and I started to feel the panic. I was breathing, watching the mind and trying to keep myself relatively calm. But her panic attack went on for a really long time. It was infectious, in my case, and it had really got to me physically, emotionally and mentally. I think it was *that thought*, that I had *no idea* how likely or unlikely a plane crash was, which had got me.

The mind had suddenly decided to *weigh the possibilities differently*. Suddenly, on that flight, death felt very possible indeed.

I tried to wake Nadine up to get a bit of support from her, but she was so sleepy that she couldn't grasp I was in a sensitive state, and just went back to sleep after a minute or two. During that time, we briefly discussed it, and she basically laughed at the idea that what we were doing was dangerous in any way. I didn't want to disturb her after that, so I just left it, but it was this issue which stuck with me. The woman's panic attack had totally changed my perception of flying itself and made me distort how dangerous it was. Nadine thought there was probably a 0.000001% chance of a plane crash, and my percentage had suddenly jumped up to about 20% or so, probably. No wonder I was scared!

When we got home, I decided to address this, because I had been so shaken by the event that I didn't want to fly ever again. It was a visceral, physiological thing for me. So I did a bit of research, and it didn't help at all. I was hoping to see that basically no planes ever crash, but that wasn't the case. Of course, I know that the chances in comparison to car crashes are so incredibly low, but it still didn't reassure me as I had hoped it might. So we had to discuss it in depth; what to do? I couldn't *never fly again*: Nadine made me see how restrictive that would be. So I had to come face to face with this somehow.

The next year, I had my chance. We flew to Ibiza for my

brother's wedding, and I felt a lot of anxiety leading up to it. As we took off, it peaked. I could feel the anxiety in my body and see the fear in my mind. This time, I did it differently. Earnestly, with all my energy, I put into practice what I had learned from the spiritual teacher I have studied the most – Jiddu Krishnamurti:

"Without the process of recognition, fear is not."[23]

I watched the whole process with as much energy as possible, but detached. I was not allowing the system to believe it 'knew what the fear was'. I wasn't allowing the mind to hook itself onto some story and spiral with it. I wasn't allowing the physiological state, the shaking, to create an even worse story. I was fully present with it all, in that moment, not moving away from it one iota. I was in real acceptance of the fact of what was happening.

It worked. The anxiety subsided, and I watched it reduce throughout the flight. Each time there was turbulence or anything which triggered anxiety, it was slightly quieter and weaker than before. No reaction from me. I wasn't feeding it at all.

That was it. On that flight, my short-lived phobia of flying died. It didn't mean I would never experience any fear relating to flying again, but the whole thing was transformed. Thank you, Jiddu! No wonder George Lucas allegedly based Yoda on Krishnamurti. He's even got the cool, Yoda-esque voice.

I have taken this same approach to listening to Elfie's cry many times, most recently just an hour ago:

You don't know what it is. Don't move away from it, energetically. Stand still in the face of it, totally open, and don't move away.

This shifts everything.

Because we have had so many health scares since Elfie's birth, we feel that there is a fine line between her life and her death; our minds have started weighing the possibilities differently, distorting them. It doesn't matter what the reasons for the distortion are; to sit with the process *without believing you know what it is*, to accept it and to watch it happen without reacting is powerful medicine indeed!

The First Six Months

<u>Friday 6th August</u>

It is one of life's great ironies that as your wife's breasts evolve, uplevelling like a victorious Pokémon, they are almost literally ripped away from you. I have created a simple graph below to illustrate this:

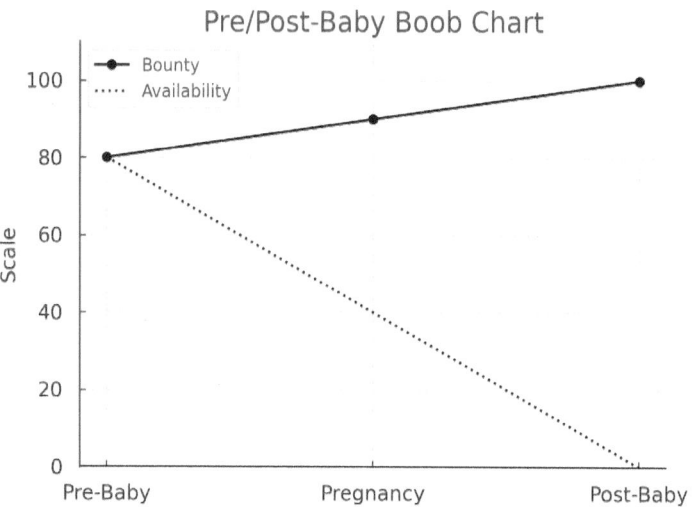

I remember our bitter-sweet journey to the mall a month ago, going to Victoria's Secret to discover that my old friends had grown by two cup sizes. I might have been rubbing my hands together with glee if I hadn't been pushing a pram. Maybe this was the universe's way of giving me a sneak peek at the lesson on the horizon.

It's been difficult for me to adjust to a sex life on hold, and this is a very big deal for men and women all over the world. In our case (and in the vast majority, I suspect), it's been harder for me than for her. Nadine's system is so wired to nurture her baby, who is *dependent on her to survive,* so her subconscious has moved sexual activity way down the list of priorities. She is also receiving a beautiful dose of oxytocin from breastfeeding and building that lovely new bond. It's not quite the same for me!

It seems that every time I so much as look at those 'warlocks', to quote Seth from *Superbad*, Elfie shoots me a look like I'm a dog about to piss on her favourite tree. She knows.

Yesterday, the question of our sex life buzzed into my mind and was instinctively swatted away like a pesky fly. Just a minor disturbance, an obstruction to my day. Ignore it, make it go away and move on. Thinking about it might be difficult and unpleasant.

But this is how things get worse, so I came back to it, opened up the door again, and I'm glad I did. This is a *big deal*. It's not as simple as swatting away a fly because, if you leave it alone, a fly will eventually go away.

Yet if my unprocessed and confused perception of my transformed sex life is not illuminated, then it will twist, tangle and burrow itself deeper, expressing itself further down the line in some more dissonant way. Frustration, resentment, depression; I presume all of these and more can end up on that timeline, as some of them already have.

I *have* been finding it hard. It *is* frustrating. I *don't want* it to be like this.

I chose, energetically speaking, to respect the inner event and give it the space it needed. As usual, what at first seemed like a small niggle became something much larger, more nuanced and *interesting*. Instead of being some 'little thing bothering me', it was revealed to be a difficult part of the human experience that literally billions of people have faced, and one to which there is no 'easy answer'.

Making this move and opening up this space changes everything. It brings new perception, new possibilities and fresh energy. It allows me to accept this as a lesson and be more open to evolving in my understanding of it as time goes on, *consciously learning* instead of *unconsciously avoiding*. This changes the relationship from one of conflict to one of harmony.

No, it isn't 'solved', and now I see that it doesn't need to be.

Witnessing what Sheldon from *The Big Bang Theory* calls the "dirty magic show – people coming out of people" can understandably change the way that people think about sex. That wonderful, sacred area, which has only been for pleasure up until this point, completely morphs in your perception, revealing all of its hand-squeezing, blood-curdling, primal power!

Ahhhh...so *that's* what that's for.

Of course, the same goes for boobs. It turns out that those soft and mesmerising cushions are for a different purpose entirely. What a hilarious prank by the universe, drawing us in like that. Clever, I admit. I totally fell for it.

But does it have to be one or the other? Can't the pleasure of sex and the actual creation of life be seen as one? Perhaps the problems we have with this in our society come back again to how messed up our ideas about sex are.

Maybe, instead of it being a trick, it's just that boobs are *actually the best things ever*, as many already suspected. My friend told me about a book by Theodore Rasbury called *Things Better Than Boobs,* which he has on his coffee table at home.

Like mine, your mind may already be whirring with the possibilities, crossing each off the list as potential candidates for this award almost immediately. Well, so was the author.

The book is *empty*.

How brilliant is that?

Anyway, apparently the change in perception of the sex act and one's wonderful partner, who just did the *most miraculous thing possible*, really can wreak havoc.

Just as above, there is no 'easy solution' or 'clever trick' for such a 'problem'. This is because, rather than being a problem to be solved, it is a complex situation asking to be attended to with energy and care. As soon as we think something is a problem, we become emotionally attached to it (negatively) and this distorts our understanding. 'It' becomes *fixed* and so does our relationship with 'it' (there isn't really an 'it' at all, because things are always changing, not being 'things' if we are alert enough to keep up with them). Then we try harder and harder to 'get out of it' whilst only digging ourselves deeper in.

Just as in the example at the beginning of this book, this is the perfect opportunity to be extra-watchful of thought. Watch its games, its tricks, its ploys, its distortions and how eager it can be to create a 'problem' with longevity, which saps our energy and is never truly seen. This last one is *so much* harder for it to accomplish if you are keeping an eye on its whispers and tales.

Yes, it must be perfectly natural for our perception of sex, and of our partner, to change for a time after childbirth, but as long as we are present and watchful, this doesn't need to go too far. With conscious attention, distorted thoughts and niggles which are dangerously twisting our perception are so much easier to spot. When we do notice them, the space will open up to reveal a new perspective.

After unpacking all of this today, I can now see some important new breadcrumbs along the trail. I can see that this difficult situation is going to require great care. It's going to require clear and compassionate communication, honesty (within and without), patience, awareness, perspective, wisdom, love and lots more of all that good stuff. And it's going to be hard.

An organic return to sexual connection doesn't need to be forced and cajoled, as if it is trying to run away from us, desperate never to return. This vision comes from the eyes of fear and control. Life has its natural rhythms, and this process is surely not an exception. Beautiful sexual energy doesn't come because it is commanded to do so, and it never has. So why force it now?

The whole process has revealed to me something new about the nature of intimacy, and made me more appreciative of 'smaller' expressions of it. It has made me see the entire sexual realm with fresh eyes, and realise how special it is, in a way I never did before. Making extra effort to try to find time, even for just a kiss and a cuddle, can create some beautiful, innocent moments which stop the oh-so-adult train in its tracks for a moment. All this is a gift, isn't it?

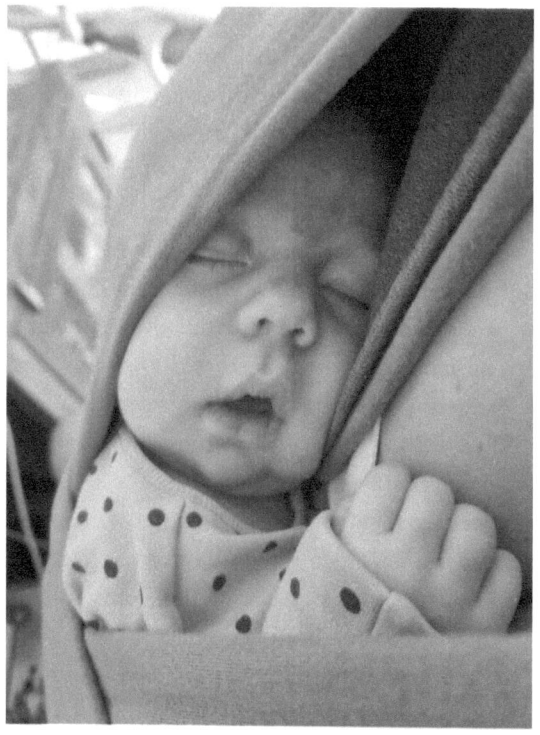

Elfie, claiming her rightful prize.

Saturday 7th August

We are used to celebrating poo in this house. We have had many rabbits, and they get sick quite easily, and the only way to know if they are OK is to monitor their poo. As soon as you see some, it's time to rejoice. They aren't dying. It's pretty much as simple as that with those lovely little creatures.

This morning we celebrated Elfie's delightful yellow poo. It has been green and bloody for two weeks now, so this was an enormous relief for all three of us. It means that one of the foods Nadine has cut out was likely causing the allergy and poor digestion, so that little nightmare appears to be over now. Thank God!

Monday 9th August

In many ways, my dadding has been average to poor, I now realise. My songs, for example, leave a lot to be desired. Ever since the first time I tried to sing to Elfie to calm her down or make her happy, the first line which came to me was always the same. Get ready for this, because it's truly inspired and has probably never been used before:

"*Who's a little baby?*"

After a few goes I was able to add:

"*Who's a little bear?*"

I was very pleased with this. Weeks later, the well, once overflowing with such inspiration, has all but dried up. The best I have been able to do is add a rhyming couplet, which would be more effective if not used at all:

"*There's a little baby, sitting over there.*"

It doesn't even make sense. She's in my arms, not sitting 'over there'.

Pathetic.

My failings came to a head today when I was setting up my Fantasy Football team for the new season. Any FPL players know that this time can be almost unbearably tense and fraught with truly consequential decisions. However, Nadine pointed out that Elfie had just started to have her 'awake time on the mat', gently and sweetly implying (as she does, with that wifely look) that it was a good opportunity for me to spend some quality time with her.

Just below the threshold of my consciousness, but available to memory later, a dreadful impulse went through me:

I didn't want to spend time with her.

I wanted to do my Fantasy Football team! It was only a small glimpse, but it was the unwelcome face of *resistance*.

I went over semi-consciously, still looking at my phone, and the way Elfie looked at me made conscience rise up and speak in its inimitable voice. I realised the stark contrast between the two worlds available to me, and that I was *still on my phone*. My lethargic, fatherly vessel had shuffled over, but the rest of me was in limbo; I had not actually decided to give her my full attention.

So I put the phone away and then really made the effort to be with her. It was magical. We had such a wonderful time. She gave me so much joy in that short time and I really felt that we had bonded.

Was being on my phone 'bad'? No, not really. Just because you're a parent doesn't mean you shouldn't spend any time on the things you enjoy. But it was definitely the wrong option *in that moment*. It was what it *represented* which was important. To me, the resistance I felt represented the difference between my old life and my new life. It is a big change to have a new being who requires lots of your love, care and attention, and that's probably – *somehow* – more important than agonising over which players to transfer into an imaginary football team.

Monday 16th August

I spoke to a friend earlier who I haven't been in touch with for a while. When I opened the chat with him, I saw a picture I had sent of Elfie after she was born. There's no dressing it up; it's a terrible photo. Easily the worst we have of her. She's totally cross-eyed and open-mouthed, like she's burping or threatening someone. No idea why I sent it; I was probably delirious and sleep-deprived, about 12 hours into her life. Nadine glanced over, saw that I had sent it and was in shock:

"*Why the hell did you send him that?! It's the worst picture ever!*"

She was genuinely annoyed, but I just found it funny. The best bit was the reply:

"Ah, mate! So cute. I can see you and Nadine in her."

Salt in the wound.

Tuesday 17th August

So I took the golf clubs out of the car and brought them back inside, unused. The end.

That tale of woe began two nights ago. As I went to bed, my mind raced with thoughts of the round of golf to come the next morning. *My triumphant return,* I thought.

Little did I know that my daughter had become a self-learning sleep-destruction device. Google's AlphaZero learned chess in *four hours* and went on to destroy the best existing chess software;[24] Elfie, it appears, is similarly laying waste to our pathetic parenting techniques.

Just when we think we have cracked it, she shows us the flaws in our system – all with a cheeky smile. Two nights ago, she simply refused to sleep in her bed; she had never done that before. Nadine took her out after ten minutes each time and tried to do 'the routine' again, but it seems the routine might need an upgrade. This meant that by 4 o'clock we hadn't slept a wink. So I messaged the golf club to cancel and took my post on the prison-cell rocking chair, keeping a watchful eye on Elfie sleeping on Nadine's chest again.

The next evening, my foolish hopes were raised again. I booked another round of golf, just in case…No dice. She had exactly the same night again. So this little monster has suddenly decided she can't sleep at night-time anymore. Is it the second 'leap'? Is it digestion? Reflux? A new problem? Maybe this weird neck thing we've been investigating? Who knows.

Everyone told me I wouldn't be able to play golf for a long time and I didn't believe them. Looks like they were right. Very much a first-world problem, I guess, that I should be thankful to have.

Wednesday 18th August

Imagine having no arms and no legs. What would life be like? Then take away your voice. Finally, imagine your vision totally distorted so you can't really see what anything is.

Of course babies are always crying! They can't do anything at all!

Today, I really looked at and listened to Elfie when she was crying hard, and I felt huge compassion for her. I realised for the first time that this is what she is going through, and suddenly all of her cries made so much more sense.

She is really, really upset.

It sounds stupid, but it can be easy to hear a baby crying without actually registering that fact. It just gets labelled 'baby crying' by the mind, and that isn't *feeling at all*. It's not love.

I wonder what impact it has when we see someone with compassion? How does it change things? Sadly, in our age, the most talked-about effect of compassion is how much good it can do *us*. I really hate that. There are all sorts of studies highlighting the positive changes in *our lives* which can come about through compassion. I can't imagine anything more selfish than that. Taking the only thing which is supposed to be *totally selfless* and poisoning it, in some sort of tragic attempt to make people 'do it more'.

I remember, when I was teaching, I posed a series of psychological questions to every class in the school, from ages 4 to 18, and included the teachers as well. One was: *Why should we be good?*

The answers were fascinating. Over 75% of them concerned *me getting something out of it*, but not in those words.

The Headmaster's reply summed it up: "Because it *feels good*."

I must admit, looking back, that it was a slightly rigged game – asking the mind to reveal the mysteries of the heart. Of course it failed.

I will never forget the answers to these questions which were put to so many different classes. Here are two more revealing ones for you to ponder. The idea is to answer them instinctively, without thought:

Are you good enough?

It was heartbreaking to see how many children instinctively believe they *aren't good enough*. Unsurprisingly, the older the child, the more this answer showed up. Adults rarely say yes instinctively. We have been sold the myth of progress, you see. It's interesting to reflect on, though. A baby, if you think about it, 'needs to improve' in absolutely every single way. They can't do *anything*.

But we see them as *perfect*.

We instinctively come into contact with that aspect of them which is eternal, whole and complete, because it isn't veiled by the debris from this world. When do we lose touch with that? It's sad, but clearly a natural part of the living process somehow. Returning to this seems to be a key part of our journey here, and I hope I can help to keep my baby in touch with this aspect of herself as she moves through this strange world. For me to do this, *I need to be standing on that ground myself and living from it*. Yet another reminder of how important it is for me to 'walk the walk' if I want to be a 'good parent' – whatever that means.

The last question which sticks out in my mind is this:

Do you go to the future, or does the future come to you?

I will never forget going into my mum's classroom and putting this to her Year 3 class – seven-year-olds. Immediately, in unison, the entire class shouted:

The First Six Months

"THE FUTURE COMES TO US!"

It hit my mum and me like a bolt of lightning and I have never forgotten it. Proof that, at that age, they are naturally mindful and present. The older we get, the more we have the sense that we are 'forging our future' and 'taking control'. If you really reflect on it, though, this idea turns to dust. I agree with the children: the future comes to us. To feel that way engenders stability, openness and a sense of adventure; again, I want to help my children stay in that receptive space as much as I possibly can, as the inevitable challenges of life assail them along the way.

Friday 20th August

How important is intention? It's invisible, of course, and like all other invisible things, it doesn't get the respect it deserves in our society.

I am amazed and slightly irked by how easy it is for me to forget how important it is. If you get the intention right, magic is sure to follow. This has been the guiding principle behind all that is good in my life. Take the example above of me putting away my phone. Committing to a moment with all that you have for the right reasons, *because you know it's the right thing to do*, opens the door to as yet invisible, unimaginable beauty and magic. We may think we are getting away with it if we are being deceitful or cutting corners, because nobody is watching. Maybe there's no higher power watching and judging us – maybe there is. But I have discovered that, by having such attitudes, we poison our deeds. We are *cutting ourselves off from that which is good*. A poisoned seed cannot grow into a tree which bears good fruit, and so how we approach things is hugely significant.

I have seen this so many times when working as a teacher. When you are really under pressure, rushing or stressed, all the decency from what is taking place can evaporate, and you can find yourself just trying to control a child or extract the right answer from them. You have stopped caring about them and any sort of real learning. Unfortunately, we are so used to giving value to end results and 'outer things' that the importance of the inner ground of what we do has become even more invisible than it was to begin with.

If the intention is impure, then all which follows is tainted with it: raised voices, frustrated tones and damaged hearts. This sort of thing happens all the time and in every walk of life. Yet if this energy can be seen and therefore transcended, in the moment, something changes. Everything you thought about that moment and that event is different and the Good comes back into view.

I don't think there's any sort of formula for creating these moments, no 'hack', but it is clear that being open and paying full attention is absolutely necessary. I think that always bringing as much attention as possible to the present moment, and making this habitual, somehow creates moments that are much more prone to insight and inspiration – like the natural inspiration which leads to a good intention. This seems much better to me than holding onto a conceptual strategy or technique and hoping it will be helpful in the imagined future. That's the paradoxical sort of logic which somehow guides me, with my little lamp, into the next moment, and this is guiding me through the early stages of the parenting journey as well.

I can't rely on ideas in this brave new world I've entered, and I don't think anyone else can either. I just have to try my best, to do my best, and be as present as possible, every single day, and in every single moment. That probably sounds exhausting, doesn't it? The idea of it might be, but I have found that living like that actually creates energy, rather than taking it away. It stops us wasting energy in all those other moments which, after all, *aren't actually real*.

The First Six Months

<u>Monday 23rd August</u>

Elfie is going through a 'sleep regression', and this led, last night, to her ending up in our bed between our pillows, because she was so clingy and needed to be close to us. Apparently, it's 'bad' for her to be in the bed with us. But if it's a problem, I can tell you it's probably the *best one I've ever had*. I woke up this morning and had no idea she was going to be there. Yet there she was, staring up at the ceiling, eyes wide, with a giant smile on her face. It was such a magical sight, especially for my 'just woken up' eyes.

Then Nadine unswaddled her and she had a gigantic stretch with both arms, looking totally blissful. She is a proper little human! I couldn't help but think back to all of the nights in bed when Nadine was pregnant, when we would look on the app to see what sort of berry or other piece of fruit Elfie was the size of today. At some point, she was the size of a pea. A PEA!

Now here she is, with eyes and a brain and joy and consciousness, lying between us in bed. How could this ever get old?

Conditioning is the simple answer. Did you know that, for every single millisecond that goes by, the brain is making all sorts of little predictions about what you are about to see or feel? Fun fact: this is why you can't tickle yourself. Your system already knows where you're about to be touched, and so it isn't shocked when it happens. Shame! What a world that would be, with everyone going around tickling themselves all the time for a laugh.

If you didn't expect the floor to be next to your bed, you wouldn't step out of bed in the morning. If reality weren't fairly predictable, we would be unable to live as we do. Unfortunately, the flipside of this is that everything needs to become *old* so that we don't *have to think about it anymore*. There is always so much to process, so anything which can be made unconscious is great for the system, giving it less to do.

This means that we don't look at the sky, the trees or the incredible eyes of our loved ones and see them as they really are.

We see them as if they are *already known*. The brain's need to be safe and secure forces it to remove the magic from the world, because you can't go to work and just stare into people's eyes all day. You'd be sacked in a heartbeat.

This sort of thing really can get you into trouble around old brains. When I used to work at the Toby Carvery as a pot-washer, I got into trouble with one of the waitresses for *being happy*. She aggressively chastised me for being in a good mood most of the time and smiling a lot. Who needs chastising there?

I can only assume she had forgotten that life is a miracle and that we are blessed with the gift of consciousness. I didn't say that to her. Then I would have really been in trouble. My brother, in a similar attempt to enjoy life – God forbid – went to work with a ukulele a few times, and it didn't go down well at all (he is actually very good). There's just not much space in this funny old world for new joy and fresh eyes.

Many years ago in school, I taught a lesson on this for the Year 1 children (five-year-olds), who are usually wonderfully alert and aware, seeing things as if they are new. But *even they* had forgotten the sky. We had a great discussion about how amazing the sky is and how often we look at it, and they realised that they *almost never did*. So they went outside all excited, staring up in wonder at the fabulous blue roof of their crystal ball, and found older children to share their revelation with. The older brains looked at them just as the waitress looked at me. The little Year 1s stamped the hands of the older kids with a stamp that said 'WOW!' and reminded them to appreciate how magical the world is. Mostly, they just carried on with their day, already so old at the age of ten, already too cool to enjoy the wonders right in front of them – or, in this case, above.

Having said that, it was clear that some of them had been touched and inspired by the vibrant energy of these little ones shaking them awake. Maybe, just maybe, they looked around with fresh eyes for some of that day.

The First Six Months

Such fresh eyes are a true gift and they are always available to us. Truly, everything is *new*. Your house might be similar to how it was yesterday, and this is great for our systems to process. But it's not *the same*. Today it *is today*. There is a freshness, an aliveness to everything around you which can only be apprehended and appreciated right now. If we miss this, we miss everything, and it is all too easy to do so for almost all of our lives. Then we are living a sort of half-life.

This is one of the blessings of having children. Their innocence and purity offer us old brains a chance at redemption, a chance to see with their eyes again.

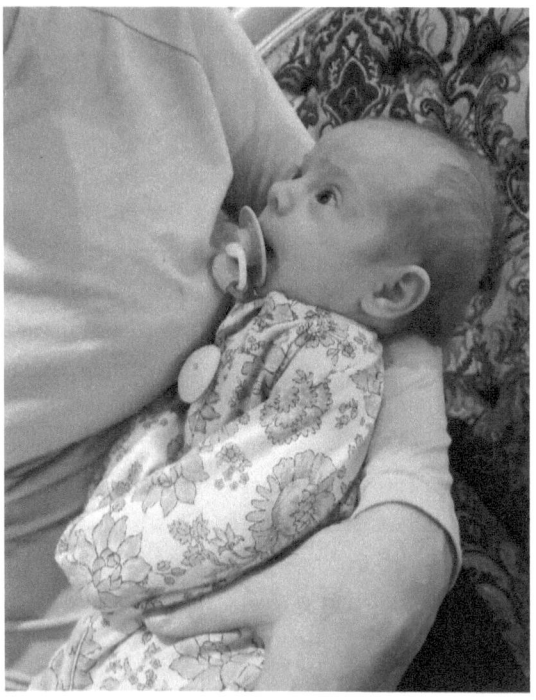

We are all just big babies, shuffling around in silly old clothes, making silly old faces and grumbling about our old world, ignoring what is actually there.

The gift of consciousness we have all been given is a miracle, just as new now as it was on the day we were born. At the core of all this old software we have built, there is this 'pearl of great price' – the saviour within – always able to see what is here and now, as if it is the *very first moment*.

"Wake up!" our babies are telling us. *"Look at that!"*

Tuesday 24th August

What a load of old crap we worship in this world. Come on, let's be honest about it. What a royal fuck-up most of this society is. We've pushed our conscience so far down that its voice is now quieter than a whisper. We see things every day that are wrong, and yet to speak up against them would demand all of our energy, so it's easier just to conform and try to enjoy our lives. Then we expect 'the next generation' to sort out the mess we've made. Poor buggers.

All this makes me so distressed that I seriously considered not having children, because I don't want them to have to live in this society. I don't want my daughter to have to conform to get along, to pretend stuff is cool so she can have friends who are just doing the same thing. I don't want her to have to sell herself out to the capitalist slavers from nine to five, day in day out, just so she can live in a tiny little house and pay off her student loan for the next 40 years. I don't want her to be made to feel less than she is by people who wouldn't know real love even if it bit off the end of their selfie stick. I want her to love and be loved, and that simple ask is a very tough one, at times, in this world.

This morning I was sitting on the sofa, and one of my cats was fast asleep next to me. He's a giant bruiser of a cat called Aragorn, as fluffy and lovely as they come. Another cat hopped on the sofa and walked straight up to him and nudged his face, asking to be licked. Arry woke up and immediately began to lick his face for ages and ages. It was a pure expression of love and acceptance. Amid all sorts of petty squabbles on WhatsApp groups about political, divisive crap, I saw this wonderful, wonderful thing. There was no judgement whatsoever between these cats, and all they wanted to do was have a nice time – everything else was irrelevant. I wish more than anything that we could find this sort of intelligence amongst ourselves.

All of my ranting and raving aside, I have always thought that everything I've moaned about is less significant than the joys and miracles which abound. Despite the nonsense of society, life is filled with magic, and we can be ourselves – if we are brave enough. So I have faith that my little one will find her way, and I hope that the immense challenges which this world brings her will help her to do so.

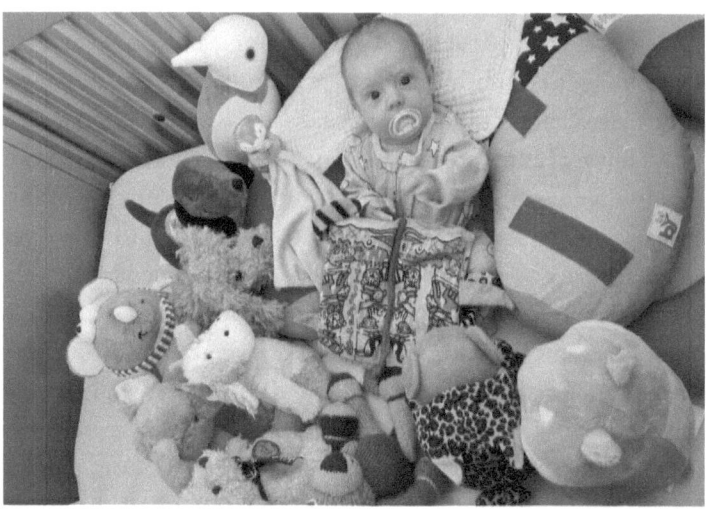

Wednesday 25th August

My hormones have definitely changed since becoming a dad. I just started welling up when someone got kicked off a cooking show, and they didn't even seem to actually care that much. *What the hell is wrong with me?*

"Just roll it into the shape of an avocado," Nadine says, gesturing to the plush Ikea throw.

I'm out of my depth here, I'm thinking. I fumble around for a while, true to form, and wait for the inevitable "Not like that!"

It's no secret to those who know me that I have absolutely no 'common sense', in a rather specific sense of the phrase. I've often wondered if the part of my brain responsible for manipulating mechanical things is damaged or even missing altogether. My friends at university used to have fun forcing me to play an online game called 'Fantastic Contraption', where you have to assemble a vehicle out of rods and wheels and the like. Most of my creations were positively deranged and couldn't accomplish the simplest task.

Perhaps the best example I have of this deficiency of mine goes back to one Christmas about ten years ago, when my sister-in-law caught me failing miserably to wrap a present. I had been staring at my foe for a full few minutes, paralysed and completely unable to see a solution. There just wasn't enough wrapping paper there; it was an impossible situation. It turned out that all I needed to do was flip the paper around so that it was landscape instead of portrait. My sister-in-law stared at me, baffled.

This ramble leads to the...

Independent Napping Battle Stages

Stage 1: Build the avocado throw nest, by hook, crook or both.
Stage 2: Sit and bob on the ball, whilst she falls asleep on your lap 'watching the vegetables' (Jazz lullabies for babies with hypnotic, slowly swaying vegetables).
Stage 3: Slowly stop bouncing until you are still.
Stage 4: Come and sit on the sofa near the avocado throw nest.
Stage 5: Place her on the nest in your arms, being very still.

**WATCH OUT: FAILING STAGE 5
TAKES YOU BACK TO STAGE 2!**

Stage 6: Remove the arm from underneath her.

Stage 7: Stay with her and cuddle her, holding both hands. Every time her movement reflex wakes her up, hold her hands. Stay in this position for at least ten minutes until she is at a solid Level 0.

Stage 8: Slowly remove yourself from the equation. (Jedi tip: Distance yourself energetically throughout this process to make sure energetic links are sufficiently severed as well.)

Stage 9: Hope that the lullabies you are playing don't suddenly play a loud and obnoxious ad about how amazing for your child the latest sugar-filled drink is. Ignore the 'happy' faces: those smiles are made of money and lies.

Saturday 28th August

Can you spoil a baby? Apparently not, but the jury is still out. Back in the day, it seems that the stereotypical 'male' approach to parenting a baby would have been quite tough, leaving them alone to cry for ages and the like. This seems to be the consensus from the conversations I've had, at least. Today, though, my mum told me about something even better – a rather inspired historical strategy for dealing with these little rascals.

A woman would be employed and put in charge of multiple babies at a time, and in a move so brilliant it would be completely illegal these days, like all the best things, they were wrapped in pieces of linen and hung on a 'swaddling board' on the wall. Loads of them together in one room. That's it. Perfect. You can go to work, eat your lunch, do a poo and have sex (not at the same time), all safe and secure in the knowledge that the apple of your eye is suspended in the air, unable to bother you one little bit. Then, when they are ready to be a respectable member of society, let them come out and join in the fun. Ideal.

Of course, this isn't really ideal, and it surely did 'spoil' these babies in many different ways, except in the fun way of having everything you want all the time. Now, times have changed. Nadine assures me that 'you can't spoil a baby', because that is what 'they' say now. She's done loads of research and so I try not to argue.

Having said that, I've always wondered who 'they' are, because they say an awful lot, and seem to hold sway in our collective mind, perhaps more than they should.

Apparently, research now shows that making a baby feel safe, secure and loved at every possible moment until the end of the fourth trimester (12 weeks) is actually very good for them! Surprising, right? Not really – love is good for us! What's more surprising is that there is an *endpoint* for that recommendation. What happens at 12 months? Kick them out of the house?!

Due to how much of a topic of debate this is in the world, this research is at least fair enough. Some scientific research isn't, though, and it can really wind me up. How about this one?

Years ago, a UK TV show spent a lot of money devising experiments to see if people *would be annoyed if you took their phones off them and locked them in a box in the middle of the living room for a week*. Hmm…I wonder what 'they' will say about that?

Or how about the totally astonishing study which showed that people who *really love going out* had a harder time in 'lockdown' than people who aren't really bothered? Aren't you so glad your hard-earned money was spent discovering that?

Similarly, also during the pandemic, *'non-compliers'* were found to be less likely to comply with Covid restrictions. Can you believe that? I almost fell off my chair reading about that study for the first time.

The ever-present voice of scientific authority makes me consider the question: do we really know the links between what happens when we are a baby and the kind of person we become? This comes up all the time in discussions about parenting, but my spider sense is tingling.

Take using a dummy, for example. When should that stop,

and how? It can be easy to make assumptions about how this will affect someone's personality, but those assumptions *might not be right*. For example, many people advise against using a dummy because it prevents the child from soothing themselves – the same logic used to justify leaving babies to cry. I can see the rationale behind this; I think resilience is extremely important for adults, and it makes sense that learning to self-soothe as a baby could help with this. But just because it makes sense doesn't mean it should be treated as some sort of a fixed *truth*. Nadine had a dummy all the time as a baby, and also slept in her parents' bed for 18 months, and she is an extremely emotionally secure adult. So, did having the dummy or staying in the bed prevent her from being strong and able to cope independently? Not at all.

Sometimes, a bit of faith in your own judgement can go a long way. So when our tiny little human – *who can't see or walk or speak or move or eat for herself* – is screaming, we have made the decision that we will go with our intuition, which happily happens to fit with what 'they' are now saying, and mollycoddle away.

Sunday 29th August

OK, this white noise is really starting to screw with my head now. In case you aren't familiar with this, it's supposed to replicate the womb noises and babies use it for sleeping; it makes a crackly noise like static from an old TV – I don't think they do that anymore, do they? They're far too smart for that now.

It makes sense as a comforting strategy, and it seems to work extremely well for the little one. The problem is that the white noise plays tricks on your imagination: I keep *hearing cats meowing and fighting in it*.

Oh dear. Says a lot about where I'm at. I've looked it up and this is a really common thing. Not the cat bit, obviously, but the distortion and imagination. So many people on the forums I visited have had to stop using it because they are being similarly tormented by all manner of auditory surprises. I have heard beautiful singing, familiar voices speaking inaudibly, as well as the cats. Isn't that amazing? When you realise that's what's happening, it's so odd to focus on it. Like crossing your eyes on purpose and realising that it means you're always seeing an image and not real life. No? Just me? Oh well.

It shows in a really clear, visceral way how we constantly and unconsciously distort reality with our own interpretations – the past relentlessly determined to impose upon the present.

Wednesday 1st September

It seems that the stress which a baby brings to your life is just as protected as the baby itself is in the womb – it *has to be stressful*. You might think that it's been cracked now, with everyone sharing their tips and successes on the internet, coupled with the enormous number of scientific studies done on every aspect of parenting. You might even have foolishly believed that *this book* might help you have a stress-free time. Ha! No way. It doesn't seem like that at all. Here's a good example of the inevitable confusion and aggravation which still reigns:

Today was the day of the dreaded vaccine, which so many people have warned us can be quite difficult emotionally, for parents and children alike.

"Should we expect any side effects?" I asked.

"Nope."

Let's go for it. So we did. Two nurses held her down and gave her one vaccination in each leg simultaneously. She didn't react – for about half a second – and then all hell broke loose, as she shouted the place down for about ten minutes. Nadine took her as far away from the other patients as possible; it was the loudest I've ever heard her cry, and heartbreaking to hear.

Later that evening, her temperature was rising and rising. The doctor had said, regarding fever, "If it's ever 38 or above (in the armpit), take her straight to the hospital." That seemed clear enough: *38 – armpit – go to the hospital.* A clear line. That's all we need. As usual, we left the doctor's feeling far too knowledgeable and secure.

Yet hours later, the inevitable confusion began. Her temperature was 37.7° in the armpit and rising, but before getting ready to go anywhere, we looked online. *Healthline* said:

"Most children don't experience side effects after getting the shot. That said, your baby may develop mild side effects, including fever..."[25]

So it's normal! Great.

Then, on *Seattle Children's*, we read the following incredibly unhelpful statement:

"Fever with most vaccines begins within 24 hours and lasts 1–2 days. Call Doctor or Seek Care Now (if) you think your child needs to be seen, and the problem is urgent."[26]

That last bit really cracked me up. The whole problem is that people don't know what is urgent and what is not, and whether their child needs to be seen or not!

Naturally, after reading the above, we thought, "Hold on a minute. Is the fever from the two-month vaccine normal or not? If it's normal, why would we need to seek care now?" Now everything was as clear as mud, yet again. So we tried to contact two doctors who had kindly and foolishly given us their direct numbers. It was 10:30pm. Poor people!

The first responded and told us that fever after vaccines is normal, but anything above 37.5° needs to be treated with meds. Oh dear, the website says not to give any medication before the baby has been seen!

The next temperature check was 38°. OK. We know what to do. The doctor was very explicit – now we have to go to the hospital. But we had this nagging question about whether this was the same even if the baby had had vaccinations. Maybe he only meant in a normal situation? There was no way to find out. I wasn't going back to Google.

(Obviously we did go back to Google about 15 times.)

Just as we were about to leave the house, the other doctor I had messaged got back to us and said we could call. On the phone, she said there was definitely no need to go anywhere. Just give her the meds, sponge her with a wet flannel and wet her clothes. She would be fine, it's completely normal. So that's what we did.

Her temperature did start to go down after a couple of hours. That was a relief. One last check on Google before bed, for good measure, made everything better. The *NCT* chimed in:

"*No need for a wet flannel.* You don't need to undress or sponge your child with water. Research shows these don't help reduce a fever."[27]

Perfect! Just the lullaby we needed. Good night, stupid phones, stupid Google, stupid world. Including, and especially, us – of course.

Thursday 2nd September

According to our friends, we have made a 'rod for our backs' by letting Elfie sleep in the bed. So what? Maybe we want a rod! What does it mean, anyway?

Apparently, we're 'supposed to be' training her – like some of them are doing with theirs – forcing them to separate from their parents (who they love) so they can sleep on their own and everyone can have a more sane time in the future, when our messed-up society comes a-knocking at 6 o'clock every morning.

Perhaps they are right, and we should be more 'militant' with our parenting, but everyone has to judge their situation for themselves. I'm sure it will come to the point when we miss her being in our bed with us. The last thing we need is confusion from another person (who, let's be honest, *doesn't know either*) trying to be an authority over us with all this. We're all just blundering along, aren't we?

I realised, this afternoon, just how special Elfie's little mat is. Her entire universe is right there. Everything. All of her ups, downs, challenges and joys are taking place right there, in that space. This means I need to make it my place as well, and make conscious efforts to get on that mat with her as often as possible. When I move into it with full attention, it feels like crossing the threshold into another realm. The adult world is left behind, and she lends me her precious way of being in the world, for just a little while.

Friday 3rd September

Have you ever been hooked? You definitely have, but you may not have heard it described as such. Our thoughts come so fast, and they represent different perspectives we can take. Their speed means we fall into them, just like little dream bubbles, and they suck up our attention and close us in, taking us away from everything else, from so-called 'reality'.

I was hooked today when I had some time off work and needed to look after the little one on my own for quite a while. I was totally out of practice and experienced a severe bout of inadequacy. It was a thought bubble, a story. I fell in, and my attention rolled around inside the bubble for a while; it *was reality*, until the bubble popped. When it did, I 'came to my senses' and could see that this was just one perspective. That it was short-term, very short-term, and I would get back into the swing of things very soon.

Another frustrating aspect of returning to work properly is the energetic shift which is required for me to shift out of work mode when I come home. I've noticed a dissonance, a block, when I try to connect to Nadine when she describes her experiences and challenges of the day with Elfie. It's just such a different world from my world of work, and even more intense, that it requires a conscious gathering of energy for me to be fully present. Without this, we are not in relationship, I am not listening, and there is no love. I'm very glad I noticed this today and gave the energy needed. It would have been much easier to half-listen, to *not connect*, and so "liking what it (the Ego) does not like" – as Gurdjieff put it – allowed me to be supportive.

Could this sort of thing be a significant cause of PPD for mothers? I'm sure it must be; we need to connect and we need to be heard. I wonder how frequently the partner who is out and working must find themselves not caring or engaging as much as they would like to, in an ideal world, if they had a choice. So we need to try to give ourselves the choice! How often will I have to make an effort to give myself this choice? As usual, awareness is my only hope.

I want to be the best husband possible. It's so demanding to be a mother at home with a baby, and if she can't talk about it and have genuine engagement and support, it will get harder and harder and will make her feel closed in and alone.

Saturday 4th September

This morning, I was a little late for work again. I was rushing a bit and it was all very stressful. Aggravation was flying at me from every angle: hungry cats, a crying baby and lots of jobs to do to get out of the house in a civilised state. I was in a whirlwind, going way too fast.

Suddenly I noticed. This noticing made me stop in my tracks. This stopping made me *really see the whirlwind*. It was there, all around me, so alive and so tense and horrible. I could feel it pushing and pulling at me and filling my world. In the noticing and stopping, it all came into focus, contrasted sharply, viscerally, with the world of the present and the world of the senses.

BOOM. Perspective. Everything slowed right down and completely changed. I breathed deeply and fully accepted being late for work, again. It's not worth that much stress; not even close.

This was another 'weather check' when I really needed it. Meditation on the move. Thank God for consciousness.

Tuesday 7th September

Elfie is just *so soft and squashy*. She has such tiny everythings: little toes, pristine and smooth; cute, rounded toenails; the softest little ears, which you can't help but stroke and fiddle with; a doughy little tummy, perfect for blowing raspberries on; and the squidgiest, pudgiest limbs you can imagine – whose only purpose right now is to be squeezed by doting new parents.

How is it possible that her existence is becoming normal? It's so strange. The further we get from the time of her birth, the more we forget the birth itself and how miraculous it is. The further we get from her *not being here*, the more it seems like she has been here forever.

We are all that miraculous. And, as Gandalf said to Frodo, "That is an encouraging thought." Perhaps we should remember it every now and then. Giant babies, everywhere, just struggling along and trying their best.

Wednesday 8th September

My mum and stepdad came to visit us a couple of weeks ago, and it was delightful; we were so excited to show them the little wonder that we had somehow made. To share her with them was so touching, and it brought home to me how difficult it has been to be separated from our family during this adventure so far. To see my mum holding her for the first time was one of the high points of my whole life.

I will never forget the moment we all shared when they very first entered the house. As we greeted them, Elfie was asleep on Nadine in the sling. When my mum noticed that she was sleeping in there, she spontaneously burst into tears. Then, at the exact moment when my mum looked at her for the first time, Elfie's big blue eyes shot open. She gave my mum the most adorable, innocent, bright smile I have ever seen, and this is no exaggeration. There was a real knowing glint in her eye, like they were long-lost celestial friends, and the atmosphere was charged with a special feeling – beyond time, somehow. A tear came to everyone's eye, and it was the perfect start to their trip. Somehow, I managed to get a picture.

My stepdad thrived on the challenge of getting her to sleep in the sling. He was brilliant at it, even inventing a little rhythmic song which always worked. Unfortunately for him, the little Ferris wheel melody which played on TV to get her to sleep was too much for him as well, and made him fall asleep every time, right on cue. We got a video of him asleep on the sofa, doing a cartoon-esque, loud blowing noise out of the side of his mouth, in time with the music. My mum thought it was bullying, but I don't agree. She gets very pranxious, you see – a word I am officially coining – but years of seeing friends hilariously terrorised when asleep have blurred the line on this issue massively for me. Do bear in mind, in this case, that it looked like he was blowing up one of his cheeks on purpose from the inside, and then letting go of it like a balloon. I had a phone in my hand – what would you have done?

It was amazing to have them with us during their stay, and very sad indeed when they left. It was always sad on previous trips, but with Elfie here it feels *very different*. The wave of emotion when we parted was far more powerful than usual, because it just feels *wrong* to be living so far away from them. I guess, unfortunately, we are going to have to grapple with this feeling a lot in the future.

Thursday 9th September

Elfie has suddenly stopped wanting to breastfeed for the last 24 hours, and it has been really difficult. Again, we find ourselves faced with the piercing sound of her constantly crying, topped with hopeless confusion about what on Earth is wrong. This has all been exacerbated by a reduction in Nadine's milk flow (seemingly as a result of the feeding troubles) which, in turn, creates a very powerful and immediate fear, which only makes things worse. A vicious cycle, if ever there was one.

Then, she appeared to be allergic to the formula that we reluctantly tried to give her as a replacement. We have ordered oat cereal formula as another substitute, and get this: it says on the box that it has wheat in it, but *also* that it doesn't. Considering that wheat is one of the allergens Nadine is trying to cut out, we have found this really helpful! We are fine with the demands of having to give all of our time to look after her; we have no problem with that. But her not wanting to eat *anything* makes us feel that we *can't* look after her, and that is a really unsettling thought.

Sunday 12th September

To get a different perspective on Elfie's health situation, we went for an appointment today with a magical healer who masquerades as an osteopath. Well, she's a qualified osteopath and craniosacral therapist, but primarily seems to focus her treatment on energy healing. My friend had recommended her, though warning that she was a 'bit voodoo', and I assured him this was fine, because I'm fully voodoo!

Having said this, even I was stunned when she began laying on her hands and assessing Elfie's energy field. It just seemed so unusual in what seemed to be a medical setting, but in the best way. I cannot imagine how freaked out many people must be by this if they haven't entertained the possibility of such things. Our society simply does not accept the idea of action at a distance and of energy transference between beings.*

The session was quite incredible. It was refreshing to witness and speak to her about her alternative approach, which I have studied a bit myself, and her conclusion was startling to us:

This is not an allergy. It is unprocessed emotional trauma from the birth experience.

I have considered this factor here and there in the last few weeks, but not as much as I should have. I blame our scientific culture for this. Why? Because our bias towards the 'physical' (a word which has actually lost all meaning because of the unexplained mysteries of consciousness and the findings of quantum mechanics) makes us ignore all the other layers of what we are. After a child is born, and the physical elements of the body have been taken care of, the doctors' work is done, and you are allowed to leave. It is assumed that, now, everything is 'fine'. But what about the mental and emotional layers? I'm not suggesting these need to be 'fixed' by doctors, but can we see how our outlook is ignoring all this? None of the 'regular' doctors we have seen about Elfie's issues have even considered the possibility of birth trauma affecting her emotions, and in turn her digestion, despite the growing body of research linking the gut microbiome with our emotions and overall wellbeing.[29]

---

* It may surprise you to hear, though, that even the CIA has extensively investigated claims of this nature. You can read about those extraordinary adventures on their website under the *Stargate* files, which include – believe it or not – hundreds of documents detailing their training program for 'psychic spies'. See: *CIA Reading Room*, 'Stargate Collection', https://www.cia.gov/readingroom/collection/stargate.[28]

Diary of a Mindful Dad

Returning home really felt like a return home. Seeing someone in a professional setting with this outlook, with a huge emphasis being placed on emotion, which I share, returned me to a holistic view of Elfie's health.

Immediately, we needed to address the issue of Nadine's milk flow and the anxiety surrounding it, and the session gave me the perfect perspective. We needed to attend to the whole situation slowly and with care and love. We needed to acknowledge how difficult the situation is, emotionally, for both of us, worrying that she cannot feed properly. We needed to speak our acceptance of this into being together.

Nadine read online all about how stress impacts milk production, and we marvelled together at the power of the subconscious to impact physical reality and the world of the body. This helped to shift some of the grit at the base of our clouded hearts, and Nadine began to pump milk with a fresh outlook. I suggested that this was the perfect opportunity to benefit from mindfulness. We noticed how fear distorts the whole process, causing Nadine (and me as well, when I'm there) to obsessively scrutinise how much milk is being produced, fretting about it and perpetuating this cycle. A watched pot never boils.* We have the choice, instead, to consciously accept that the flow is reduced, *for now*, and face what is happening with consciousness, love and faith. Love for Nadine's body, love for Elfie, and faith that this, too, shall pass.

The whole atmosphere started to change and Nadine had the most successful pumping session in over a week. She is far happier now that we have spoken about all of this together and refreshed our energy. It's amazing how powerful a conscious change of perspective can be – in this case *directly* impacting the physical body – when we *face* the inner instead of ignoring it.

---

* Pots being the most quantum of all the kitchenware, of course…Physics joke, anyone? No?

Wednesday 22nd September

It's been over a week since Elfie's visit to the energy healer, and she has undergone a significant transformation during that time. Nadine has also won the breastfeeding battle, at last, and this has been a huge factor in the shift. Now Elfie has forgotten the bottle exists and so she is far more settled whilst feeding. She has had the happiest and most settled week of her whole life, perhaps except for one week at the beginning, when she just slept the whole time.

This is excellent timing, because Nadine's mum is visiting and has now also met Elfie in person; again, this has been so lovely to witness. It represents a big shift in their relationship, a new chapter, now they are both *mums*. It feels like an ancient and almost mystical *rite of passage* to watch Julie helping Nadine in various aspects of her new role, and I guess that's because it is!

Ever since visiting the healer, I've been reflecting on a 'holistic' outlook to health, and this has had the unexpected effect of making me far more aware of the state of our house and how it *feels*. When times are stressful and busy, it is only natural for us to let things become more of a mess, inwardly and outwardly. Yesterday, the energy of the house was *all wrong*. I stopped to notice, and realised that the cats had suddenly started fighting each other a lot as well, over the last few days, which is very unusual. It all felt horrible and something needed to be done.

In the normal way of thinking, there's no way this could be related to the waves of fear we've been riding, or to our state of consciousness at all. If our 'inner' world is stuck inside our head (the story we've been sold), then of course it has no relationship to anything 'outside'. But is it? If, instead, we exist in the shared field mentioned previously, then it *must all be related* and could not be otherwise.

In light of these reflections, I began to 'smudge' the whole house. This is a Native American tradition (burning sage) in an attempt to clear stagnant and negative energy from a space. I was surprised to see, recently, that smudging is becoming a little more common these days, as Western culture starts to entertain a larger story about the invisible world we inhabit. I've been doing this for many years, ever since I attended a remarkable sweat lodge – another Native American tradition. The last time I smudged the house when the cats were going through a bad patch, they immediately stopped fighting for weeks; it was truly remarkable.

At the same time that I was smudging, my mother-in-law spontaneously began cleaning downstairs, and we ended up having an unexpectedly wonderful afternoon. We cleaned! We cleaned the whole garden, which hadn't been tended to properly for months on end, and it was refreshing and therapeutic. I found it interesting to note that we bonded more during this time than over any fancy meal, or evening drinking – though we are partial to those as well! After the cleaning, we went for a celebratory swim, and it was all just a delight.

It prompted some general conversations about 'energy' and what is meant by it, and these exchanges, with both Nadine and her mum, have reminded me, again, of just how far the current paradigm is from a *holistic perspective*. For example, why are we always told that any disturbance the baby has is caused by wind or poo or food? Why do we still instinctively exclude the possibility of emotional triggers, emotional wounds and other 'inner' factors? We hear about a mysterious condition called 'colic', which has no definition whatsoever, except for *constant crying*. Is this insight?

I cannot shake what the healer said about how significant the birth trauma is. It reminded me of 'Identity Therapy' (the powerful form of therapy mentioned earlier in the book) which, like the work of Stanislav Grof,[30] traces some of the dissonant aspects of our personalities and lives all the way back to birth, and even beyond: to our experiences in the womb, and even the emotions which our mother felt during that sacred time. I remember how powerful it was for me to see this in relation to my own past, and how much it opened up for me.

As I reflect on all this, at the same time as doing my best to deal with Elfie's situation, I am seeing the wallpaper of the mainstream paradigm cracking over and over again. It's like when you buy a new car, and then start seeing it everywhere. Now, whatever happens is perceived through the lens of its potential hidden, noumenal causes, and I cannot stop seeing this every time Elfie is crying or having trouble feeding or anything else. Yes, of course, sometimes she is just tired, and babies cry when they are tired. But how much that is invisible to our eyes, and all of the physical senses, are we each going through every day? What about her?

This has shown me how far this is from the normal way of thinking, and how difficult it is to discuss with people. We are so entrenched in our mechanistic, reductionist conditioning that it is close to impossible to step outside of it, or even to see its borders. Yet it seems like every comment anyone makes about health comes from the *assumption* that everything is physical, that the inner world has no relevance, even though we are all *experiencing and speaking out of our inner world all the time!* This absurd situation, believe it or not, goes to such an extreme, in defence of the standard scientific outlook, that some prominent neuroscientists, psychologists and philosophers have denied *that consciousness exists at all!*

I tried to discuss Elfie's health with a friend, when we were all considering what might be upsetting her, and the disconnect we have been sold between mind and body is so strong that even to *suggest* she might be experiencing emotional difficulties, as a result of her traumatic birth, sounded so odd and was met with enormous resistance and bemusement. I believe it would be the same if I mentioned this to most people. Yet how can we possibly be so shocked by this idea, considering how traumatic birth obviously is??? Isn't it just as traumatic (or perhaps even more so) for the *being* experiencing it as it is for their body?

Thankfully, the total refusal to acknowledge the inner world, which our culture has suffered from for so long, seems to be giving way at long last. Rupert Sheldrake's work to expose his ten dogmas of 'scientism'[31] has now been bolstered by the excellent work of Bernardo Kastrup[32] and many others, and there are plenty of signs that the tide is beginning to turn, with a brave 'new' world coming into view. Both Kastrup and Sheldrake have spoken separately of the number of prominent scientists who are coming around to these alternative views in private, but are not yet ready to publicly be associated with them. Over time, to do so will hopefully become easier, and science can be released from the shackles of materialism (the belief that everything is made of *matter*), once and for all.

Sheldrake's tenth dogma is: "Mechanistic medicine is the only kind that works." He's right: this *is dogma*, and it certainly might be false. If it is, the implications are immense. Perhaps it's time we, as a collective, start opening our minds to these possibilities and not seeing them as so strange, once and for all.

Thursday 23rd September

Nadine and I have found, over the years, that it's much better for us in every way to eat together at the table, instead of sitting and watching TV. Not every single time, but mostly. Now we have been able to go back to doing this, and I noticed resistance to it.

It's so much easier to just sit and watch TV. We are so tired. Etc. Etc. Etc.

Because it hasn't been our habit for a while, the whole timeline of the universe pushed back against me when I imagined it happening. I was forcing myself into a new timeline, effectively, where things were quite different from the current one. That's literally what the resistance is – the mind sensing how different that future is, *how far away it is*, from the one which is expected, the one which is most probable based on the past. But then I remind myself that *the mind is an idiot* and that it *doesn't know that future*. Its idea of that future is just that, an idea.

Unsurprisingly, going back to the table has been a blessing. Everything is so much calmer, quieter, more peaceful and more intimate. It really is *quality time. We are truly together.* In the age of overstimulation, the phrase 'quality time' has lost a lot of value and credibility. If we watch 1,000 TikTok videos every day, it's not going to be possible to have quality time with nature, for example, because the consciousness of trees and streams and flowers is in a completely different time zone. You just won't be permitted access to the true beauty of that world. Sadly, this is impossible to understand if your consciousness has only ever lived in the 'TikTok time zone' (I would also like to coin that), and this is the situation for many children and young teens growing up now. It's simple: it's all speeding us up, so we will miss out on everything which requires a slower state of mind to appreciate or experience.

If we, as partners, are rarely together during the day, and then sleep for a third of our lives (I wish), and we don't eat together, looking at and speaking to one another, then what sort of relationships are we really having? Are we in relationship at all? Or just shuffling past each other, exchanging a few thoughts on the surface?

<u>Monday 27th September</u>

At the beginning of this book, I mentioned how we protect ourselves from thinking about how incredible and strange the miracle of birth is, because it's simply too much to properly perceive the reality of it. I wonder if the same happens when it comes to sleep and dreaming? I remember, at university, I suddenly became aware of how incredibly odd it is that we become unconscious every night, like phones charging their batteries, and imagine ourselves in situations which we believe are real. What was really throwing me was the fact that all of this *just happens* to 'us', whatever we are, and there's nothing we can do about it. It meant that whatever *we are* can exist in our imagination, with *no connection at all* to this world. It meant that we, the very essence of consciousness, are a total mystery – yet we go on with our lives as if everything is totally normal.

I had a similar experience in a Neuroscience lecture, during a period of particularly acute existential crisis. I saw the lecturer speaking blithely about the brain and pointing repeatedly to his diagram on the board, with all the other students semi-listening, and I just couldn't believe it.

Was it not freaking him out to see that, according to the normal view, he was speaking *out of one of them*? Or, stranger still, that he *is that*? There is a brain inside your head right this second, apparently*, and it has always been there, though you've never seen it or felt it directly. How bizarre this was suddenly hit me in the lecture, in the same way as the insight about dreaming, and I was well and truly freaked out. I guess the crux of it could be described thus: we don't understand what we are, or what's happening here, but we've deceived ourselves into thinking that we do because it's less scary. We have deceived ourselves into thinking that life, sleeping,

---

* In case you think this 'apparently' is outrageous, that *surely I must be taking the piss now*, consider the following: First, the idea that what we see is objectively 'real' and independent of *our perception* is fiercely debated – philosophically and now scientifically (just ask *Schrödinger's cat*). Second, what we think things *are* really just means how they *appear* to our limited, 3D, physical senses. So what we call the 'brain' is merely one peculiar part of what a human being looks like *in this dimension* – and even then *only if you cut their head open!* Kastrup has often summarised his view by saying that the brain is just what consciousness *looks like* from inside the body (see The Idea of the World, 2019)."[33] This also means, for example, that the Earth isn't round at all – not in 4D, anyway. What we see is just a *spherical cross-section* of something stretched through time. Its full 4D shape would be much more weird and 'wormy'. Feel free to keep that one and share it with the next 'Round-Earther' you come across. :)

dreaming, waking, brains, all of this, *is normal*. But is it? That picture of the brain didn't seem very normal to me. What the hell is it?

I am writing this because I heard Elfie crying hard as Nadine was rocking her to sleep. Why does she so badly not want to go to sleep? It's almost certainly *not this*, but could it be possible that she is freaked out about becoming unconscious and disappearing from this world? How does she know that she will ever wake up again? Is she crying because she thinks she might not see Nadine or me again? What a horrible thought – I hope not! Perhaps this is why most people would rather not think about this sort of thing. Cypher's steak, in *The Matrix*, was pretty tasty, after all.

Friday 1st October

Elfie's breastfeeding has been better since the events a couple of weeks ago, but now she is only feeding from one side. Due to this, today Nadine is doing another kind of 'reset': 24 hours, just in the bedroom, no chores, nothing but skin-to-skin with the baby, feeding and playing. A bath is also on the agenda, and it's called 're-birthing'. This was a recommendation from a lactation consultant to help Nadine refresh Elfie's relationship with breastfeeding in a powerful way. Going into the bedroom, it feels really nice, safe and special. This is exactly the idea, and I can see how this could make such a difference.

I was on the phone to a friend earlier who has just had a baby, discussing why the crying is so unbelievably triggering. We both feel the same about this, and of course he wanted a solution, but there's no solution for caring! I told him my approach to the crying, which seems to be helpful in some strange way, a lot of the time. I try to attend to my own reactions as well as the external situation – to feel it all fully and not 'run away' inwardly. Does it 'work'? Well, it doesn't make the crying stop, of course. Neither does it simply make everything jovial and great again. So if that's what he meant, then no.

But does it stop the *fighting*, the battle between me and the experience? Yes. This *is great*. Does it also stop *time*? Yes, and this is even better. It stops the *mind from creating time*, and this artificial time is where all the problems start. This is the sort of time that creates a drama about how it's all so 'hard for me'. Without this added stress, we are only in this moment, and this moment is never as bad as the mind says it is. Does it also regulate my nervous system, giving the message to Elfie that everything is OK, which in turn helps her to regulate hers? For sure. Does all of this transform the experience? Yes.

If that is it 'working', then *yes, it works.*

Tuesday 5th October

Many religious traditions hold that creation starts with vibration or sound. Whether it's 'the Word' of the Bible, the ancient Hindu *mantras* (which have an incredibly fascinating backstory) or even Tolkien's mythological 'Music of the Ainur', the theme appears again and again: *words are pure magic.*

Every time we use the perhaps primordial (literally meaning 'existing at the beginning of time') power of speech, we are vibrating the air and sending our inner world symbolically through space so that it can be beheld by another. Do we realise that? This *is magic.** Perhaps if we stopped using this sublime gift so thoughtlessly, we would be more aware of how powerful and remarkable it is.

Despite this, however, there is also a sense in which words can *get in the way*. I remember, when she was just a couple of weeks old, I had been sitting with Elfie quietly for a while before I began to talk. I noticed, after a few attempted sentences, that the symbols of language, the encoded vibrations, on this occasion, were acting as a *barrier* between us. The act of speaking meant that I could

---

* Ever wondered why it's always a magic *word* or a magic *spell*?

not *be with her* as directly as before. So whilst words can be immensely powerful for communication, they can, paradoxically, sometimes also block a more basic and instinctive form of it, a simple *being with*. How often do we engage in this '*being with*' in our relations with others, and how healing might it be? It is much simpler to do this with trees or other parts of the natural world which don't speak back (through language, that is). It is also perhaps rarer than it should be to have this simple communication with pets, as it is so natural and enjoyable to talk to them.

Yet this evening, and yesterday, this is how I had bath time with Elfie: in silence. There we were, both just being with one another. It was really beautiful on both occasions. *Still, calm, present.* Communicating deeply, without the need for words.

Friday 8th October

The joy which comes out of that little being and into my heart is truly indescribable. I cannot believe how elated she makes me feel just by looking at me and giving me a cheeky smile. She is genuinely happy to see me every single morning when I eventually have the energy to sit up and look at her for the first time. Such moments are blessings beyond measure.

Now that she can understand so much more, there are songs to be sung. Nadine and I have both been primary teachers, and in that setting there's a lot of that sort of thing you're supposed to do. I couldn't hack it, personally, talking to the kids in baby voices and the like. My ex-head tried to force me to wear a 'pinny' in the playground containing Phonics cards, and to go around ruining the kids' break time by shoving letters in their faces, but I vehemently refused and thankfully won.

Nadine is very good at all this performative, nursery sort of stuff, but I must admit that the songs I'm hearing leave a lot to be desired. Please feast your ears on the lyrics of this particular masterpiece:

"The grand old Duke of York, he had 10,000 men,
He marched them up to the top of the hill and he marched them
  down again.
And when they were up, they were up,
And when they were down, they were down.
And when they were only halfway up, they were neither up nor down."

Sorry. What? Is anyone listening to this crap? It's embarrassingly bad. Whoever sang that for the first time would be amazed if they knew it had stuck. It might even be worse than my pièce de résistance that I showcased earlier. I know it's the 'rhythm that's important', but seriously – come on. A little effort wouldn't hurt, now, would it?

Monday 11th October

I have quite an odd relationship with birthdays, because I've spent a few hours annoying children in classrooms about it. Instead of giving them the 'you're so speshul' treatment, I often go the other way, although always in a spirit of jest. I gently remind them that the calendar, with its months and days, is a human invention, and therefore June, or August, don't really exist. I kindly remind them that the Earth isn't even in the same place as it was a year ago, because the entire solar system is revolving around the centre of the galaxy. If I'm in a really annoying mood, I will offer the suggestion that their essence has never and will never age and that, therefore, they are both infinitely old and infinitely young at the same time. None of these ever go down too well, but it used to give the class a bit of a laugh.

My 32nd birthday was yesterday, and whilst Elfie was an absolute delight, in the evening the universe gave me the gift of an emergency vet trip for our four-year-old cat who hadn't been eating properly. This has happened before, so we weren't too concerned – but we were wrong.

It turns out that he has an enormous tumour in his intestines, and the potential surgery to remove it would be an unspeakably expensive 'Hail Mary' more than anything else. The entire small intestine was glued together, so the surgeon had to cut out the tumour, untangle the entire intestine and then stitch it back together. *What?!*

Thankfully, she is considered one of the best veterinary surgeons in Dubai, so there was hope. She told us that she had only attempted this once before, and it had failed, but that it *was possible*. 50/50 then. Great.

As the surgery was beginning, Nadine and I both did some creative visualisations at home in a desperate attempt to help in any way we could, just in case it could make any difference. As usual, the imagination surprised me and we saw and felt all sorts of wonderful things. This time, his intestines became an extraordinary water slide, and Nadine and I were sliding down it with Elfie on our laps, full of joy, sending healing water rushing through every twist and turn. It was incredibly vivid.

Three and a half hours later, we received another call to say that it was done – and it was a resounding success! We were unbelievably relieved. Now it's time for him to recover and, unfortunately, spend at least five days at the vet's.

Wednesday 20th October

My dad has just left, after coming to visit us for a week, and we had a lovely time with him and his fiancée. It was so emotional for me to watch him with his first grandchild, just as it was with my mum and Nadine's mum previously. Elfie was on pretty good form on this visit, but we had to take many trips up and down the stairs in the evenings to keep putting her back to sleep when she woke up. This gets old fast.

During the day, when she was awake, she was charming them both with her lovely smile and playful spirit. I watched my dad's heart melt a little when he spent time with her, which I haven't seen too much in my adult life. They were both really helpful and encouraging, and pleased to see the three of us in good health and coping with it all reasonably well.

During their visit, we had to go and visit Elmo, our cat, every day and take Elfie with us. This caused a lot of stress because she was being a bit of a nightmare most of the days after we had been at the vet for half an hour. At least we got a nice video of her turning the pages of a cat encyclopedia with her feet. That's the sort of little boon we need to appreciate with this little wonder, it seems. Her energy does seem to transform any public space which we enter; I guess that's her job?

The vet told us that Elmo was lucky to be alive and he had recovered really well so far. She also added that the surgery had been videotaped, because vets often do so for training and sharing amongst other vets. Some of the other vets who received this video thought it was a *post-mortem;* that's how 'out there' it was. I asked her, "Are you proud of yourself for the surgery?"

She wasn't at all ready for such an emotionally intrusive question, and has a reputation for not being the most socially comfortable. (I doubt extraordinary surgical and social skills go hand in hand.)

"Yes, I am actually!" she replied. She then became very animated and told me that I could watch the video if I wanted! I genuinely considered it, but said no in the end; that's a bit much for me, I think. She told me that the results had come back from the pathology report on the tumour; it wasn't cancer. That was great news. So what the hell was it?

Her answer was not a surprise to me.

STRESS.

Imagine that. The stress of a new baby, most likely, had given our lovely cat a *gigantic tumour* in his intestine and almost killed him. It's likely that the cats being shut out of our bedroom now, when they weren't before, has contributed to this.

He also suffered a lot of trauma when he was a kitten, when

The First Six Months

we had to rescue him from underneath a climbing frame. His very first interactions with human beings were being chased out of the only safe place he knew, grabbed by the scruff of the neck, put into a carrier and then driven somewhere unknown in a car. We didn't want to do this, but were forced to, otherwise he and his siblings were going to be *poisoned* – believe it or not – by the unnamed organisation where they were found. Can you imagine the level of trauma for a kitten? Ever since then he has been timid, shy and prone to sickness.

Like early human trauma, these events can deeply affect long-term health – not only by leaving unprocessed stress in the body, but also by shaping how we perceive future experiences, creating a vicious cycle. For example, Elmo has an irrational, powerful fear of visitors who come into our house and have no intention of harming him. All of this creates an undercurrent of stress existing just below the surface of his consciousness all the time, as it can with us, and these movements eat away at our energy and our lives.

When Elmo returned from his major ordeal, he snuggled up straight away on the sofa with Elfie for a 5* cuddle, both hiding away together from the traumatic and scary world!

Wednesday 27 October

We had to go to a government building today to transfer ownership of our car to an insurance company, after it had been crashed into a couple of weeks ago – ironically, while it was at the repair shop! I tried to do it on my own so that we wouldn't have to take Elfie, because it's a bloody hassle to go anywhere with her. In the end, this wasn't possible, so we had to go on a family trip, as Nadine is the official owner of the car. The difficulty with leaving the house is that, if it isn't timed correctly, it ruins Elfie's day and, in turn, ours. If she doesn't sleep at the correct times, she is incredibly grumpy and cries far more; everything is so much better when she has her routine. Towards the end of the visit, she reached the 'end of her useful life' (as we say, but probably shouldn't) and started to cry loudly at the desk. There were around ten government officials nearby, and many people sitting on chairs around us waiting for their turn. Nadine had to stay there to sign documents, and after she had done so, I urged her to go and walk around. Normally, this soothes Elfie and stops her crying.

"No," Nadine said. And she rocked and rocked and ignored her whilst she cried. We were both triggered by the situation and felt the instinctive, archetypal embarrassment of ruining the previously quiet atmosphere. I looked around and saw that many people were looking at us, bothered by her crying. Nadine said, "We have to get used to her crying in public."

I saw that she was absolutely right. Now was the time. 30 more seconds of crying and I carefully looked around again, wondering, with fresh eyes, *is this really bothering people?* Upon this second survey, the answer seemed to be no. Everyone had clearly labelled this disturbance 'baby crying' in their mind and filtered it out; they were all continuing as normal, as if she weren't there. This was a great moment. Sure enough, after a while she did stop crying and it was a lesson learned. We have lots more visitors coming in November, and big plans have been made. The little one's going to be out and about all over the place, hopefully, so we have to get over this sort of thing.

One of the ladies on duty came over to us and said, quite insistently, as Elfie was crying, *"Maybe she is too cold here?"* The look on her face said that Nadine was 'doing it all wrong', and that's how it came across.

Nadine replied, "No, she's just tired." And she was right; she knew what was going on. Was this lady trying to be annoying? Of course not! She was just caring. Her parental instinct had reacted to the crying, and she wanted to make it better. Unfortunately, as we saw before with the cleaner, this helpful intention from other people rarely lands as intended.

Thursday 28th October

Last night Nadine said, "We really need to WD40 that bed." Unfortunately, this isn't because we've been waking up the neighbours on account of our having such a great time. No. It's because it apparently takes her 'literally three minutes' to get out of bed every time she has put Delphine down to sleep. This is exactly the kind of thing which it's so easy to forget, or not bother to do, isn't it? So we probably won't bother to do it now, either, even though I'm taking the time to write about it. Ah, the human condition. Absurd!

This evening, something quite scary occurred: a loud alarm went off to tell us that Elfie had rolled onto her front in her swaddle in bed. It's amazing tech that Nadine has sourced, and I haven't given a moment to trying to understand what it is, where it is or how it works. All I know is that when we hear that alarm, it's not good at all. Nadine ran up the stairs to sort the situation out as quickly as possible, and then it happened again two hours later and it was my turn to rescue her. And so the era of swaddling comes to an end.

Nadine then showed me the magnificent next step we have to take, because it's unsafe to swaddle a baby at night once they are able to roll over. When they can't be swaddled anymore, their 'startle reflex' is likely to wake them up over and over again, and so *this* comes to the rescue…one of my favourite photos I've ever taken:

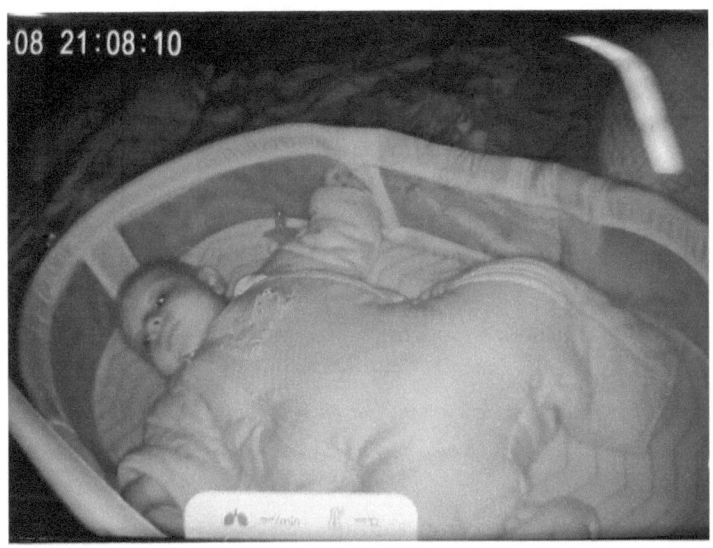

Yes, that's right. A sumo suit. I don't know what it's actually called, but we all know that's what it is, and it's bloody hilarious. Just look at the state of her. Try rolling over in that, little one.

Check.

Your move. If you can…

Friday 29th October

I can't believe I wrote 'Check' last night with such a positive attitude, like it was going to be that simple. Obviously, she had the worst night's sleep ever. She hated being a sumo wrestler in comparison to being swaddled, and couldn't get used to it. After a pretty good stretch of a couple of hours she was up, down, crying and all sorts for most of the rest of the night. Not fun. Nadine told me the different options we have: continue with this, try without anything or try a sleeping bag. We have decided to give the sumo suit a few more tries and see where it goes, partly because that's the least it deserves in return for the comedy it has brought us.

As soon as Elfie came downstairs in the morning, she hit a wonderful milestone. As I was reading a book to her, she reached out with both of her little hands and I gave it to her to hold. She held it up on her own for a few seconds and then it fell flat on her face. I told Nadine, and she was excited because Elfie had never done this before. Then, she reached across and turned the page with her left hand as I held the book for her. I shouted to the kitchen, "She's turning the page!"

Nadine misunderstood me and replied, "They can't do that for another few weeks, I don't think."

(Before moving on, let's just take a moment to appreciate her casual and total dismissal of what I have apparently just witnessed with my own eyes whilst she is elsewhere.)

I said, "I've just seen her do it!"

"Whilst holding the book?" she called out, incredulously.

"Obviously not, that's *impossible*. She would have to have three hands," I responded, matter-of-factly and far too quickly. Oh dear…remember what I said about my common sense?

"Well, how do *we* do it then?…" came the inevitable reply.

I could almost hear my lovely wife hitting herself in the forehead with her hand. Then I heard an exasperated, but not altogether surprised, "Dom…"

Personally, I think what I said is perfectly sensible, and just serves to demonstrate how ingenious fingers actually are. Tell me you haven't already tried to imagine how we do it, and sympathised with me just a little…

Diary of a Mindful Dad

Saturday 30th October

She's so bloody lovely it's unbearable at times. Nadine just brought her down from her nap and she was in the most docile, still, watchful mood – just staring at me sweetly. I picked her up and squeezed her tightly, carrying her around the house, and felt like I never wanted to let her go. *I want to squeeze you until the end of the world,* that feeling said in my mind. This is the love a parent feels which makes people keep popping out these little critters.

Sunday 31st October

With no time in the day as a new parent, apparently important things like exercise disappear immediately from the world. Luckily for me, though, it never appeared in the world in the first place, so that's one thing I don't have to worry about.

It's hard to build new habits, isn't it? Just ask my obese cat, Aragorn, who has already made a couple of cameos in this book. He entered the 'Biggest Loser' competition at our vet (a genuine contest for pets in the community – and guess what the prize was? Food. Seriously.) and he failed miserably. It was our fault. We were good at starving him a bit, but couldn't commit to exercising him enough. Life was too busy and still is. So here he sits, as big as ever.

His exercise habits are very similar to mine. He gets very excited about it and ends up in 'Child's Pose' within a few minutes (this is essentially just lying on the floor). That's about it. I have genuinely done this more times than I can count, and it draws a great chuckle of mockery from Nadine every single time.

However, I am improving. It's been one of two major blind spots for me in terms of my overall health since I've been an adult – the other being glorious sweets, chocolate and alcohol. Oh dear, that's three more. Well, one at a time, eh?

With exercise, at least, I have now seen the light at the end of the tunnel. I realised last year that my bouts of exercise get longer and longer each time, and during the last one I exercised every day for a month or longer, without having any external motivation. That was a big step for me and I see now that I'm almost there.

When we fall off the wagon, we think just that – we've fallen off. But not necessarily. It's just the natural see-saw of our energy with regards to that life change. We dramatise the trough of the wave and it makes us freeze, energetically, preventing us from finding the motivation to start it up again. We think we've gone right back to the beginning, but actually we haven't. In just the same way, we get over the top about things at the peak of the wave, thinking the brilliant enthusiasm we have for something will last forever. Ever seen a kung fu movie and been convinced you will take it up and become good? It's OK, we can admit it – I literally do that every time.

In fact, due to this particular quirk of our species, in combination with my 'elf-like' tendencies, in my house we have the following:

⋄ A contact juggling ball I was definitely going to learn to use (that's the weird thing David Bowie is beguiling people with in *Labyrinth*)
⋄ My left-handed electric violin – played once, slightly drunk, by someone else
⋄ A 'diabolo' I was definitely going to master after seeing a performer using one at a dinner event – also used once, this time by me
⋄ Three unused books on how to draw
⋄ Loads of exercise equipment, mostly unused

The list probably goes on, and I can't be bothered to mention all of the different careers I have said I wish I had moved into, always met with a mocking laugh by my lovely wife.

Reflecting on it, I went through this same rollercoaster when trying to learn to meditate. But I had experienced such wonders from it that there was no way I was going to lose it as a part of my life. This is the same thing which has happened to lots of people I know with exercise, and maybe the same will happen to me soon, and hopefully my big fat cat too!

Now that meditation is solid for me, I am very thankful to my past selves for the efforts they made. During the last couple of months it has, of course, been very difficult to keep this going to the same degree. This is to be expected, though. I do miss being able to get that time each day, but it's also good for me to get used to not relying on it, and therefore finding balance and grounding in the midst of daily life only. Babies are, for sure, the most ruthless mindfulness trainers I've ever encountered.

Nadine said, earlier today, that she knew she wasn't going to be able to 'do anything' for six months, and so she hasn't let anything she is missing bother her – even showering! Her stability and serenity continue to amaze me.

Monday 1st November

Without full attention, there can be neither romance nor intimacy. Last night, I gave Nadine a massage. It was 'nothing big'; I just decided to do so for 20 minutes or so after Elfie had gone to bed. It was lovely. We relaxed and chatted to each other the whole time about any random thing which came to mind, and the act of massaging seemed to change the atmosphere and what was possible. Perhaps it was just having time to ourselves without phones, TV and other distractions, and perhaps the massage was a key part of it. But it felt *special*. I felt like it was the first time we had *really communicated* in far too long, because life just gets so busy. It doesn't seem too harmful to be on your phone, or to watch TV together, but it's easy to lose this real deep contact with your partner if you never have time without *any of this at all*.

It reminded me of how short life is, and how important it is to carve out such times.

Thursday 4th November

Oh, God. No food for dinner, I thought, looking in the relatively full fridge. "How come there's nothing for dinner?" I asked my lovely wife.

"Because you said you didn't want any of the normal things because they weren't healthy enough. But then you don't know how to cook anything."

Ah, yes. Right again. She's good, isn't she?

We were both surprised, looking at the monitor, that Elfie had slept for two hours straight immediately after 'going down', and I said to Nadine, jokingly, "Are you sure she's alive?"

"I went upstairs and checked," she replied. Oh dear – even with a monitor telling us her breathing and heart rate on the phone! I guess this gives an insight into the new-parent state of mind.

Friday 5th November

Yesterday, Elfie was in the most amazing mood from start to finish. We went to IKEA in the morning, and she was going around in the buggy, happy as Larry the entire way, without a single sound. All day long, she was totally still and present, like a little sage, and such a delight to spend time with. We are both stunned by how much she has changed and how much more fun she is now. Everything you do provokes a response from her, and it's a completely different ball game from the first few months, which were described as 'just about survival' by a friend of mine. Her experience was fairly similar to ours, and this is a great description.

"We're insufferable, aren't we?" Nadine said to me in the evening.

"Yep."

We've done it. We've become those people. I think that basically everything she does is the cutest thing any being has ever done and I cannot believe how much I love her all the time. It is quite ridiculous. Looking at the baby monitor yesterday evening, I genuinely heard myself say, in response to Nadine asking me to check her temperature, "Oh my god, she's got a little body and it's got a little temperature. That is so cute." I've literally become that exact guy.

I am trying to curb my 'baby-spamming', but it gets the better of me at times. I sent a video of me flying her around in the air to the song 'Walking in the Air', because in the moment I thought there was no way anyone could possibly see it as anything other than absolutely wonderful. But I'm pretty sure I was wrong. I think I received a total of zero replies. It's hard to tell at this point what other people think is cute/interesting and what they don't. Just to mix it up a bit, I sent a picture into my family group this evening of a bath filled with water and poo; that ought to throw the cat amongst the pigeons.*

Oh yes, this reminds me: Elfie shat in the bath. That's ten minutes and an ill-fated game of rock, paper, scissors with Nadine that I'd rather forget.

When it comes to other people's babies, I have always thought nothing more of them than that: they are other people's babies. If they are doing something particularly cute, I have always appreciated it, but the general media of them doesn't provoke that much of a response from me. I think this is a fairly well-known phenomenon. Will this make me stop sending people pictures? I doubt it. Maybe I will just accept my subjugation to

---

* A phrase which, by the way, we should consider retiring, like many of the other unnecessarily horrible ones – more than one way to skin a cat? Is there? None in this house, thanks.

this cosmic law: *people want to send you pictures of their baby, and you don't really want to see them as much as they think you do.*

Monday 8th November

Nadine's determination has, once again, come good for us. Elfie wants to wake up at approximately 6:30 every day. Many mothers give in and their day begins then, but not my wife, lover of sleep that she is. She is so determined not to let this become our routine that she manages to get her back to sleep every single morning. She really cares about this extra hour in bed and I'm so glad she does. Just before 8:00, the little one wakes up again and gets plonked in between the two of us happily, the door is opened, and all the cats rush in and jump up on the bed. It's like we have a viewing platform for a mini zoo *every morning,* and Elfie is unsurprisingly entranced by it all. She watches them, rapt, for 15 minutes or so, and we all have a lovely wake-up together. Thank you, Nadine!

Tuesday 9th November

Ah, milestones. There are a lot of these to look out for when you have a baby, and they can easily be a source of angst if your child is not 'hitting' them. 'Hit' is an interesting verb which we use for that, and quite an apt one, as this is the attitude many of us have regarding progress and 'making waves' in life. The desire for our children to 'hit' their milestones 'on time' (or early) goes far beyond babyhood, and our society is full to the brim with this sort of thinking.

Mindfulness is often perceived to be against progress and, in a sense, it is. The attitude of mindfulness cautions us against an unconscious and unquestioning desire for 'progress' in the *ordinary sense,* which could also be called 'blindly following others or society without awareness of what you are doing'. This means that what society currently regards as progress should be examined and brought into question. What if we are wrong? What if what we really need is somewhere else? Krishnamurti often used a metaphor to illustrate this point: "You have been walking North for thousands of years, and someone comes along and says, 'No, go East.' What will you do?"[34]

We have sacrificed wisdom, peace and harmony on the altar of so-called progress and now, in so many crucial ways, we are lost.

People want fame and they can't explain why. Everyone wants to be rich, but they don't know what they want the money for, beyond a house and a car and not 'having to work' (which is supposed to be our contribution to, and participation in, the whole). We crave a promotion because we are sick and tired of being enslaved by a system which only cares for its own survival, and we spend lots of the money we earn buying clothes which have a recognisable little picture in the corner, mainly so other people know we earn a lot of money. We have made a real mess of things.

When it comes to babies, the meaning of progress is rather straightforward: walking, talking and the like. Walking forward, the true meaning of progress, would be a fantastic thing to see your baby do! These skills can be broken down into stages (e.g. crawling) and we can see, generally, how quickly most babies do this and compare them to our own. The fact that these milestones are just a guide, an estimate, is so easy for parents to forget.

Of course, if your child is very far behind average in a certain area, it may demand attention. Perhaps there is something you can do to help, and your intervention may be necessary and beneficial. However, how easily can this balanced approach be lost, and should these milestones be a cause for anxiety? In a world where competition is king and it can easily determine our quality of life, we see here the seeds of worry planted very early indeed. As usual, the conditioning of society plays a significant role in this. Nobody is *telling you to worry*, but I can see how easy it could be to do so.

The way we approach milestones for our babies is a good indication of our general approach to our child's place in society and, therefore, presents a good opportunity to consciously find a perspective that we are happy with.

All too often, in my career, I have seen the negative effects of pressure on the psyche of a child. It *squeezes them* and *dulls* their natural light, despite this being the opposite of the intention. *The negative emotion of the experience of being pressured constricts the flow of their natural intelligence.* This can be seen in mathematics perhaps more than any other subject, partly because the 'problems' (interesting word to use, isn't it?) are either right or wrong, and it is seen as a 'clever-person subject', but this same energy is manifesting all over the place in more subtle ways.

This has shown me the enormous importance of not allowing the seeds of this pressure to take root. As Elfie develops, I am ignoring any flutter of mind which tells me that the time when she does x or y actually matters. This leads naturally, and without consciously creating it, to a much more beautiful perspective, a real connection with the moment, *as it is*, and my child, *as she is*.

Those flutters of mind are *seeds*, and the seeds are made of *fear*. Fear of your child not being good enough, not fitting in, not achieving what they want to (or, more accurately, what *we want them to*), the list goes on. Make no mistake, these fears are going to rear their ugly heads frequently as our children grow up, and if we act on them unconsciously, they will produce poisoned and poisonous fruits. Some of these challenges are going to be incredibly difficult; far more difficult than thinking they are a week later than others to sit up. What if, God forbid, they suffer from a disability which dramatically reduces their opportunities in life, or they don't fit in at school and are bullied?

There is so much more to these fears than meets the eye, and, as usual, they deserve a lot of attention and investigation. This means that we, as parents, have the *responsibility* of rooting out and transcending the fears existing *in us* which might negatively affect our children. What are you afraid of for your child? How can you even know and find out? Do we see how these fears affect both us and them, or are they in our blind spot? It takes a lot of effort for us to even notice these fears, let alone to transcend them.

The good news, though, is that *if we can* do this, we learn a great deal about ourselves and we help our children to grow organically. Such transcendence is also a healing action for the *community at large*, filtering into society in unforeseeable ways. Perhaps this is a little more like *real progress*, and the direction we should all be moving in.

I have a client who had many bad experiences at school and, as a result, his parents eventually decided to homeschool him. These parents had seen the negative effects of pressure on his psyche, and they had had enough. Working with them has been such a breath of fresh air, in comparison to working within a school environment, where pressure and stress are so normal that they can no longer be seen. He is now permitted to mature and develop at his own rate, and this has helped him immensely, although he may have missed out on some other aspects of school life.

If you want a plant to grow, do you need to rush it or force it to go faster? Of course not, you simply give it what it needs, including the right environment. Take the avocado tree, for example. It can take up to six weeks even for a little root to appear, and between 5–13 years to bear fruit. All those grown in good conditions produce fruit in the end, but with an enormous variance in the time frame.

So why pressure your baby or your child?

The First Six Months

Friday 12th November

When did everyone start wanting you to take a survey? I received two calls yesterday, in the middle of trying to make food for Elfie as she yelled at me, specifically for *surveys about calls that I had already taken earlier that day*. What? Don't companies realise that asking you relentlessly for feedback on their customer service makes their customer service much worse? It is bizarre.

In other news, I now have the perfect excuse to try to be the best human being I can be. The excuse is that *she is watching my every move!* She is learning so much so quickly, and I have just been reminded by watching *The Secret Life of 4 Year Olds* that she is already doing the worst thing imaginable: *imitating me*. She is going to do this more and more until she can *tell people what she thinks*, and what she thinks – and how she expresses it – is determined hugely by the two of us who are raising her. This is a big problem for me, because I say a lot of outrageous things and my 'filter', if it is in place at all, has not been installed altogether properly.

For example, one of my clients gave me a very generous belated gift voucher to celebrate Elfie's arrival, and I said – perfectly innocently – that it was *wonderfully timed* because Nadine needed some new bras! It was only when I got into the car and called Nadine to excitedly relay all of this to her that I discovered that the money was supposed to be used to buy *Elfie* something nice, so I had to quickly make amends with some well-placed linguistic manoeuvres later in the day.

One thing we both want is to spend less time on our phones. We've always aimed for this, with varying levels of success, but having a baby makes you see these bad habits from a whole new perspective. Her existence and presence give me a *direct external reminder* when I am doing something which I don't think is right. Pretty handy, really. Wise people might pay good money for that sort of service!

Friday 3rd December

It is so difficult to write this book now, being back at work and looking after the little Elf, as we now call her. What am I thinking? How could this be a good idea? It's hard enough just to try to live all this, let alone to write it all down.

Despite my misgivings, when the energy is there, the energy is there, and I am trying hard to make sure I sit down when it rushes in. Inspiration: literally when 'spirit enters'. What will you do? It needs to be used, or it will depart as swiftly as it came. That's what this whole book has been like for me, and even if the mind can't understand it, it *feels right* to ride the waves of inspiration when they appear.

Do we live in a magical reality? It will be clear to you now that I think we do. What is going to happen in the next moment? We don't know, and so often this is a source of delight. Just as I wrote that, our fluffiest cat Pippin jumped straight up onto the table and leapt across the screen of the laptop. Delight incarnate!

Are you ready for wonder, for magic in your life? The idea (and it is just that – an *idea*) of a mind *'in here'* and a world *'out there'* removes the possibility of magic from the lives of so many of us, duped as we have been by the saints and saviours of the scientific so-called 'Enlightenment'.

A *magical reality* is one in which not only is the universe *alive,* but it is mysteriously, wonderfully and magically linked to *your consciousness.* It is one where our experience, as we blunder about the world, is responsive to flow, to blockages, to attention and intention. One where the life you see is a reflection of yourself, with neither of the two taking centre stage. As Shakespeare noticed, it's one which is a little bit more *dreamlike* than the solid one we've been sold.

So many of the children I have worked with are simply *not ready for magic,* even though most of their schools have Roald Dahl's quote, "Those who don't believe in magic will never find it", stapled up somewhere. There's something about *stapling quotes to the wall* that seems to kill them a bit, isn't there? Not really surprising, I guess.

Tragically, the story we have been sold about this world we live in has destroyed our readiness for, our *openness to* magic, and so Dahl's words fall on deaf ears – the door is closed. We have all been sold the lie that *we understand life and the world, in principle*. Nothing could be further from the truth, and nothing can do more to douse the flames of wonder. This pernicious, invisible belief closes the door to the *new* and the *surprising*. This is probably the most important thing which I want to ensure does not sully the consciousness of my little Elf. A self-fulfilling prophecy of the worst kind; creating boredom and a sort of half-life, inner death for oneself. If we cannot find the magic in *this moment* we are living *right now*, then *there is none*. Sometimes we are lucky enough to see this, and if we can catch onto a feather, we can glide along with it for a while.

What if a change in perspective changes the world you live in? This is impossible in the materialist worldview. Most of us still see our perspective as essentially irrelevant to the 'reality' of things, despite quantum mechanics showing this to be false over 100 years ago. In *Science Ideated*,[35] Bernardo Kastrup demonstrates the need for us to finally accept what nature has been telling us for all these years: that the line between 'I' and 'the world' is much more blurry than we have been led to believe. Even 'physical' science seems to be telling us that *half of the magic comes from the eye*.

Unfortunately, this has been interpreted by the collective mind of our modern age into a mandate for 'manifestation', a prescription for making demands of life to fulfil our every wish. It is symptomatic of our age to take the understanding that we live in a responsive and alive reality as an invitation to *demand more*. If only it could have been interpreted otherwise. If only the fact that we are at one with reality, connected in a magical dance, could be seen as a reminder to *listen, to pay attention*.

Diary of a Mindful Dad

If we are always grasping, demanding, how can there be the 'flow' everyone is talking about? Again, it is typical of our age, when hearing about flow, to turn it into a 'flow state' which can be *had*, or *achieved*, forgetting that it is *blockages which restrict flow*. Flow is the natural way of life; it is the blockages which need to be seen and attended to. This is the 'way of negation', in spiritual-speak. See the stains in the mind and wipe them clean; then the mirror of consciousness will reflect truth. We don't need to 'go' anywhere, because what we are seeking is not somewhere *else*, something *extra*. Rather, the *natural magic of life* – which is our birthright as human beings – is *here* and *now*, but clouded over by a misty haze of desires and fears. Like Eckhart Tolle once said so concisely, any spiritual 'instruction' worth its salt should have the effect of *removing content*, not adding more.[36] But this is not at all sexy or exciting to the modern mind, so full as it is of achieving and accumulating. It's content *creation* which gets the plaudits in our world.

People are told to imagine they already have whatever they want and to *really feel it*, and then it will happen. The irony of this is that *we do already have it!* The gift, the miracle of *life*, of *consciousness*, is right here, right now, and no experience or achievement will ever be able to trump it. If we turn in *that* direction, the direction so many saints and sages have pointed to over the years, things blossom in the most unexpected way.

If we let them, babies can instantaneously transport us out of our personal, isolated dream and into this sacred remembrance, into a space of wonder and magic *right now*, in the games they enjoy so much. We have been playing the old classic 'Peekaboo' with Elfie lately, and it's such a beautiful example of the *aliveness* of being, the beauty of connection, of how the mischievous spark of consciousness can transform the moment. It's the simplest game imaginable, trying to alert us to the ever-present miracle of consciousness itself.

"*Where have you gone?*"

The First Six Months

"Here I am!"

No wonder they get so excited. Each sudden appearance is a 'Big Bang', the essential mystery, experienced and marvelled at over and over again.

As we grow up and out of 'Eden', there is not so much which *seems* new, which perhaps makes it harder for us to feel magic and wonder. Yet does this left-brain lie have substance? Is this moment, *right now*, not perfectly, wonderfully new?

Saturday 4th December

After writing that last night, I drove to the shops this morning and my words were thankfully ringing in my mind's ear. (Or ears? How many do you have? Don't worry about it.) I was looking at the same old road I drive down regularly, and then it hit me, as it sometimes does: I was looking at the *same old road*.

However strange it seems to say, this really means you are looking at your memories, or at the very least looking *with* your memories. *I already knew the things I was seeing.* The street signs, the lanes, the view.

As usual, as soon as you 'wake up' like this, everything is *new*. It was no longer the same old road. Everything I could see took on a new quality and became *interesting*. Somehow, everything was *sparkling*. Not visually, but giving off a sense, a feeling of *aliveness*. This is a good example of how we co-create the reality we perceive, how what we see is our *interpretation* of reality, rather than simply something 'out there'. It is also a quintessential experience of what is often called 'Beginner's Mind' in mindfulness.

It is tremendously satisfying, enjoyable and simple to live when seeing with those eyes, which can bring the magic out of anything in life. Nisargadatta Maharaj said something wonderful on this topic. The questioner asked:

"There is something exceptional, unique, about the present

event, which the previous, or the coming do not have…What makes the present so different?"

He replied, "Obviously, my presence. I am real for I am always now, in the present, and what is with me now shares in *my* reality."[37]

Doesn't that seem so simple and obvious when it is said? The 'stamp of reality', as he calls it, which the present seems to have, is in *us*. We are not only present, but *presence itself*.

Sunday 5th December

A lot has become easier as the little one has approached six months, but it seems that for everything which has become easier, something else has become harder. This feels like a pretty neat and tidy little cosmic law of experience. For example, we are nowhere near as worried about her health now that she has been alive for longer and her body has acclimatised to the world more. However, she now does gigantic proper turds (one of which I just had to walk around the house holding in a nappy whilst I did urgent jobs for her bedtime), and she needs to be entertained 24/7 like a tyrannical little monarch.

Latest nicknames: Tyrannosaurus Elf, the Tyrant, the Elf, the Gremlin, and Little Elf.

She gets bored SO QUICKLY and then just makes this awful moaning noise, which isn't loud enough to really annoy you, but just grinds you down over time. Quite a short amount of time, come to think of it. This is towards the end of 'Leap 5', a long one which entails starting to understand the 'relationships between things'. If only those things were 'how to not annoy' and 'my parents', we might be in better shape.

A key development for Elfie is realising that she *wants things*, and *experiences*, and that she can *kind of get them some of the time*. It is this understanding which gives birth to the terrible droning sound mentioned above, which is the background noise of our house these days.

The First Six Months

<u>Monday 6th December</u>

I sinned against my baby today, for the first time that I am aware of: *I told her off.* She has disturbed, annoyed and disrupted me millions of times already, but this is the first time that I have ever directly given her a negative reaction to any of this. I just wanted to lie down for five minutes – that was it. I had worked solidly all morning and was just about to start again. But the drone just got louder and louder. I can't even write it; the noise is so annoying that it defies any sort of lettering. She was right next to Nadine and me, and we had been entertaining her relentlessly. I was lying next to her when Nadine quickly went on to her phone to do something.

"*Babyyyyyyyy! STOP!*" I something'd. I don't know what it was. I definitely didn't 'say' it, and I definitely didn't 'shout' it. If saying is 0% and shouting is 100%, then this was about 35%.

She didn't even register it, so I don't think it had any effect on her whatsoever. But Nadine put me right in my place and showed me why she was doing it. She picked her up and held her, and she immediately stopped. "See. You just have to work out what she wants. She just wants to be held."

Told. Parenting 101.

I felt bad about this, obviously, and drove to work. On the way, I digested the experience and realised the significance of it. It might sound like a little thing, and as if my reaction was justified. But I was unnecessarily unkind to her, because of my own situation and emotional state. Although it was the first, it definitely isn't going to be the last time this happens.

How can I do better? Do I need to? Is it possible? I try pretty hard already, and nobody is perfect; I don't want to be unrealistic about that sort of thing. Obviously, millions of times, she is going to do something which she *actually shouldn't* when she 'should know better' and sometimes discipline is going to be necessary. I can't beat myself up about ever being stern or firm with her as she grows up. Years in teaching make this abundantly clear. But this wasn't one of those times, I don't think.

The best thing I've learned in the past is to make efforts as often as possible to be as present as possible. That has saved me from blunders and arguments more times than I could possibly count. I don't think there can be any formula or strategy for this sort of thing. You can't plan how you should act when you're tired or stressed because, *when you actually are tired or stressed*, you don't have the energy to remember and act on those things. Your best chance, in my view, is conscious presence, as often as possible, and this is what I will continue to stick with to be the best dad I can be. I'm open to seeing that I've been an idiot, and I try hard to apologise and forgive with equal speed and consistency. Preachy? You love it!

Needless to say, I apologised to her when I came home from work and bought her a third iPad (one of those two things is not true). Hopefully, I've learned my lesson.

Friday 10th December

Last year, we went to the community pool and saw something I hope I'll never forget. This guy was tanning himself whilst his kids were swimming in the pool. They kept coming up to him and shouting, and he was fobbing them off with expert ease; we were somewhat in awe and enjoying the show. Then it took a hilarious turn. He shouted, "OK, OK. Swim to the other side and I'll give you 100 AED."

What? That's 20 quid! Either the guy is absolutely loaded or he REALLY wants them to piss off for a minute. Or both. Sure enough, they did – they pissed right off. But I had seen the flaw in his plan. Can you spot it?

Time. Time was the fatal flaw.

What do you think happened next? His worst nightmare.

They swam back.

The First Six Months

Check, I heard the universe think.

What happened next we couldn't believe. Realising his blunder, he sat up and said with a totally straight face, "OK, OK. Swim all the way around three times and I will give you 500 dirhams."

This was unbelievable and we were loving it. Sure enough, they did this and it gave him a whole ten minutes of peace. His smile looked like it might have been worth the full amount. Kids, eh!

Wednesday 15th December

Ah, leaving the house – one of life's great non-events, until you have a baby. My friend Jimmy used to say to me, "Leaving the house, mate!!!" with an exasperated face to match his tone, to explain how hard it was to have kids. I didn't get what he meant.

Now I do. To leave the house with a six-month-old, this is what we need to do:

⋄ Prepare the nappy bag with toys, food, wipes, nappies, muslins, change of clothes, and something to cover Nadine with so she can breastfeed
⋄ Change the nappy before we go
⋄ Plan the trip perfectly around Elfie's many precious naps
⋄ Put the buggy in the boot (don't forget this and realise it halfway and drive home)
⋄ Change Elfie's outfit again because she has been sick again two minutes before we leave

There's probably loads more I can't remember right now, and it takes forever and always somehow goes wrong. It makes you see whatever you're leaving the house *for* in a totally different light. Is it really worth it?

Thursday 16th December

Last night Nadine asked me to get a bodysuit out for Elfie, forgetting that I obviously don't know what that is. Apparently foolishly, I got out something which *covered her body* and was met with utter ridicule.

"That's not a bodysuit!"

After being shown the error of my ways, we had the inevitable discussion of why it's called a bodysuit if it doesn't include the whole body, and I was fobbed off with some strange logic about limbs not being included in the clothing definition of body.

Then, tonight, I get this:

"That's not a bodysuit, that's a romper!"

Nadine exclaims this with glee, not even slightly seeing the uncanny resemblance between the two.

"What the hell is the difference?!" I bravely replied.

"A romper has frilly arms and funny legs."

Well, that's that then, I thought – I'll close this door and try to never open it again. It's a bit like the ever-enigmatic concept of 'going', which I have tried to fathom for the 15 years we have been together.

"No, they don't go," she declares, about a wonderful outfit I've fashioned. Granted, harem pants and trilbies aren't usually seen together, but *give them a chance*, I urge her. Ever tried chilli chocolate? Historically, these arguments tend to fall on deaf ears. I pick my battles and move on.

Friday 17th December

We are convinced about the science behind the 'leaps' now, because we've just finished Leap 5 and Elfie has been constantly whining and trying to learn new things ever since it began. Now the leap is over, according to the app, she had three of the best days (emotionally speaking) that she has ever had. It's visibly obvious that she has mastered so many new skills, and now she is just enjoying using them, rather than desperately learning something else. She seems to be truly content and relaxed for long periods for the first time in a while. Of course, the timings of these leaps will be different for different babies, but generally, from our perspective, the dates on the app have been very accurate. Quite handy, really. Finally, science and technology pay out in the parenting journey.

Saturday 18th December

Bollocks to all of the above – she's back to normal now and it was a horrendous morning. A couple of days of not learning and being stimulated relentlessly is all she can handle, it seems. Nadine's job – being at home with her all the time – must be so hard, and I think it's much harder than what I'm doing. It's just relentless. As Elfie is only napping for 30 minutes at a time, Nadine has to fill all of these breaks with housework and barely gets a chance to shower, cook, eat, etc. Certainly very little, if any, time to relax.

"Why do we keep going to bed so late?" she asked me the other day. It's because it's the only time we both get when nobody is pressuring us in any way. Elfie is sleeping and I've finished work; it's our time to wind down. Unfortunately, this fact is on a collision course with perhaps the worst thing about having a baby: you have to wake up at the same time *every day*.

Last week, we had friends over in the evening, and we were having a really good time until it hit 11:30 and I saw the time. The significance of it seemed to loom over me like a phantom: *every* bit of enjoyment I have from this point on makes me feel *worse* come 7:15am. We can't sleep in. How crap is that? So socialising needs to be earlier from now on – lesson learned. It's just not worth having five hours of sleep and trying to keep her occupied and entertained all day. It's too hard and then I'm more grumpy with her and that's not good dadding at all.

No, we still haven't given in to the sirenic call of *CoComelon* (the ultimate in hypnotic, addictive and lobotomising programming), but I can see why people do. Just to get a bit of peace! I found my peace during her 30-minute nap this morning, when I had a really nice long meditation. Bathing the mind in the ocean of awareness truly is the most wonderful, wonderful thing.

Sunday 19th December

Yesterday was my last day of work before finishing for the Christmas holidays, and it started terribly. Both of us were with Elfie on the bed, and Nadine walked off to do something else. This meant that I was now *in charge of her life*, but I hadn't quite taken that fully on board. I turned around for literally five seconds to tell Nadine something, and when I turned back around, I was horrified. In that tiny space of time, she had rolled about four times to the side and I saw her hanging off the bed, almost standing, and then she fell. The floors in houses in Dubai are rock solid, not carpeted, and she landed on the floor on her front. I think she had instinctively put her arms out to cushion her fall, thankfully, and for a second she made no sound. Then it came: the horrendous shriek of a baby in a lot of pain. I had got to her by this point and picked her up. Nadine and I were both terrified that she had really injured herself. After a minute or two, she had calmed down and seemed fine, but we hadn't and didn't.

I had to quickly shower before work, and of course I felt like the worst human being on Planet Earth. I had let my baby fall off the bed and really hurt herself.

As I drove to work, I noticed my mind trying to process the trauma of the memory. About three times, my mind replayed the memory and glitched when it came to the moment when she hit the floor. I could hear the thud reverberating around my psyche. Just like when I remembered the birth, the system seemed to freeze at that moment and could go no further.

The next time I flashed back, I consciously made my mind replay the entire memory, breathed deeply and accepted what had happened. It was really interesting and did seem to help. I was able to see everything which had happened, including the fact that she seemed totally happy and normal now. Imagine how many of these events we each have locked up within us, unprocessed, frozen and probably causing some sort of trouble.

I wondered if everyone else's mind would have also been doing the same thing, or am I just being oversensitive? I spoke to Nadine about it, and she relayed lots of moments in her life when she remembers this same process taking place. One difference is perhaps that because of how much time I have spent watching the mind in my life, I will be more likely to notice this process happening when it does.

Take this for an example of why I think this is so handy: when we went to the last baby class, our little one was on superb form and causing all sorts of trouble, whilst the others just sat like little angels/zombies – not doing anything at all. Elfie had just developed a strange, gremlin-like noise which seemed to be an attempt at a laugh, and she had no shame in sharing this with the group. The best way to describe the noise would perhaps be a *threatening, throaty cough*. When she expertly combined this noise with a maniacal glare, she had great success in scaring the hell out of the other babies and parents.

The instructor loved her, and it was clear that she was her favourite that day because she was so animated and lively. She threw a few compliments her way and intimated that she was very advanced. After the class, I asked Nadine if she had had the same reaction as me: a flutter of pride and feeling great about myself. I watched this foolishness dart across my mind in real time and found it funny immediately. No, it's not *me*. It's the software of humanity operating in mind. The thing is that by *seeing it* in this way and therefore *not identifying with it*, you don't fall into the trap. If I hadn't seen it, I probably would have gone around for a while thinking my baby was better than all the other babies.

That which starts with a seemingly innocent little flutter of 'Ooh, isn't my kid great?' can morph over time into something far more pernicious. Maybe, in time, you will be disappointed with your child for not constantly excelling in everything, because you've got used to enjoying seeing them in that way. Maybe you will reduce them in your mind to just a little 'achievement device' to make *you* feel good about *yourself*. Maybe they will put way too much pressure on themselves as an adult, and never be able to find peace, and not realise it's because so much was expected of them as a child, and it all started with that *one bloody baby sensory class*!

When I returned home after work to start my holiday, I embraced my little Elfie – six months old tomorrow – with a bit of extra squeeze because of the events of the morning. It was very healing to see that she was perfectly fine. There's nothing like a brush with severe injury to remind you how much you love these little mischief makers. Half a spin of the giant marble, and we are all still alive. That's got to count for something, hasn't it?

4

Six to Twelve Months

"Realise deeply that the present moment is all you ever have. Make the Now the primary focus of your life."

— Eckhart Tolle

Thursday 23rd December

It's been said that the sexiest thing a man can do for his wife is the washing-up. When you've had a baby, though, this is no longer the case. When you've had a baby, it's far sexier to have done the *washing*.

If I went upstairs right now and told Nadine I've put a wash load in, taken it out, hung it up to dry, folded it all and put it in the cupboards, I think she would look at me with a passion Juliet only burned with once or twice in her lifetime.

Sadly, this isn't the case. I'm not as sexy as I would like to be, which means I haven't done that; there are clothes hanging up all over the house. Bedsheets hanging on doors, towels on chairs, and muslins as far as the eye can see. We are trying our best, but 'uphill battle' doesn't even come close to describing it.

We went to the doctor last week, because Elfie had the symptoms of a virus. When the topic of her 'reflux' came up, he said, "Oh don't worry, that's just a laundry problem for you. As long as she's gaining weight, it's fine."

Yep, she is, and hell yes, you can say that again: *the laundry is IMPOSSIBLE*. Today, she was sick probably 30 times. That's not an exaggeration, and it means clothes being washed on a constant basis. For us it has just become the norm, comfortably settled in our subconscious, but my mum pointed out during her visit quite how much it disrupts everything. For one thing, it means that other people can't enjoy picking her up and cuddling her, because so often she is *sick on them*. Anyone really determined to run the gauntlet has to weigh up that desire against mild terror about their clothing and the sanctity of their face. Every ten seconds, it seems, we are bending down to clean up a sick or shouting to the other for a muslin. An old wives' tale my mum is adamant about is fennel tea, so Nadine is going to try this and see if it can reduce the reflux.

Next year, we desperately want the house to be in order more than it has been, so we've invested in a tumble dryer to make life easier. We won't have to spend hours every day hanging everything up all around the house, and we are very excited about this. Imagine being excited about a tumble dryer? I am so old.

Delphine has given us a potentially fantastic Christmas present this year and decided to sleep for longer than half an hour sometimes. We have made the classic mistake of getting ahead of ourselves and thinking it's a long-term change. Then, predictably, she sleeps for half an hour again as soon as we think it.

Having said that, we do seem to be lucky about her nights. One of my friends just said to another, who is about to have a baby, "Say goodbye to your sleep!" but it hasn't really been like that for me, as you know if you've managed to keep reading until this point. Bless your heart.

Nadine's watch, which monitors her sleep, tells her that she isn't even waking up when she knows that she is woken by Elfie for a feed. This happens three to five times a night and it means she is only waking up *just enough to do the deed*, fooling the apparently 'smart' watch (self-named, you see), and therefore still having a good amount of rest during those times. Thankfully, then, it appears that she is getting at least six good hours on most nights.

Every evening, after Elfie 'goes down', we have the rest of the evening to ourselves, with the exception of the odd feed which Nadine has to quickly run up for. It's only five minutes each time, so we have still been able to watch a few films and read, and that has been an absolute delight. Six months in, it feels like we have a relatively good routine going. The utter madness of the first week and some of the challenges of the first three months seem like a very distant memory now. We joked that we are ready for another one! That, my friends, is absolutely absurd. The power of biology.

Friday 24th December

Time is very odd, isn't it? I can't help but annoy Nadine when she says things like, "God, it doesn't feel like it's been six months, does it?!"

"Yeah, I think it feels like it's been exactly six months."

Real conversation killer, that one.

It is a well-known phenomenon that in meditation, dreams and other changes in our state of consciousness, our perception of time is liable to change too; in deep sleep, for example, the perception of time might be non-existent – if we could remember it. We can't remember, and this makes it feel like no time has passed at all. Questions like Nadine's one are more than fair then, and point in the direction of something enigmatic and fascinating.

Time is one of the central mysteries of our existence, and its many enigmas prompted a rather unhelpful quote which I was disappointed to discover *wasn't Einstein's* after all: *"Time is what keeps everything from happening at once."* A guy called Ray Cummings, apparently.[39] Isn't that a shame? Do you know how many Einstein quotes aren't really Einstein quotes? We just seem to really want him to have said all of these things. Is it the hair?

We don't have to go far to hear about the shenanigans of quantum particles which seem to be living just like that, casually mocking linear time as they go about their quantum business (see some interpretations of the 'Delayed Choice Quantum Eraser experiment', for example).[40] Rob Bryanton's mind-melting *Imagining the Tenth Dimension*[41] and many of the world's spiritual traditions suggest that this might just be par for the course in higher-dimensional realities.

Yet the strange, illusory nature of time is not restricted to sleep and the quantum realm. What does six months feel like?

Six to Twelve Months

'Feeling like it's been six months' is a feeling of how 'big' a vague package of memories feels right now. You can't remember six months' worth of stuff right now.

You are always in the present.

Have you ever really thought about that? *It's always now.*

Even if you had a time machine and went back to the past, it would *still be now.* How weird is that?

Every memory you've ever had has been *now.*

But the mind has the curious and dangerous ability to make us feel as if the *unreal* moments it presents to us in our minds are *actually in the past or the future.* But they aren't.

We move around this world we all share whilst also inhabiting a private, imaginary world, *right now, and right here,* which is pretending to be behind us, or in front of us, in time. It gets very messy in there and takes up a lot of our time and energy.

You can see why Nadine sometimes regrets saying casual, 'normal' things like this to me.

You might also think that this is just idle philosophising, but it's not. In fact, what I'm saying is the *central mystery and insight* of meditation, mindfulness and the like.

In this first picture, our energy is being drawn, *in the present moment,* into the imaginary realm of past and future created by the mind. This magic trick makes us lose sight of the present moment, which you can only make out in the background if you look carefully. This resembles how the present is apparently veiled from us by the mind from moment to moment. Living like this is fundamentally unsatisfying, because some part of us knows we are missing something vital.

In contrast, the picture below shows what it is like to 'live in the present':

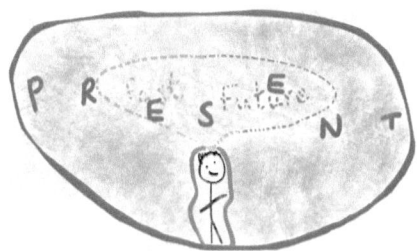

The mind is still there, and it can still offer us glimpses of the imagined past and future, but it is felt and understood on an instinctive level that *this is still happening now*: mind is *not in the driver's seat*. We are aware, throughout our lives, that we are here, and now, and that is where we place our energy. This is a simple but powerful way to understand what 'conscious living' is all about.

The most amazing thing we discover through meditation is that *full attention* has a curious ability to *stop time*. As it embraces the totality of what is seen, without effort, there is nothing but that. That moment, and everything in it. This state of attention brings us into the 'Eternal Now' of Hindu philosophy, and it is deep nourishment for the soul. In this sort of presence, there is no fragmentation between different parts of ourselves, nothing 'taking us away', and no duality between this moment and any other, remembered or imagined. In that moment, we feel truly whole, at peace, and at home, because we really are at home, because our home *is the here and now*.

This morning, when I sat at the breakfast table with Nadine and Elfie, I enjoyed simply witnessing her eating her food and participating in the moment fully. There was wholeness and I was there – *all of me*. I felt a deep sense of contentment. How can there be a sense of lack if there is total presence? There are no cracks, nothing is being lost. Breakfast for the soul.

Six to Twelve Months

Thursday 30th December

Nadine's mum Julie has just left, after coming to visit for Christmas, and we had a wonderful time. Elfie's first Christmas was truly magical. She had a couple of good days and a couple of bad days, but for Christmas Eve and Christmas Day itself she was absolutely brilliant. She is capable of so much more now and this makes it way more fun to spend time with her. You can easily see what she enjoys and what she doesn't, and she is so much more animated about everything. She has a real little personality now and it's amazing. This was encapsulated perfectly in a picture we took on Christmas Day, which embodies the wonder of Christmas and is easily my favourite picture of her so far.

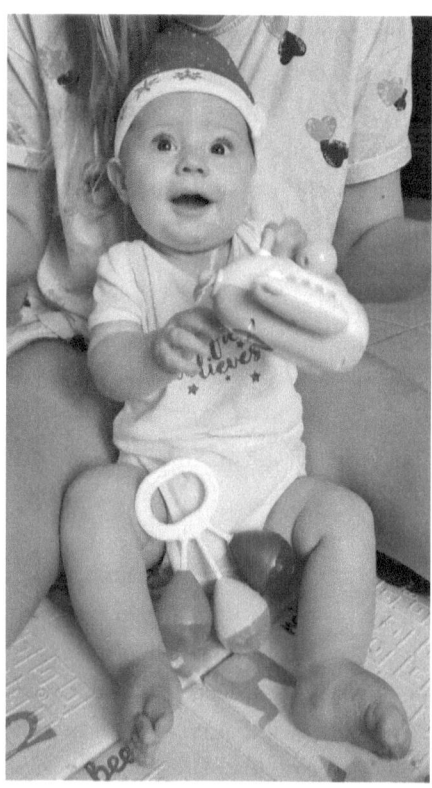

We went out to restaurants for a few evenings, and this was difficult to start with. On the first evening out, she went berserk crying just before we left. It was bedtime and all she wanted was her normal routine, but she could see she wasn't getting it. We felt so bad for forcing her out of her routine and I had the thought of cancelling the dinner. Nadine made a very good point: if we had turned back then, we would have been accepting that we can't *ever* go out. So we needed to go through the pain barrier and get her into a routine of not always having a routine. 'Mummy's intuition' was right: as soon as she got in the car, she was quiet, and then she was sleeping soundly all evening. "*Sorry, not sorry,*" Julie whispered to her as she slept, "We wanted a nice evening out!"

She slept in her pram next to the table and then, every so often, she woke up needing to feed. She flew out in her Zipadee-Zip (a strange, winged sleep outfit), looking just like a sugar glider, and looked around whilst in the air before latching straight on. Then she went right back to sleep. Nadine even managed to get her to sleep inside the noisy restaurant without too much hassle.

The night went by like a dream, with Elfie in her own little dream. It's great to know that we can do this and we are going to try to go out at least once every ten days, partly because it's good for our sanity, and partly to keep Elfie able to sleep outside of the house.

At the end of the trip, we all found it very tough to say goodbye, and it reminded us again of how lovely it would be if Elfie could see her grandparents and uncles more often. I'm not as close to my grandparents as I would like to be, because they've always lived abroad, and I feel that's a bit of a shame. We have resolved to do more video calls with family back home from now on, though, so they don't miss too much of these early years. Previous generations never had that luxury and I'm very grateful for it.

Six to Twelve Months

Sunday 2nd January

This morning, Elfie gave me a cheeky smile as she threw my wallet on the floor. She is starting to take the piss out of me already. Oh dear. I thought, in my innocence, I might be able to enjoy the illusion of being in control for longer than this.

The question of discipline is a huge one when it comes to parenting, of course. One of the advantages of being in the world of teaching is that Nadine and I have seen many different parenting styles and the types of behaviours and personality tendencies they play a part in shaping. As we have also done so much tutoring, we have seen an extra dimension to this – the student's life at home – which many teachers never see, and which perhaps helps us to connect the dots. The aligned stance we have come to (theoretically, of course!) is authoritative, not authoritarian (like Chairman Mao), nor laissez-faire (let them do whatever the hell they want all the time).

This means that, despite being the least intimidating person on the planet, and having a strong urge to be 'good cop', I probably can't get away with that.

We want our child to grow up with clear boundaries and to understand that there are consequences to her actions. I think I'm going to find it very hard to deliver on that, as I'm such a sap, but I know Nadine won't. In the classroom, her discipline has always been impeccable and none of her kids have ended up taking the piss, but they have all still loved her. When I was a teacher, it was a very different story. There is a phrase in teaching: 'Don't smile 'til Christmas' – the inference being that you need to be pretty strict for the first few months, so your class doesn't walk all over you and ruin your year.

I was never able to stick to this, even for a day, and it definitely resulted in some piss-taking over the years, and then me having to be more angry and mean than Nadine ever was.

In our experience, unfortunately the laissez-faire style (which would be my ideal way if it worked) doesn't seem to 'work' at all. This might come from a place of love, but I think it's a naive sort of love. It's exactly what I would do if I had never been a teacher.

The intention is always lovely: we don't want our children to be hurt or upset, so don't do things which make them sad! What could be kinder than that? Unfortunately, what's kinder than that seems to be caring about their future self just as much as their present self.

The present self often doesn't want to do boring and annoying things, like cleaning up and working hard on something tough, which doesn't give up its secrets easily. So what if your child doesn't want to do any of that?

Well, if they never clean up after themselves, for example, then they are quite likely to become lazy and irresponsible, surely? It also stands to reason that this will have the effect that they do not *care about things*. If you don't have to put your toys away because someone else does it for you, then you lose a precious and almost imperceptible sort of respect for them. This, over time, makes you lose that vital quality of respect for *everything*!

I used to ask classes of children, 'Would it be good to have everything you want?' – and this is basically the same thing. It comes down to a misapprehension of what 'happiness' is. The answer is, quite clearly, no. What if what you want is extremely bad for you? Who's deciding what you want?

What our children want is decided largely by the impressions they receive from the outside world, including parents, friends, teachers, adverts, music videos, CoComelon and everything else that enters their precious consciousness.

So if we always let our children do whatever they want, shying away from the difficulty of discipline, then really all we are doing is leaving them to the wolves, I think. Letting the worst of the world have its wicked way with them, without giving them the tools to be independent in their consciousness.

Self-discipline can guard us against instant gratification, which is very important in an unashamedly consumerist, dopamine-hunting, selfie-taking, "I've got more than you have but inside I'm empty" society. How can a child learn self-discipline if everything is always easy? They can't.

This will probably mean tears, tantrums, arguments, sad faces, and many instances when I'm going to think I'm a terrible human for denying her something she wants, or taking her toys away. But it seems like the only reasonable choice!

There you have it. The 'ideal' approach I want to take. Let's see what actually happens as she grows up. I've seen far more capable people than me get walked all over by their children; I might well be the next one on that very long list.

Wednesday 5th January

One of my favourite things about having Elfie is that she's the perfect excuse. The excuse I've always longed for to *not go to things*. Gone are the days when I have to make up a lie or go to events under duress.

"Ohhhhh, no. *I've got a baby.*"

I've become so lazy with it that now I literally just say, "Ah, mate, baby." Everyone just says, "Yeah, of course. Fair enough."

And *it is* fair enough. The best thing about it is that it's *actually true*. It's way more annoying to go out and do anything when you have a baby in tow. But…

Bit late for something?

"*Baby.*"

Really want to sit around and do nothing instead of socialising?

"*Baby.*"

Just can't be arsed?

"*Baby.*"

OK, that last one is pretty similar to the second one, but you get the idea.

One thing I would advise against is actually *telling people it's the perfect excuse*, especially almost immediately after *making* said excuse. Unfortunately, that's what I did a couple of weeks ago, and it really killed the momentum of the whole charade. Something about the way it came out made it quite clear what was happening. I think I need to learn to keep my cards a bit closer to my chest, but that always just seems to feel a bit *squashed*.

Thursday 6th January

I love her so bloody much it's a joke. Every time I come home, the feeling I get when I first interact with her is indescribable. It feels like it's getting stronger and stronger as time goes on, and now I understand what everyone meant when they told me, "You can't understand until you have your own." She's so excited to see me when I get home from work and she can feel my excitement shining back at her. When I pick her up, she kicks her little arms and legs frantically, with a beaming, celestial smile, and it's almost too much to take. *Pure, unadulterated, unconditional love.*

Friday 7th January

Why are we not talking about how weird teething is? Well, I guess *we* are – right this second – but you know what I mean. It's a bit of a design flaw, isn't it? It's caused absolute mayhem in this house, which I will get to in a minute, but couldn't those rather vital parts of the body have grown in the womb, like everything else? Imagine if you had to let your baby's eyes pop out as soon as they hit one year.

"How's the baby?"

"Yeah, not too bad. Eyes really popping through now, though – she's fuming."

Or how about if the entire head had to burst out from the neck a few months in? I bet that would cause a few scenes.

"How was the flight?"

"Oh, God, I had this baby sitting next to me who had just started 'heading' – it was an absolute nightmare."

It would be like a scene from *Alien*.

Upon reflection, I assume it's because babies breastfeed, but they also breastfeed after the teeth have come through, so that doesn't seem too watertight as a reason either. Whatever the method is behind the madness, it doesn't seem fun at all. I've never heard our little one scream like she has been for the last few nights, and it has completely destroyed her sleep.

Her yowls of pure agony have been awful to witness, and we know there's basically nothing we can do. Calpol, of course. As the doctor said to us a few weeks ago, "Why does every Brit just use Calpol for everything? It's literally only good for bringing down a temperature."

I don't really have an answer to that, except for: "Have you tasted it?"

Saturday 15th January

We have become past masters at 'fobbing her off' of late, and it's been a source of mild but frequent amusement. Fobbing her off means giving her something to do so we don't have to look after her for a minute. One of her current favourites we call 'The Wheels of Neglect' – basically just a little car she can ride around in. You chuck her in and get five minutes of peace! Hallelujah!

I discovered this morning that Nadine has built up an arsenal of strange little objects on the bedside table for these morning emergencies. I have been wondering how she is keeping her distracted so we can lie in a bit, and this was her secret. It's about eight or nine things which she gives her, one by one, when she is still half-asleep. A tiny little roll of Sellotape which she can't undo but really wants to, a hairband, a little empty pouch of some sort – the list goes on.

Now *that's parenting*. Not Instagram parenting, no. No filter!

Wednesday 26th January

I saw yet again, this morning, that stressful times require seeing if this moment is *actually bad*, and disconnecting from the projected story in the mind *over and over again*.

Just take the next step.

As shown in the pictures before, we need to bring the present strongly into focus. Slowly but surely, that antsy mind music gives way to something more clear and balanced.

After a tough time, I was able to go for a beautiful walk around the local lake with Elfie and enjoy all the fresh energy this brought. In one school of Hindu philosophy, particularly the Sāṅkhya Yoga tradition,[38] time in nature is said to cultivate *sattva*: the redemptive energy of consciousness, peace and bliss, and I certainly felt that today.

On these walks, I'm using language as well as I can to speak to Elfie about what we can see. I'll never forget a training session we had at school on teaching phonics (learning to read), where they showed us a fascinating study. It was meant to compare how kids develop language when their parents talk to them a lot, versus when parents just let it happen naturally. The number of words that the first group knew was so much higher and it had helped them in many ways. This reminds us of the power of language, and that in many moments we could be helping our children more than we realise. At the same time, though, it's important to find a balance here, and not just mindlessly babble all the time – forgetting to enjoy the silent aspect of being as well. I've been trying my best to walk this line, to enrich her vocabulary without speaking over the birds and the sounds of the water all the time.

One surprising boon on our walks is that one of our cats follows us all the way to the lake, which is close to our house. Elfie *absolutely loves this*. It's delightful to see how much it brightens her up. She leans her head around so far in the carrier (my current favourite object in the world) to try to see her following behind, running in and out of the houses to keep up with us.

Friday 28th January

There we were, the picture of harmony. Me lying on the floor, Elfie hovering in the air in my arms, a manic smile adorning her face. My arms were dead straight, giving me a good opportunity to get a cheeky stretch in for my shoulders at the same time as being a good dad. I was winning.

All of a sudden, a *gargantuan torrent of vomit* spewed forth in the slowest of slow motion. Like a man at war, my senses were heightened to their limit as it fell towards me, like some sort of demonic waterfall, but nothing could save me from this particularly delicious twist of fate. There I was, on my back with a puddle of hilarious shame all over my face, neck and chest. I mean *all over*. But the worst part of all is that a significant chunk of it had ended up in my mouth. Yep.

I have never heard Nadine laugh so hard. I really was totally covered.

Thankfully, the comedy of it was immediately apparent to me as well, because I had known this day was coming.

Just a few hours later, Nadine said, "This is my favourite age so far!" and I agreed straight away. Such is the madness of parenthood. Even on the fateful day of Chundergate, I still can't get enough of her.

Diary of a Mindful Dad

Tuesday 1st February

I don't know how Nadine does it sometimes, looking after her all day. I had a couple of hours' break between sessions today, and I had a lovely time looking after Elfie, generally – but she is beyond relentless. Even if we put her in the Wheels of Neglect, it's only two minutes before she's making the droning noise again. Now it's even worse, because she can reach out with both little arms and make a sad face, asking to be picked up! How can I say no?

Friday 4th February

It's curious how the same facts can support completely different stories about the world, and how easily we forget that. We naturally assume the usual interpretation is the only one.

Take, for example, the theory of Darwinian evolution. We're used to hearing that survival is a creature's main motivation, hence the phrase 'survival of the fittest'. To survive literally means to 'live on', but I feel like this instinct is normally interpreted as a desperate desire *not to die*. There's always an undercurrent of *fear* in it.

But doesn't it feel more true, and beautiful, to imagine that everything really wants to *live*? Because *life is so precious*? It's such a strange and subtle shift in interpretation, but perhaps you can sense how significant a difference that could make in the way we feel about life and the world.

Similarly, I was thinking this morning about the phenomenon of parents being biased towards their own children, with the implication often being that they always see them as better than they actually are.

But maybe it's not that we see them as *better* – maybe we're simply allowed to see something others can't? Because we have sacrificed and given so much to take responsibility for their lives, maybe we've earned a kind of closeness that lets us see their essence more clearly.

I refuse to buy into the idea that when I see my child with the eyes of unconditional love and wonder, it's just some kind of evolutionary trick, some built-in bias. Again, the implication lurking in the background is that what I'm seeing isn't real.

No. I'm seeing something that *is* real.

I'm not referring to blindly believing everything my child does is fantastic and that they can do no wrong. I mean the simple perception of their essence; that glimpse of wonder might be a kind of high magic, a sacred gift reserved for those who are closest. Wouldn't you rather look at it like that?

Perhaps the real question is this: is it possible to see *everyone* with those eyes? Isn't this the ecstatic love of the Sufis? The unconditional love of Jesus and other prophets and saints throughout the ages? It's easy to dismiss this kind of seeing as unrealistic, but maybe it's not as far away as the mind believes. Surely love is the most natural thing of all? Maybe this kind of seeing, this simple recognition of the essence of being in another, is what it means to see *through God's eyes*. Can you imagine a world where we all looked at each other like that?

Saturday 5th February

Today I had Mark from *Peep Show* in my head: "Butter the toast, eat the toast, shit the toast. God, life's relentless."[42]

That's exactly how I felt. I only get one day off on the weekend and I just want to sit down, lie down, relax – somehow. But there's *no day off*. It's simply not a thing. Ever since this little menace arrived, it feels like we've *constantly* been on duty. I knew we were going to a swimming pool with our friends who have a baby the same age, and there would at least be some relaxation time by the pool, so I felt like an ungrateful sod not feeling up for it, but sometimes that's just the way it is. It's the getting out of the bloody house again! I just dread it sometimes. All I really wanted was to have nothing at all to do, *zero pressure* from the (allegedly) external world. Four hours later and I've read just two paragraphs of the book I so optimistically brought with me, I've been sicked on again, and I've been weed on as well for good measure. Oh well.

We did have a lovely time in any case, and it's great to see the two babies try to interact with each other. Their interactions are so odd and interesting to behold. It's like looking after two drunk friends, who are constantly falling over and creating a very real fear in the atmosphere that they might, at any moment, *bring public shame upon us all.*

The contrast between the babies was stark, and it reiterated for us the pattern we keep seeing: our one is a lunatic. She is always on – either up or down, but definitely on. Our friends' baby was so quiet and well-behaved, just taking it all in, and Elfie was causing constant trouble. They don't know how easy they've got it in comparison! On the other side of the coin, though, it takes them an hour to get theirs to sleep every day, but Elfie is out like a light within ten minutes consistently. It shows that just as each baby can cause different symptoms for a woman during pregnancy, they also come custom-built with their own unique set of tests for their parents once they're out in the world.

Monday 7th February

Sean Lock, the English comedian – may he rest in peace – once gave me a fantastic life hack to use when you open the dishwasher and see that, God forbid, it is full of CLEAN THINGS.

Just turn it on again.

I've never actually done that, but just the thought gives me a smile every now and then.

On that note, have you ever noticed that tidying up and cleaning is just hiding things? Cupboards are literally hiding places. It blew me away when my friend told me that.

Anyway, for me the trouble with the dishwasher starts when there are loads of *tiny objects* in there which need to be put away. This is so much worse now with a baby, because there are all manner of strange things, the homes of which I have never got to grips with. I only consciously realised this today, and then saw how feebly I have subconsciously decided to deal with this situation over the years. I just confidently and delicately place *all of the troublesome items* onto the draining board, right above the dishwasher, and move on with my life.

How do I decide what's troublesome? Well, I know where lots of things go. Teaspoons are the smallest object I will entertain; they are a safe bet. As I'm writing this, I now realise we have these weird small forks which I always put in the same place as the teaspoons, and I still have absolutely no idea what they are for. I've never even wondered. *Just get it done.*

I've just asked Nadine and she says she uses them all the time, they are for 'when you want a fork, but a *small fork*'. Very insightful, and a lot to unpack there, but I just don't have the bandwidth to probe any further.

All the rest, anything *small* or *weird*, just goes onto the draining board – simples. I can't believe Nadine has never called me out on this before; she's just been subconsciously putting the items away herself all these years, never wondering how it all got there.

Wednesday 9th February

Probably the most significant parenting challenge of this time (between six and eight months), in our case, is the issue of separation anxiety. We've hired someone to come round sometimes to get to know Elfie a bit, so that ultimately they can look after her when Nadine returns to work. But after a few days of trying this out, Nadine is now going off this idea. We have decided that, rather than allowing Elfie to have childcare at home, we would prefer for her to go to nursery, where it is much more stimulating and she can increase her social skills. We think that would be much better for her in the long run.

We are going back to the UK for a wedding in April, and my dad and his fiancée are going to be looking after Elfie for the day whilst we are at the wedding. This, understandably, has caused us a little bit of anxiety, apprehension and uncertainty about how it's going to go, because she has never had to be with anyone else for a long period. People might criticise this, perhaps, and say that we should have made more effort to give her to other people before, but we simply haven't wanted or needed to. We've been lucky enough that Nadine has been able to give her her undivided attention, and we think that has been good for her. It does mean that the experience of separation might be a little more difficult for Elfie than for other children who have experienced it earlier, but that's just the way it is. We are lucky that we have a cousin living here in Dubai, who is eager to help us begin this process of separation. Just like so many of the other challenges that we have faced, this challenge involves a great deal of resistance, and it requires conscious effort to *go against the stream of resistance and begin a new cycle.*

Having seen this process so many times during this parenting journey alone, we are now full of confidence that we understand how it needs to go; provided that the transition is staggered, it should be fine. Yes, there will be tantrums; yes, there will be tears; yes, Nadine and I will be very upset at times, but it needs to happen, and we are ready to take the plunge.

Six to Twelve Months

Friday 11th February

Elfie has started crawling over the last week. She has been so desperate to interact with the cats that it's as if she has forced herself to learn to crawl as quickly as possible. She follows them around like a possessed puppy, making accidentally threatening noises, and they react just as you would expect them to. A mildly horrified acknowledgement of the situation, a majestic leap to a safe vantage point and a quick reset.

This morning I thought, in my naive innocence, that I might go to the driving range – just for an hour. Nadine is at home all day with Elfie, and so I asked her first if she would mind; she said not at all. Yet when the time came, it was all wrong. She was trying to set up a Zoom call with her friend, I was eating my lunch, and Elfie was constantly moaning for attention. Non-stop. I knew, in that moment, I shouldn't go. For me to go and practise golf for one hour meant Nadine was going to have a terrible hour herself. So I stayed.

Instead, I went for a lovely walk with Elfie in the 'Bjorn' – a brand of baby carrier. She loves it just as much as I do, and as soon as I put it on, her little face lights up and she crawls over to me as fast as possible. She puts her arms out eagerly and tries to climb up my legs, desperately asking to be picked up.

When we go for a walk, she is always enthralled and entertained the whole time, and it is a precious bonding opportunity for us both.

Her new favourite thing is nicking the sunglasses off my face during these times. As soon as I put them on, she turns her head around and pulls them off to play with. If I take them back and put them on, she will do it again without hesitation. It's hilarious and another reminder of how 'civilised' we are. "Those are mine!" the mind says. Err...no. They're not. They're just sunglasses on your face. I'll take those. Thanks.

So now I take two pairs out.

Check.

Her reply is to always want *whichever pair is on my face.*

So we've ended up in a ludicrous situation in which anyone seeing us walking around the local lake is treated to a strange comedy sketch, with a steady and continuous exchange of sunglasses between the two of us. We barely even see the lake, and we both bloody love it.

Saturday 12th February

This morning, Nadine and I were discussing a social occasion we weren't very keen on, and her eyes lit up as she realised, "We've got her – she's our secret weapon!"

I thought she meant that we would just bore everyone by talking about parenting, as we usually do, and I would bang on about my book and people would pretend to care.

"We get to just chase her around the whole time!" she ventured.

Aha, yes. The secret weapon, allowing us to escape from any dull conversation, even, and especially, if it's been made dull by us. Dear me. What has become of us?

Tuesday 15th February

Something truly remarkable happened today in the car. Elfie was suddenly so overwhelmed and upset that she was crying incredibly hard. Louder than I've ever heard her before. Normally we use a dummy in these times and it works to calm her down, but we didn't have one, and we knew it would be a long time until we were home. I suddenly had the thought to play the song we used to listen to every day during our meditations when Elfie was in the womb. For some reason, we have stopped listening to it, even though it used to be a daily thing. The *second* she heard it, she stopped. It was as simple and amazing as that. The same thing happened again, in the afternoon.

The melody, the rhythm, the tone, all of it is familiar to her on the deepest level possible, associated with the relaxed breathing and loving vibrations of both of her parents, as she nestled in the best bed nature has ever designed.

It makes sense, doesn't it?

Wednesday 16th February

It is SO different entering Elfie's world after a day of work. Completely chalk and cheese, and it takes some time to adjust after coming home. One effect of this is resistance to entering certain aspects of this world. For example, I noticed some extraordinary resistance tonight, and I have a feeling that the episode in question might be quite consequential for me as a parent.

I had come back from a long day at work just in time to put Elfie to bed, and we did our usual routine. Then at the end of the routine, I realised that I always leave the room and leave Nadine to put her to sleep. Why?

It's just become a habit, as it has been this way right from the beginning. I see, upon investigation, that some aspect of mind thinks it is good for *me*, because 'less effort'. But that's a total blunder. I had the thought of staying and doing it myself this time, and there was just this block. This resistance. I watched the feeling and it was actually really strong. So I went against it and plonked myself back on the bed, in protest against this gremlin of short-sighted laziness. As I sat down, all of the energy which wanted to be wasted in doing nothing of value downstairs was just there, bubbling around, confused and not knowing where to go. I realised that I had *absolutely no good reason not to do it*.

Unsurprisingly, when I did put her to sleep myself, I had the most wonderful, magical time. We connected in a totally new way, and I saw a whole new dimension to her day: *the very end of it*. When you think about it, this is a remarkable and important time. Consciousness, that wonderful mystery, slowly but surely slips and fades away, into the unknown, and the day is over. Surely this is just as important a time in which to connect to her, to be with her, as any other?

It was one of the first times I have been able to share this experience, this energy, with her. It made me care for her anew and see her in a new light. It reminded me of how precious the gift of consciousness is, and how fragile she is. When she looked into my eyes, slowly blinking her way out of the day, she was fully present with me, giving me enormous love, and I was there, protecting her, gently allowing her to pass from this realm to the next.

It showed me, yet again, how the mind had hoodwinked me – made me a slave to another of its tricks. How many other things have I decided not to do, things that might have been enriching, interesting, even lovely, just because of some shitty, vague 'reason' that didn't really exist? A great many, I suspect.

Thursday 17th February

I just found another one. Food time. Nadine is in charge of this because I'm out working, so it's just something I've never taken the lead on. Why not? Probably the same reason as above. It's a lot of effort. It's *another universe*.

So I did it today. I sat directly in front of her, whilst she was eating, and then I realised that this was the *first time I had ever even done that*. I always sit in the other chair! Just *sitting there* already felt interesting: she attended to me *differently*; we connected *differently*. I loved the whole adventure and saw, yet again, that Nadine is granted privileged access to so many wonderful areas of life that I have never shared with Delphine.

I was enthralled by the way she eats, and I saw that I had never really observed it properly before. Now that I was in the 'main chair', I could see it all as clear as day and I had such a funny time. I can tell you that they wouldn't want her type in a 5* restaurant – she's a bloody disgrace!

Six to Twelve Months

Nadine had kindly made her pancakes and she just stared at me, picking each bit up extremely slowly and chucking it on the floor. Over, and over, and over, and over, and over, and over again. Is she taking the piss, or what?

Friday 18th February

Did you know that approximately 75% of UK children nowadays spend more time inside than prison inmates?[43] You could be forgiven for forgetting, in this world, that we are wild creatures, deep down. Looking around at our neat little boxy shelters and our orderly, tidy coverings, it's easy to be fooled. Yet one more meal time with my baby has shattered that illusion again, in an instant.

We are wild.

She chucks her food out of the high chair with a mischievous glinting grin. She wipes hummus all over it, hands becoming filthier by the second, with reckless abandon. Whatever was on her plate is all over her face and tummy…and she doesn't even notice. She spends the whole time chucking, spitting, grinning and occasionally a strange sort of growl comes out: it's bloody fantastic.

The whole thing makes me think that we are all so embarrassingly civilised, aren't we? Nadine has been encouraging her to 'experiment with textures' recently, and what this means is to let her chuck stuff all over the floor…more. The mess this makes is out of this world, and almost every move is such a trigger to my subconscious cultural sensibilities. I feel a sort of revulsion; an instinctive, societal grimace edging out of me. How sad is that? What she's doing is great!

She gets to really explore all sorts of different food and have the visceral experience *of that food*, with more than just her sense of taste. Obviously, she loves it!

Don't get me wrong, it's great to tame this madness so you

don't have to spend your entire life cleaning up to get back to the pretence of being civilised. But there's a deep lesson, a potent tonic being offered here: the spontaneity and freedom of being wild. Why have we gone so far away from it? Where is the line, and when did we cross it?

Once, at my first school, my heart sank lower than it had been for a long while. I was running an after-school Meditation and Philosophy Club and the weather was beautiful. So I announced to the group that we would be going outside for the session. As we got to the perfectly trimmed grass, one student said with abject horror, "Mr Watts, I can't sit here! It's *dirty*!"

I replied instinctively, "No. It *is dirt*!"

Or how about when I wanted to take the class *just outside the school gate* to the lovely grassy patches on the other side? I was forbidden. I would have to create and complete a risk assessment first, and have it signed off by the Head.

What about rain? God save us from the rain! In the same school, in the same week, two children in my class were not given permission from their parents to attend the school field trip to the cinema (the irony of this being the 'field' trip is not lost on me) because they were going to have to walk about 200 metres *in the rain*. Sorry, they *might* have to, *if it rained*. That is 100% true.

In case you were hoping this sort of thing might just be about that school having silly rules, how about this one? Nadine was teaching elsewhere, and an unexpected shower precipitated an email (see what I did there?) to all staff, saying the kids had to stay inside for morning break time. Fair enough, perhaps? Well, then the rain *stopped*. All of the classes went out for lunchtime, but Nadine's year group wasn't allowed. The Head of Year refused to let them, because she *hadn't been sent an email by the Head confirming that they were now allowed out*. Wow! Please let that one sink in. That year group stayed inside for lunchtime because it USED TO BE raining. I really can't imagine anything more embarrassingly, and painfully, civilised than that.

In light of that, and other examples like it, we remind ourselves that we don't want to 'wrap her in cotton wool'. Yet just as I write this entry, Nadine is buying her a helmet for when we go on bike rides. I've just looked, and it *literally has cotton on the inside*. Ah, parenting, you've got us again.

Saturday 19th February

This morning, I saw something extraordinary: *Elfie's first telling-off*. She was breastfeeding and then she bit Nadine's nipple really hard. Nadine gave her the 'teacher face' for the first time ever and exclaimed, "NO!"

Then all hell broke loose: she WAILED.

But it was different from any cry before because of the context. We knew there was no pain or anything like that, and it really got me. I never want to make her feel like that!

Suffice it to say, my callous wife was just laughing at her! I couldn't believe it – I thought she would be feeling like I did. So the lesson has been learned: she is officially Bad Cop. Works fine for me!

The womb song worked an absolute treat again this evening, taking her from hysterical crying to absolute silence in about five seconds. It's incredible.

Monday 21st February

I'm a messy cook. I tried to help out for 30 seconds this evening and, by the time I was done, Nadine had to clear up eight pieces of food from the stove which I had chucked about the place. I'm almost as bad as Elfie.

I'm not doing it on purpose, though, like my stepdad does. He pretends he is inept at all household tasks so that my mum takes over, and he does it to great effect. He is a past master. I have tried to emulate this, but my tendency to overshare makes it so obvious that this is what I'm doing. Essentially, *I will immediately say that's what I'm doing*. This really spoils the charade and eliminates a lot of potential 'getting away with it' from my life.

Tonight, the resistance to putting her to bed myself showed up again. When the moment came when Nadine asked me if I wanted to do it, I was quiet for a while and I observed my reaction. *I didn't want to do it*, and there was again *absolutely no good reason for this. Not even a reason at all.* There was no *reason* because it's an *emotional block*, emotional resistance to something which isn't 'the norm'. So I did it, and it was fantastic.

Wednesday 23rd February

"You know there's still piss over there, right?"

"Yes, darling – I told you I was trying to clean it when you said I had to come in because she had her hand in the toaster."

This sort of day has had us thinking, "How many times do you have to get shouted at during the day before you're allowed takeaway?" Of course, you can never really know the number, you just have to instinctively gauge how shit your day has been. Or you could use *actual shit*, of course, which tends to make for quite a clear barometer. How many times has someone done a shit on your floor before you're allowed takeaway?

This afternoon, Elfie laid an absolute monstrosity on the floor, rubbed her feet in it, and started eating a wet nappy – all at the same time. This took place in about five seconds. Does that qualify? I think so.

If the baby is having a bad day, you really are screwed. That's it. Your life has no significance whatsoever, except for helping them sort out theirs. This must be what makes people say, "Make the most of life while you can!" when someone says they're thinking about starting a family. So, if you're reading this and haven't started: *make the most of life while you can!*

Thursday 24th February

I'm currently sleeping separately from Nadine and Elfie, though in our case it's because of the cats more than the baby, because of a difficult situation which has arisen between them. One has had to be temporarily separated from the others and it's pretty annoying. It does mean I'm not waking to the sound of the baby, mostly, and that's been great for my energy levels and my ability to work. Sleeping separately from Nadine is very strange, though, as we have only been apart for a maximum of a week for our entire relationship, and we always share a bed. I haven't even been relegated to the couch after arguments in the past, like the people on TV. We just do the 'angry-huff-and-turn-away-and-then-think-about-it-all' in bed instead.

I think I underestimated how much a baby can dramatically change a couple's relationship, but now I am understanding why. The upheaval of your sex life, the possibility of sleeping separately, and the lack of time you have for one another throughout the whole adventure are just a few factors which contribute to this. On a fundamental level, you have *far less time and energy* to give to one another. It's no wonder that relationships easily and often suffer as a result of this. Think about it: beforehand, your energy is totally directed towards the other person (provided you don't hate each other's guts – in which case, don't have a baby!). Suddenly, *all* of that energy goes in a completely new direction. It's no secret that I absolutely adore my wife, and I have ever since we met when we were 17. We have given each other an enormous amount of energy, attention, affection and love for 15 years and then – all of a sudden – there is something else which is attracting all of that energy. This is a monumental shift in the dynamic.

It's very hard for us to find time for each other and, even when time *is* found, it can be difficult for us to give ourselves to one another, because in the short amount of time which we have for ourselves we just want to rest! There are jobs we need to do, the house needs to be sorted, we have messages to respond to on our phones, and so on and so on.

Little faces of this challenge pop up every now and then. For instance, yesterday, on Valentine's Day morning, I went into the bedroom and Elfie was there waiting for me with an unbelievable level of excitement. I gave her the same amount back, and Nadine said, half in jest, "Oh, I don't even get a good morning any more!"

This was a wake-up call, both literally and figuratively. She was right. I had only focused on the little one. I always normally acknowledge them both equally, but she was just so bloody excited this time that it was harder to do so. Such 'little' things can happen *so easily*, but what happens if there are 100 a day? This can really add up, and it had better not go unnoticed. It was a reminder for me of how important it is for us to make the necessary effort to *pay attention to our relationship too*, when we can.

My approach to this has been the same as usual – lean into it, rather than ignoring it through reactive fear. As I've been noticing it, this noticing itself has naturally opened up a different world. This is what Krishnamurti calls 'choiceless awareness': as long as you properly notice, the rest takes care of itself. This is a massive relief because I haven't got time for anything else!

In this case, non-reactively noticing what was operating has organically led, today, to little conscious efforts to give Nadine an extra cuddle, be present with her, look her in the eyes with all of my being, to see her as she is, *apart from the baby*.

I think it's important for us both to be seen, to be *remembered*, in this way. We are more than just parents. I think that little conscious efforts like this, regularly, can go a long way to staving off a gradual decline in a couple's affection for one another. Having spoken to friends with babies, I know that this is something everyone must address, somehow. The babies change so much for us. It's impossible for this not to affect the dynamic of a relationship *in every way*, and it's natural for it to do so. But I want to see, as often as I can, how much I love my wife just for her, just as I always have. Soppy, I know.

Our relationship doesn't need to be *the same* as it was before; I can accept that, I think. That is a kind of death, in a way, and it needs to be honoured and treated as such. But all things give way in time, and it's another good opportunity to *appreciate what has been*, and look consciously, and fearlessly, at what is here and now.

Tuesday 1st March

"So from 4:30am we both sleep basically like that with my boob in her mouth," Nadine says, bluntly, like it's probably not what she 'should' be doing.

"What does everyone else do?" I reply.

"I don't know!"

Who bloody cares? is the answer. Why should we care if other people don't think she should still be in our bed? Other people are annoying.

Not you, of course. You're great!

My favourite T-shirt used to be one with a rainbow on it and the words '*I hate everyone*' emblazoned beneath. We all do sometimes, don't we? Conformity is a killer. 'Never do as others do' was the motto given to Gurdjieff (the first mystic I studied) by his grandmother on her deathbed.[44] It served him very well.

Yet although it doesn't matter what others think, sometimes it can be nice to find out you aren't alone in your eccentricities. I discovered, this evening, that we aren't completely mental for often watching media of Elfie in the evening after she's in bed. All of our friends who have babies say they almost always do the same. It's just such a nice way to enjoy them, without any stress of having to do anything to help them. It's a treat!

Do you want to hear something cute? Every time Elfie goes to sleep in the car, she is holding a toy magnifying glass, like an adorable little inspector. It wobbles to and fro until it finally comes to rest when she is asleep. It melts us a little bit, I must admit.

Thursday 3rd March

I was quite shocked to discover, at the age of 21, that I didn't know how to listen. It sounded like quite a vital skill, in principle, that I had been missing out on. I thought I knew how, of course, like everyone does. But that was when I heard it.

My mother-in-law.

Don't worry, it's not what you think – she's lovely. But that is the truth. I was sitting around the dinner table with Nadine and her mum after work one day, having just watched a Krishnamurti video on listening. It had struck an incredibly deep chord within me and I was still reckoning with his words as the evening progressed.

Suddenly, at one point during the meal, everything became SO LOUD!

Honestly, I wanted to physically recoil because of the intensity of the conversation (which was just a 'normal' one). Giving *absolutely all of my attention, possibly for the first time, to listening* was blowing my world into pieces. I didn't physically recoil, thank God, as that would have been a bit inappropriate.

I was being hit by so much: not just the voices and the words, but *the layers of thought and emotion behind the words as well*. Each time either of them spoke, their *entire being* was there to behold, and was entering directly into my own – so much so that it really was all too much.

Since that day, I have never been able to listen in the same way. It showed me how important it is to give *everything* to listening, and I would say it is now one of the most important aspects of my life.

Normally, when we are listening to someone, our attention is centred *in the mind*. But *we don't realise this, because it's all we really know*. Even when we're not lost in personal thoughts, the mind is still *reacting*. It starts making associations – comparing, relating, judging. And in those small moments of inner commentary, we lose touch with the person in front of us. We're no longer fully with them.

But there is *another way*. When we give our full attention, without trying to think, something remarkable happens: the mind becomes quiet. And yet, understanding still flows. We don't need to analyse; the right words just seem to come. We don't have to search for them – they just appear, *as if the space itself is speaking*. The conversation becomes truly *alive*, and we connect in a different way. Somehow, mysteriously, we stop being separate.

This is why the experience I had was so jarring and shocking. I could suddenly feel the full presence of the people I loved, and it overwhelmed me. I could see, by contrast, that I had never actually listened before. This was not a nice thing to realise, but I'm so glad I did. Now I give others my full attention as much as I can, and it feels like it's opened up a deeper layer of living. I'm sure it's also helping me connect with Elfie in a way I never could have before that fateful video.

When I *pay* full attention to her, I always *receive* a gift – a *blessing* – in return.

Diary of a Mindful Dad

<u>Monday 7th March</u>

The question of separation anxiety has come to the fore again in recent days. How should we approach this issue? The first thing we are doing is noticing the wrong things. For example, I had the idea of sneaking out of the house so she doesn't have to see me leave, but this is doing more harm than good. Yes, it saves me from having to feel like I'm leaving her, and feeling a bit sad because of that. But what about her? Elfie will suddenly notice that I'm not there, and not know where I've gone. The idea of sneaking out is just avoidance of something difficult. It's resistance again. Resistance to facing the fact: the *fact* is that sometimes parents need to leave, and then they come back, and she has to get used to it. There's no need to run away from the fact. Just do what needs to be done, no matter what it brings up.

We are all *sitting with the feelings*, and it's hard. When Elfie cries because she knows I am leaving, we're trying our best to *stop*. This is much easier said than done. We are opening up a big, silent space, even just for five seconds, to not immediately react in the way the mind wants us to, and just to *be with* the difficult thoughts and feelings which arise. They arise for all of us, not just Elfie and, as we recognise this, we face the situation together, energetically supporting one another through the invisible web which connects us.

In that space, that silence, we all have the opportunity to see ourselves, and the situation, clearly. We suddenly *see*, instead of running away:

Oh. This is sad. This is difficult. We don't like what's happening, but it's still happening.

That space is where the real magic happens. The power of this stopping amazes me again and again, as it consistently transmutes the energy of a moment in a surprising way, even if it only lasts for a short time. It creates a mysterious little opening.

As usual, this is difficult work and takes a lot of intention and attention!

I remind myself, every now and then, that there is *no separation*. Not really. I believe that the essence of us is a total mystery, and I am not at all convinced that we are as separate as we can sometimes feel. The ancient 'consciousness-only' model of reality, which I have alluded to a few times already, rests on this understanding: we are each like fingers of a hand – seemingly separate, but inextricably connected in some deeper, unseen way.

Certain experiences over the years have shown me this directly, and that means that this entire movement of tests relating to *apparent* separation always has something slightly illusory about it, from my perspective. When I return to the recognition of our *shared being*, it strangely and quite beautifully feels like going home.

Wednesday 9th March

As awful wars rage around the world, entering our consciousness more intimately than ever before through our wonderful little machines, I am reminded of Krishnamurti's talk at the UN. He went to speak on the topic, 'Why can't man live peacefully on the Earth?'[45]

He illuminated the minefield of barriers between humanity and world peace in his inimitable style. Then, right at the end, when asked by one of the audience, in near desperation, what people could 'do', he replied emphatically: "*Change completely.*"

Oh. That's not what they were hoping for, really.

They wanted an idea, a strategy, which could be implemented 'out there' to bring harmony. Not something which would be incredibly difficult for them as individuals and shatter their normal existence. If we can just fix it all 'out there', without it changing us, that would be ideal, wouldn't it? Nice and neat and tidy.

Krishnamurti, throughout his life, urged us to ask the most difficult questions about our own lives, and to sit with them until we really understand what on Earth is going on. He emphasised the need for us to totally eradicate conflict within our psyche and in our relationships. His bottom line was that it is only love, real love, total selflessness, radical love for all things – including ourselves – which can truly set us free. Yet to find this, he maintained, demands going beyond all that we know, and all the systems and ways of living we have created. He always repeated that we cannot solve this problem using *thought*, and that is a very difficult pill to swallow. After all, in that grand old hall in New York, *thought* had arranged the meeting in the first place. *Thought* had put on its suit and tie and sat there, waiting to listen in a very thought-like way, and learn something *it* can do. Nothing, comes the answer. Certainly no 'technique', no 'hack'. Just good-old fashioned, greasy, muddy *soul work*. Oh dear.

On the same day as reading this, I was sent a video of a group of football fans brutally attacking an opposition fan for celebrating his team's goal, whilst sitting in the 'wrong' stands. There couldn't be a better example of Krishnamurti's points. Nations are glorified tribalism, and this energy goes all the way up and down society: that football fan crossed a border. The energy which creates war is operating at so many different levels and all age groups every...single...day. My eight-year-old client today recently demanded to fight another boy at school; this is starting a war as well, isn't it?

The Dalai Lama allegedly said, provocatively, that "if every eight-year-old were taught meditation, we would eliminate violence within one generation." How?

Well, Krishnamurti similarly spoke about a radical *inward revolution* which *is* possible and which could lead to a totally 'new mind' – one which has completely gone beyond the 'me', the self born of the past. This new mind is always fresh and generally *empty*. Krishnamurti likened this mind to a drum: finely tuned and totally silent *until it is struck*.

Can I raise my child to have such a mind? Should I even try?

I have benefited hugely from his teachings, and I have also spent a lot of my career trying to share these principles with the children in my care, with varying levels of success. It is understandable, then, that I would want to raise my child with his radical vision partly in mind, but there are some huge problems with this.

The first is that *I have to live it*, because hypocrisy doesn't really work. How inconvenient! That is a significant problem because of how difficult it is to live in this way. To give just one example, Krishnamurti held that when we live with an 'image of ourselves' (similar to the idea of the 'ego'), then we can never truly be in relationship with another, and there is *no real love*. He said that only when there is *no image*, which also means, psychologically, *no sense of the past*, can we go beyond the cycle of disorder, trauma and conformity, and be truly secure. Does that sound easy to you? It means, for parents, that if we want to truly relate to our children, to *really love them*, we need to go beyond the ego. This gets right to the heart of what 'conscious parenting' is all about: *do the inner work*. Can we see our ego operating? Are we willing to? Can we live without it?

The second problem is the matter of our children *fitting into society*. No, I don't want my beloved Elfie wasting her energy in tribalism, superficial ambition, conformity, vanity, competition and all the rest of that business (including business, which comes from an Old English word meaning *anxiety* – believe it or not). But that *is* the world we live in and the collective 'mind' she is being born into; do I really want her to be totally different from everyone else, to be an outsider? To what extent? In principle, yes. Yet, in practice, it must be very difficult for parents to deal with a situation in which their child is ostracised by their peers and stands alone. To step away from social media as a teenager, for example, puts you in an extremely isolating position, even if it *might be* the wiser thing to do in many ways. To step away from anything you know is *wrong*, when to do so causes lots of other problems, is a fraught affair and demands huge courage; even more so when you are making that decision for *someone else*.

This brings us straight to the third problem: the small matter of what *she* actually wants! Ah, almost forgot that one. Of course, I can only try to guide her as best I can, and I must stay aware enough to give her the space to find *her own way* – not mine, and not Krishnamurti's.

There she is, upstairs, sleeping soundly, dreaming of boobies and bath time, whilst I ramble on down here about world peace and what her life will be like in the future. If only she knew! I know what she would do…just what her mum does: laugh at me.

"*Silly daddy! What's he doing!?*"

Thursday 10th March
==

"It's good to pretend to be blind sometimes," I assure Nadine, when she asks me why I'm fumbling around the bedroom with my eyes closed.

I've been watching a great YouTube channel made by a guy called Tommy Edison,[46] who was born blind and answers questions from viewers about his experience of the world. I have found his material fascinating and inspiring and used it for many lessons recently, to evoke appreciation, empathy and gratitude in my students. It has allowed us to appreciate one of our ultimate gifts, vision, with 'fresh eyes'. However, it's simply too difficult to properly appreciate them because we use the eyes *so much*.

Just how significant the eyes are in our lives helps us to understand why so many children are scared of the dark. Elfie has stopped being able to go to sleep easily at night, and it seems to be because she is more aware now and understands what's going on; she has a renewed appreciation for the stark difference between day and night, light and dark.

Tonight was particularly hard, though. Her crying has *changed completely*. It's a far more *communicative* cry; you can hear the content of the emotion in it, *what it means*. She's really asking us to stop and not to force her consciousness into another dimension against her will. Understanding that makes it so much harder to deal with. Nadine said we are doing all the things we have been 'told not to do'. But she can't just stand there for 30 minutes or more, listening to that wail, without doing anything to help, and I couldn't either. She's getting in the cot to help her sleep and picking her up and rocking her again. Right, wrong, whatever. Does anyone really know for sure? Who has told us this and who should we listen to? Many people advocate the 'cry it out' method, and assert that it is *definitely not traumatic at all*. I've read some stunningly poor justifications of this in various articles online. It's convenient to believe, if it's going to help you train them to sleep in a way which is convenient for *you* and *your life* but, let's face it: it can't possibly be true.

Attachment theory, originally pioneered by John Bowlby and Mary Ainsworth,[47] is a foundational theory in many modern therapeutic modalities, and it shows us the importance of *secure attachment*: for babies and children to *know they are loved, unconditionally*. Maybe one of the reasons our society is so messed up is because so many of today's adults were left to 'cry it out'. I know I've certainly met a few who could do with a big cuddle. Yes, it makes sense that there can be a healthy balance here, but surely we need to show her, to some degree, that she is being heard and understood? We are just doing the best we can in the moment, and I'm sure it will be good enough. We have heard about sleep training, which attempts to find some middle ground between neglect and overdependence, and maybe we will need to go down that road eventually. Our current stance, though, is simple: *if in doubt, love*.

Diary of a Mindful Dad

Friday 11th March

There's nothing life loves more than to make you eat your words. I'm eating some of mine this evening, and they don't taste great.

Ten days ago, I was waxing lyrical about the power of conscious listening. Yet today, I failed to listen to Nadine in an important moment, and had to apologise to her for it later. In the last week I have had a lot of extra work to do after returning home and it has been quite stressful. Nadine tried to speak to me about our plans for her to work one or two hours with a client of mine, but I was in the middle of working, and I didn't listen to her properly.

I know, in theory, that she can plan it all herself, and I was busy, so my mind was saying, "Why do you need my help with that? I've got to do this." I know how capable she is, and I was busy, so I let her get on with it, psychologically, and was not supportive. We didn't return to it after this, and so subconsciously I probably thought it was all fine. But my mind had only seen what was there *on the surface*, and it takes a deeper quality of attention to reveal the deeper layers of what's in front of us.

Later on, though, conscience rose up in its inimitable voice and I *remembered*. What my lovely wife was *really asking for was my energetic involvement, my support*. My attention, care, presence, *love*.

When I really stopped to notice, I realised that this was a far more delicate situation than the mind had led me to believe. Nadine was understandably anxious about any sort of return to work, even just for an hour or two. She was concerned not only about the sort of work she would be doing, but even more so about the separation from Elfie, and everything it entails. She felt uneasy, uncomfortable and afraid.

Yet I was too absorbed in my own difficulties, the demands of my own life, that I *missed it*. I didn't turn my attention fully towards her. I didn't *see her*, I didn't *feel her*, I didn't *listen*.

When we are feeling like Nadine was, we need support and

love. I didn't give that to her, because *I wasn't really listening* in the way I mentioned earlier, and she could *feel it*.

This is a good example which shows how hard it can be to do this, and why it really matters. Truly listening involves the entire being, not just the ears or the mind. It really is the essence of love, and it is easier said than done, especially when modern life is so fast and, at times, overwhelming.

Sometimes it doesn't matter that much if we don't listen properly. Scores of stand-up comedy routines include the stereotypical man not listening to his wife. I forget what Nadine asks me to get from the shop just as much as Micky Flanagan does. Weirdly, it just seems to be a cosmic law of marriage, and I think that *is funny*. Even if it's just three things, it's as if the weight of all of the men in history who have forgotten what they were asked to get from the shop is on my shoulders, and I *must write it down*, in a flurry of fear that I'll be the next on the list.

But sometimes listening *does matter*. A strong relationship is surely woven from many little moments where we give the other *everything* when they need us, even when it's hard for us to do so. I couldn't do that today, but I'm glad that I at least noticed it after the fact.

Eating my words tastes a little less bitter now, when I remember that it is seeing these moments of 'getting it wrong' – and caring about it – which tends to create more of the 'getting it right'.

Saturday 12th March

At the moment I'm working 5.5 days per week, and this makes Saturday my only full day off. No, this isn't really OK, but it's how it has to be for a little while longer.

When we woke up this morning, we were both ludicrously tired and gathered our things to take Elfie out for the day to a swimming pool. As soon as we got in the car, I started remembering a few of the significant jobs we have to do, which we simply haven't had time to do over the last few months. This is partly because I'm not getting two weekend days, and on the day I do get off, I really need to rest. A few other concerns have been floating around my mind, and I have realised that I am enmeshed in a huge cloud of negativity. I suspect it is also partly because my emotional well has run dry, after a very difficult day yesterday. Whatever the reason, the energy has been there and it has distorted everything.

It is one of those clouds which is excellent at drawing really annoying events towards it; it also seems to be adept at creating this kind of thought: *Oh, the weekend is almost over!* at 1pm.

Meanwhile, Nadine is experiencing a wonderful state of heart which is allowing her to see all the magic of Elfie when I am temporarily blocked access. It's another good example for me of how our state of consciousness determines what we can see, and why it's important to try to keep our energy as fresh and free as we possibly can. If we can keep an eye on our state of consciousness and harmonise and regulate *that*, then everything else flows in accordance with it.

Isn't it interesting that we talk about 'states of mind' but never really think about what we are implying? We're implying that they are somehow analogous to states of matter, and indeed they are. Solids, liquids and gases have tremendously different characteristics and are capable of totally different things – so are states of mind. If a child has been running around outside for half an hour, they won't be in a 'fit state of mind' to sit down and write something. Something needs to change, to shift, to bring about the correct state of mind for this. I always use this example because it seems perfectly apt to me and, when I meditate, I feel these shifts strongly. It is as if, when you meditate, all of the energy in the mind gathers, opening up a different world for you to enter and exist in, and then you can use this more refined energy afterwards for whatever comes up. When you are a parent, time is at a premium, though, and so I don't have many opportunities to properly meditate. Thankfully, meditation is just *purposeful presence, and we can do this any time*. Yes, it can be more powerful with your eyes closed, but such is life.

As such, I am not identifying with this cloud and the beguiling stories it brings. This means seeing that it is a cloud in the sky and not the sun beyond, the true focal point of my being. That's where I want to take my stand!

Returning to this again and again seems to clear the sky, burning up the clouds. I see, during this process, that the grumpiness is all related to not accepting reality as it is, here and now. Part of me is still *fighting the day, wishing it were different*. As I continue to perceive that this is what is happening, the poison transforms. It is this seeing, this insight, which heals and, as all of this goes on, I feel everything becoming a little bit lighter. Then I try to watch out for the little moments of grace which can move me, like a cheeky wave or grin from my Elf. They always come, eventually, and the sky is clear again.

Thursday 17th March

As so often happens, I am reminded today of how quickly she grows and how much of a constant challenge that is. I want to savour it, not to miss it, but I have to go to work. On the other hand, for half of the time when I am at home, she is yelling or doing something else which causes me stress and difficulty.

Every time I want her to go to bed, or to not have to look after her because I'm tired or busy, I feel bad for wanting this – like I'm forgetting how precious every moment is. But at the same time, surely this sort of guilt can be crippling and unrealistic? I'm only human, and I get worn out and annoyed and sometimes just need to rest. I guess this is one of the unavoidable paradoxes of parenting, and I can only do my best.

Soon she will be out of Eden and into the often cruel, callous world; then I will wish I had savoured as many moments as possible. I would definitely prefer to err on the side of too much love, rather than too little. Somehow, I need to come to terms with the infinite ambiguity of this journey being both chaotic and beautiful.

Wednesday 23rd March

The last few days have been the best of Elfie's life. She has been delighted almost all of the time. This morning's breakfast was idyllic, with the three of us just making farting noises at each other for most of the time.

My own fully engaged participation in it reminded me that we are either present or we are not. It's as simple as that. However much we would sometimes like that not to be the case, it is.

Delphine has become the ultimate mindfulness trainer now she is a bit more aware and understanding of this strange new world she's living in. Every time I am on the carpet with her, she knows if I am with her or not. Being present only with our body isn't enough, for anyone. Not for our friends, our family, our colleagues, or even so-called 'strangers'.

To be totally present, *completely attentive*, is becoming rather special in this world, so full, as it is, of distractions – the word literally meaning to 'bring away'. To just do *one thing* is now a revolutionary act. I would say that it's this simple truth which is the most important thing that I have learned about parenting during this whole journey. She has retaught me the essence of mindfulness, just when I needed it most. As soon as Nadine or I are fully present with her, she perks up, she smiles, she shows her appreciation. If my mind is somewhere else, but I am looking at her, she knows I'm not really there. Of course she does; she can feel it.

It is a constant challenge to be truly present. I have a client who told me today that they dearly miss one of their parents because they are away on holiday too much, and it was very sad to hear. Although it may seem in some ways like a 'win' to get some time 'to yourself' – and indeed we all need this to an extent – what good is time to yourself without love? Wholeness? Without wholeness and the capacity to be fully present, we are never even *with ourselves* when we have time *to ourselves*, so it's not really 'time to ourselves' at all.

Friday 25th March

Earlier today, I ordered some food whilst out with a couple of friends, and my friend asked, "So what is falafel, Dom? Is it just all the vegetables?"

Classic. That's exactly what it sounds like, isn't it? Vague, bland *health*.

Then we moved on to discussing if Elfie is going to be vegetarian or vegan – ever the fun topic. I have had a colourful history with this subject, mainly because *everybody wants to talk about it*! Nadine and I have both been vegetarians for many years, and have gone back and forth on veganism. I wonder what you think of that? Chances are it makes you immediately dislike me, or strangely gives us a renewed kinship because you agree with my life choices. Cows have best friends, pigs can play video games; those are *good reasons* not to eat them. That's my story and I'm sticking to it.

We have a mug in the house (which was just broken this week, actually) which says 'In case I haven't told you today, I'm a vegan'. Also classic.

How do you know if there's a doctor or a pilot in the room?...
They'll fucking tell you!

That's how the joke goes, I think. It's supposed to be a bit like that with vegans, hence someone buying us the mug – also as a joke, I hope.

When people ask us this question about Elfie, we try our best to skirt right past it; it's an emotive topic and doesn't usually lead anywhere fruitful. People are usually only asking about it because they are annoyed about it, and that isn't normally a recipe for a good exchange. For example, I argued with my brother about this and he ended up saying that it's *cruel* to make a child a vegetarian. *Cruel.* Cruel for the child to *not* eat the animals. I understood what he meant, but there's a case to be made in the opposite direction as well.

I became a vegetarian suddenly one day because I love animals and didn't want to eat them anymore. Is it anyone else's business what our child eats? I'm not sure. Maybe, maybe not. People say 'live and let live', and I'm inclined to agree, but I also think we are more closely related than it seems, and that what we all do matters. Live and let live has a line, and it's actually a little bit blurry if you look closely. Would it be anyone else's business if Elfie were eating shoes, cars or other humans? Probably? So people have a right to be interested in this topic and ask about it, but I guess we also have a right to decide for ourselves, at this young age, within reason. If I see her looking peckish in the shoe shop, don't worry, I'll probably step in.

Sunday 3rd April

We realised recently that her reflux has almost completely stopped now. Obviously, within one minute of us saying it (literally), she was sick about three times in half an hour.

Over the next few days, though, we have continued to observe and it has indeed reduced dramatically. It's amazing how quickly this has happened and how unaware we have been of the transition. It's just like when you are ill and you suddenly appreciate health, but as soon as you recover, you forget. In the same way, we have realised just this evening that the rash she always used to have all over her face has vanished, and we were, again, completely oblivious to it.

Speaking of illness, my brother arrived a few days ago for a holiday. The day before he arrived, all three of us had caught an incredibly unpleasant stomach bug. When he arrived, we were all in an absolute state and very much contagious – just the welcome he was looking for.

One thing which I realised is that I had never considered both of us getting ill *simultaneously* and what it would mean for Elfie. We were *so close* to not being able to look after her; it felt like an almost unbearable struggle. We felt so sick we could barely move, and she is *so* demanding. I think she let us off a bit during those days, but it was still no fun at all.

Quite unexpectedly, mindfulness helped me *a lot* with vomiting. I had forgotten how awful vomiting feels. I could see my mind making a huge drama of this as it was happening, and I saw how much of a pointless waste of energy that was. The second arrow of Buddhism, as clear as day. Noticing this without fear seemed to transform it, and after I had finished being sick there wasn't a drama about it at all. It reminded me again of how much unnecessary suffering the adult mind always adds to illness. Do we need to moan about it or have any of that 'poor me' stuff? Elfie just sporadically shouts really loudly and, other than that, gets on with her life, teaching us another unexpected lesson in the process.

Tuesday 5th April

My brother's recent visit reminded me of the power of 'mirroring' in relationships, and just how vital relationship itself is for the psyche and soul. When two different energies meet, there is always a reaction and, on a human level, it allows us to see ourselves afresh, from the outside (if we *want to*). It's easy to dismiss and take for granted the validation we are receiving from other people on a fundamental level regarding every aspect of the way we live. This applies not only to body language and emotional responses, but our conceptual perspectives too.

My brother and I have a particularly intense relationship, and it has been very edifying for both of us. It just seems as if we are supposed to discuss things with great intensity. Any differences we have in our perspectives, when they manifest themselves, light up and call for attention. This is a constant source of gifts and insight we give to one another, and if we are vulnerable and open with others, every relationship can offer such gifts. We can learn so much about ourselves through the mirrors of other beings. Is anyone in your life offering you lessons about yourself at the moment which you are ignoring or pushing away? (Clue: usually, it's *annoying*.)

On his last evening, I said to him, "So what do you think of Elfie then?"

"Yeah, she's nice," he replied.

"*Is that it?!*"

"Yeah. What do you want me to say?"

"That she is absolutely magnificent beyond measure and that one look into her magical eyes makes you see the infinite glory and wonder of consciousness and feel the pure joy and miracle of existence," was approximately my response.

Not really his vibe, my bro. He's very deadpan. As you know by now, I'm a bit different. Effulgent and effusive, I think, are some of the right words. I was once criticised by the same brother for 'calling everyone an absolute legend', a comment which I saw quite quickly afterwards is absolutely true. There's something in me which takes seeing the good in everyone to quite an extreme.

My brother has reflected, after this week, that he could never have a child without full-time assistance, as he simply can't handle the 'bad bits'. The nappies revolt him beyond measure and he can't stand the crying and losing all of your own time and sleep. OK, when you put it like that, I'll admit it doesn't sound great. Nevertheless, we had a great discussion about the subtleties of both points of view and what is really in it for parents, based on our experiences so far. I don't think he was convinced!

Side note: When Elfie is in a good mood, cuddling her is the *best thing ever.*

Wednesday 6th April

This weekend was extremely difficult. We were told, out of the blue, that we had to leave our house in three months. We have been renting it for three years and we absolutely adore it; it truly is our home and we have had no intention whatsoever of leaving.

It was a tremendously powerful shock; I felt like the rug had been swept out from beneath me. I had forgotten that it was not *our house*. I had forgotten that it could be *taken away*. What made it worse is that the rental prices have changed hugely in the last few years, and to rent somewhere half as nice is going to cost us so much more. As the only person currently winning any bread, I felt a lot of pressure closing in on me, and we were both feeling angst about what to do. It was a powerful reminder of how contingent external security is and how much we subconsciously rely on it. We both pivoted relatively quickly that day to the realisation that all would be well, but it was not an easy shift.

This week, since that news, the theme of financial instability and external security has continued to loom large, as I've discovered that a large portion of the work I've booked in over the next few months is no longer possible – for one reason or another.

This was a huge shock for me too, even though I know my job is fundamentally insecure and things like this can happen out of the blue. This 'hit', combined with the enormous costs of moving house, was very difficult to take.

I had to process the situation for a long time this evening, and Nadine found it hard to see me under so much pressure and clearly experiencing difficult emotional waves; naturally, she just wanted it all to go away. But I was allowing myself to be in that emotional space and *purposefully feeling it as much as possible*. What I was feeling was absolutely natural and inevitable. As weird as it sounds, once it was there, I *wanted to experience it*. I didn't want to pretend I didn't care. I do care. I've been feeling really good about being able to support us and still having some money left over because of my hard work.

Just before bedtime, I said to Nadine, regarding the difficult episode, "Wow! I really enjoyed that!"

Of course, she thought I was joking and gave a little chuckle, knowing it had been a 'hard time'. But then I had to explain that I was serious, and I had never enjoyed something as difficult as that as much as I did tonight. Why?

As I have mentioned previously in the book, my relationship with money has been a rich source of life lessons for me, and this was a significant event in that journey. I had been very attentive and allowed myself to totally feel and process what was there to be experienced. I was understanding my whole relationship with money with fresh eyes only because of this 'bad' news, and the inner waves – which lasted for a long time – truly felt like something growing naturally and then dying an equally natural, beautiful death. That's the best way I can put it into words. Krishnamurti calls this 'flowering'; a wonderful phrase which feels very accurate. It was as if the life lessons had been allowed to do exactly what they were supposed to, and they had been integrated fully.

At the end of the evening, rather than feeling worn out and upset by the whole episode, it was quite the opposite: I was energised and genuinely happy, despite how 'bad' the external reality was, or *seemed to be*, in comparison to just a few days before.

So I guess the question is: how much would you pay to transform distortions and tension in your relationship with money? In terms of the anxiety, fear and insecurity money can bring into our world, I suppose such insights are worth quite a large sum! Isn't that a nicer way to look at it?

Six to Twelve Months

<u>Friday 8th April</u>

We needed to get Elfie out of the house this evening, so we decided to put her into her first pair of shoes and cycle to the supermarket. We didn't want to buy anything; we just wanted her to have a ride in the wheely basket they have. The last time we did this she bloody loved it and it caused such a stir for the shoppers and workers alike.

This time, again, it just gave everyone who noticed her the biggest dose of joy. The fact that she was inside the basket in a bicycle helmet made it even better, because some people probably thought she was in the helmet just because of the ride in the basket. We created the vibe that she was in a theme park so effectively that one of the shop's employees, after enjoying waving to her for a while, blurted out, "Have a great time!" as we walked away.

Is that a normal thing to say to someone in a supermarket? Not really. But he knew. He knew that we weren't in a supermarket, and that somehow, *somehow*, his place of work had a mysteriously fun side. That it was a secret theme park. His smile said it all. Obviously, at the checkout I took her out and popped her on the conveyor belt ready to be scanned, with a sticker for bananas on her back. It gives her a mischievous, wondrous glint in the eyes, and the lady scanning items seemingly had the most fun part of her day when trying to scan her, and not knowing what she was supposed to do when Elfie finally reached the scanning bit.

Imagine if everywhere you went there was something unusual like this going on, with people in your community being drawn into some fun, spontaneous game! Wouldn't it be amazing?

Unfortunately, on exiting the shop, I saw someone wearing a T-shirt which said:

'Meditate, manifest, repeat.'

Really killed my vibe.

Translation:

'Close my eyes, move towards the deep essential peace and unity of all existence, *get whatever I want*, do it again.'

What could be less 'spiritual' than that?

The whole modern spiritual movement, unsurprisingly, suffers from existing within our capitalist society; it is inevitable that the shadow side of capitalism must poison it somehow. I'm reminded of the wonderful term 'McMindfulness',[49] which refers to the way mindfulness can be seen as just a spiritual 'quick-fix': to get a *new kind of pleasure,* and *fast*!

As I've already alluded to, we learn about the magic of reality – that we live in an *interactive universe* – and all we can think is, "Oh, great! Give me everything I want and give it to me now!"

But surely 'spirituality', if we have to use that loaded word, is about love, understanding and harmony more than achievement, ambition and desire? 'Manifestation' is usually self-centred, and what if the self in question only wants pointless, empty things? How do we know that what we *want* is the same as what we *need*, or what is *good*? It may not be right to demonise self-centred desire, but why put it on a pedestal? I wonder what the Buddha would say about all this, if he were alive today. There he sits, in so many houses, in the form of a statue, or up on the wall, often just another *thing to be had*, his essential message going as unnoticed as the present moment.

As everyone loves to point out, though, not everything self-centred is *bad*. Nisargadatta Maharaj said, on the subject of people seeming to become more self-centred when they go down a spiritual path, "Good. Let them think about themselves for a while."[50] His point is that it is only by becoming passionately interested in ourselves that we can clear up our mess and move into a more harmonious way of being. This rings true to me and accords with my experience, and it makes me feel less grumpy about it all. I try to tell myself that 'manifestation' is just the start! People waking up to the magical nature of reality has *got to be* a good thing.

Six to Twelve Months

<u>Saturday 9th April</u>

Sometimes it's obvious when you're supposed to be learning about something, because it keeps popping up everywhere. For me at this time, it's generosity and charity. It just keeps coming up. Elfie, at breakfast, is constantly offering us whatever is in her hand, and it's so endearing. Why does she want us to have it? *'This makes me happy, so it will make you happy too!'* This is very instructive for me, as I can occasionally get slightly 'Gollum with the ring' around delicious food.

Simone Weil, an extraordinary mystic, was apparently told by her rabbi when she was young that neglecting to give to charity is equivalent to causing harm, because a poor person might die without assistance.[51] The simplicity of this argument blew me away, and I was surprised I had not heard it expressed before. But what place does charity have in society? In our hearts? Do we do it because we have to? Do we do it because the BBC said that kindness increases the areas of our brain associated with kindness? Or do we actually feel it in our hearts?

Sometimes the mindset which prevents charity is that we need the money for ourselves and, when we have it, then we can start giving. Yet how can we be generous if we are waiting until we have enough?

Weil said that the ultimate act of charity is giving attention, and I quite like that as well, because we can and do withhold it each and every day. To truly be attentive to someone is a beautiful gift, a blessing, and the essence of love.

<u>Sunday 10th April</u>

Back to the supermarket again today for a quick ride, and this time Elfie wanted to go in the normal basket instead of the wheely one, just to mix things up. She drew even more looks from the surprised shoppers in that guise, and you can imagine their reactions. Actually, you probably can't, because I was surprised to notice three different categories of them:

1. Noticing her, then instinctive confusion and blocking it out of consciousness.
2. Noticing her, then *grumpily disapproving*. (Hint: don't be in Group 2.)
3. Noticing her, then feeling an outpouring of unexpected joy and smiles. (Yes, best to be in Group 3.)

Seeing as she wanted a bit of a change, we did too, so we put a cheeky barcode on her: 'Pitted Olives. 8.25 AED.' Absolute bargain. Oh, and yes, that is her vomit on my jeans.

It's getting very difficult to eat or drink nice things around her now, as our empanada from Costa was too hot for her and so was the tea. So, as she justifiably tries to reach out her little paws to enjoy what we are enjoying, she is savagely rebutted and becomes very sad (even though she has lots of her own biscuits and things right in front of her to eat). How horrible is that, considering that she always offers us whatever she has? I noticed this and felt terrible. Does that mean we should always be offering her everything, otherwise we are encouraging her to be selfish and greedy? What an awful (and probably true) thought!

Later, at bedtime, we had messed up the timings a bit so she was a little more cranky than usual and very fed up. This means lots of moaning, groaning and crying during the bedtime routine. Taking off clothes, changing the nappy, putting on new clothes – all of that becomes a real slog. Each second becomes ten, psychologically, and it was draining my energy, as I already felt tired. Then Nadine asked me to try to 'put her down' (a phrase we should probably retire) and I felt the standard resistance. When tired, obviously it's more difficult to go against resistance, but I managed to get my arse into gear and do my duty.

We are staggering this transition, so Nadine still stands next to me and we put her to bed together. We hum our standard song, 'Can't Help Falling in Love', which Nadine started humming to Elfie many months ago at bedtime.

As we were doing it, I felt so tired and drained, and then I noticed that this was preventing me from being present. In fact, I don't think that's quite right. Just like pinpointing why you 'woke up' from a dream, that's close to impossible. You weren't there! So how could you know? You were in the dream! I don't know exactly what happened. It wasn't that I 'tried to be present', no. I think I looked *properly* at Elfie and Nadine, and that jerked me into the moment and began to move me out of the funk. The vibration and energy shifted for me in that instant, and I was able to see how precious the moment was. *Remember to love her!* I thought.

Just as in meditation there are phenomena called *nimittas* – clear shifts in perception or experience that signal a transition into a different state of consciousness, like crossing a threshold – the same thing happened in this case, as it always does when we 'wake up' or come into presence. Something brings us to presence, and then the *moving out* from confusion and inattention is felt and experienced as the energy changes. Often this is happening too fast to be consciously noticed, though, so we don't see the process for what it is. It happened gradually, as I kept attending properly to everything, and I watched the confusion disappear and be replaced by 'higher' perceptions. I felt deep love for both of them and for the moment itself. I could feel the beautiful, shared energy of us as a family unit having an intimate moment, whereas before I had just been 'getting through it'.

Another interesting insight came to me during this event: I saw how incredibly magical what we were doing was. We were both creating vibrations from our throats, which went up and down melodically, in perfect resonance with almost every previous day of her life. This is entraining her brain to associate the vibrations with a relaxed state of consciousness and bringing such a state of consciousness into being. It truly is a magic spell! How often are we preventing ourselves from bearing witness to such insights by believing in and fuelling the draining and limiting stories of the mind? How much are we missing when we are asleep?

This example illustrates something vital. We often mistakenly believe that there is 'reality' and we are always seeing it when we look out at life. Not true. There are different levels of so-called reality and we are always seeing a certain interpretation of what is before us; distorting it with a certain psychological lens, just as gravity distorts light.

These different interpretations are available simultaneously, and some are far more *profound, insightful, significant, meaningful, interesting and magical* than others.

The brain, rather than being the generator of thought and consciousness, seems to be more like a radio receiver, tuning in to different stations. The question is: what station do you want to listen to?

Monday 11th April

Sometimes you know you've just got to 'get' her. What is this and why is it so bloody fun? The conclusion I've come to is that it means that you're about to take over her personal universe. When we go and 'get her' in her little tent (which is undoubtedly her new favourite thing to do with us), we are totally dominating her experience and she absolutely loves it. Forcing her to experience being tickled, or being nuzzled, or snuggled, or kissed or cuddled. It's pure joy!

Truly, the most wonderful developments so far are occurring at this point, and I cannot possibly imagine how they could get better. Cuddling! Actual bona fide cuddling, and a lot of it. That's definitely some pretty good payment for all the energy which is expended in making sure she remains in this plane of existence.

Her lust for the cats is getting pretty out of control now, though. She makes goblin noises *on sight* and it's having exactly the opposite of the intended effect. Have you ever seen an animal feel genuinely socially awkward? We have now, hundreds of times. They immediately run; all except for our big doggy cat, Arry. He simply can't be arsed to try to escape and, therefore, he is her favourite by far. Bless his heart! She has proper cuddles with him now, every time she sees him, and he is so patient that he just sits there and lets it happen. In fact, if she moves away, he actively seeks her out to continue. What a hero.

Diary of a Mindful Dad

<u>Wednesday 13th April</u>

I've had an enormous delivery of energy today for creating a course in time for the official opening of the company I work for, the Free Spirit Collective. It's been another profound demonstration to me of a principle which has guided me so much: when the energy is there, it is there and you *must act. Go with it. Open the gifts.*

As I sit down and begin to write, the energy just streams through and more and more comes, as if the 'floodgates have opened'. Where is it coming from?

Another energetic mystery came to the fore last night, when I had an unexpected (as they always are) Jedi parenting trial – settling Elfie back to sleep for 45 solid minutes. Unfortunately, it came during a Liverpool Champions League match! Isn't she selfish?

I could feel the subtle vibrational shifts taking place, over and over, guiding me on what needed to be done next. Nadine and I discussed this mysterious phenomenon later on, and she agrees that Elfie can feel her energy field when she is putting her to sleep. She said that if they are no longer in physical contact, but she takes one small step backwards, Elfie immediately reacts. On some level, she can feel the energetic shift: Nadine's energy field separating from hers.

I have been keen to discuss this with Nadine for a while because, although a large percentage of people might laugh and scoff at such a suggestion (surely not you, beloved reader?!), this ancient idea has enormous implications and deserves serious consideration. It opens the door to seeing that these subtle interactions are occurring between all of us all the time, and not just when we are standing next to each other. Looking at human interaction in this way moves us, bit by bit, into a whole new world.

When I explore this mysterious energy with a group of

children, by showing them how to create an 'energy ball' using Qi Gong, it's amazing to see how many of their eyes light up as they declare: *"I can feel it!"*

It's approximately 75%, I would say. Placebo effect, perhaps? Could be. But if you feel it for yourself, the strange tinglings, pins and needles, magnetic sensations which occur almost immediately upon doing these exercises with the right attention, you might change your mind.

I introduced this to a lovely client last week in a one-to-one session, a 14-year-old, and he was dumbstruck. He simply couldn't believe that he could feel energy emanating from his own hands within ten seconds of doing something so simple that he surely ought to have done it before. But we don't! When do you ever move your hands around extremely slowly and pay careful attention to how it feels? What place does that have in society? None! Not this one, anyway.

Thursday 14th April

Learn mindfulness from your baby: lesson number 2123

I had the most wonderful afternoon with Delphine today. Phone: off and away. That's how every truly delightful time seems to start for me. I sat with her on the floor and didn't realise I had sat down for a mindfulness lesson. Then she began, in her inimitable style, giving me a guided tour of what will henceforth be known as her 'Box of Boring Wonders'.

Slowly, she removed a small charging cable, and then did the most remarkable thing: she *attended to it*. She inspected it carefully for 30 seconds or so, the longest 30 seconds of my life (in a good way); it felt as if she had completely stopped time with this simple act of attention. Her eyes were aflame with intrigue, and nothing could have stopped her from examining every part of this previously dull object. Then, when she was satisfied, she gently and consciously turned her head, handed it to me very deliberately, with a smile and a nod, as I took it from her hand.

The smile and nod told me not only that it was my turn, but that this object was *special*. I handled it as she had, inspected it carefully, felt the weight of it in my hand, noticed and appreciated its simple being. It was utterly transformed, all of it. Me, the charging cable, the room – *reality itself*.

Then, she showed me a blue shoelace – I had been wondering where that had gone! A boring object, right?

Wrong. Boring is in the eyes, not the objects. Her eyes aren't boring at all, and she was lending them to me, for a precious time.

We went through this same sacred process over and over, with the same perfectly simple attention, and we were both totally enthralled. I didn't want to be anywhere else in the world. Each object, equally ordinary, became perfectly extraordinary, one after the other: a battery (oops), a small roll of Sellotape, a pen lid, a coin, a paperclip. It felt as if she was blessing them, bringing them to life with her consciousness, and I was then given the chance to do the same. This marvellous little box, the equivalent of which is ignored every day in households the world over, had been transformed by her wonder, by the *power of wonder itself*.

Who knows what she will teach me next?

Saturday 16th April

Can you be fully present with your partner after giving enormous energy to being with your little one? That's one of those tiny, mighty, beautiful challenges a parent must face day in, day out.

I watched the mind encouraging me to retreat into myself earlier today, after a full-on stint with Elfie, and that was when I saw her: *my wife*. She was there, *right there*, and I knew I had to move in the opposite direction to where the mind was leading me. Reset, refresh, attend, again and again.

Monday 18th April

Last week we took our first trip abroad as a family. We flew back home to the UK, as we always do, but this time with the added wonder of introducing Elfie to any friends and family who had not met her yet. It has been especially difficult for our close family to see her so infrequently, so this was a much-needed trip and we were very excited. As usual, we ignored the negativity from others about how awful the plane journey would be. We knew that we could handle it together, and there's no point in feeding a negative picture of a scenario which hasn't happened yet. That's just not my idea of fun.

Our casual attitude probably went a little too far, though. As we arrived at the airport with about 500 bags, we realised we hadn't weighed any of them. Uh-oh. We laughed and somehow got away with it, despite them being quite a bit over. The universe provides!

The flight was uneventful, thanks to the Emirates bassinet seat and my extremely capable wife. Elfie's separation anxiety kicked off during the only time Nadine left to go to the toilet, though, and it was quite horrible because she was crying a lot whilst I held her, waiting for Nadine to come back. She's never done that before, so we assumed it was because she had no idea what was going on and was travelling through the sky in a giant metal shoe. Oh, and trying to make me look like a shit dad, obviously. All perfectly plausible reasons, I think.

The best moment of the journey came about five hours in. I hadn't communicated with Elfie in about four hours because she had been asleep all that time, and Nadine took her out of the bassinet to feed her. As I looked over, I noticed that her eyes were open, and we caught each other's gaze. I was so happy to see her, and at that exact moment, she slowly, consciously raised her little hand (which was completely covered by a Zipadee-Zip) and gave one slow-motion, solitary wave. Then a smile. It was incredible. I called it the clam hand because it was one of those hand-closing-and-opening waves, which just made it way cuter. My heart melted.

Our plan for the trip was, quite frankly, ludicrous. It had been so long since we'd been home, and we only had a week, so we packed far too much in. We knew this going in and were prepared for the constant to-ing and fro-ing.

Upon arrival, we unpacked and tried to get Elfie used to the surroundings. She loved it...as long as we were there. Like...*right there. Exactly there.* We had been warned by Wonder Weeks (an app which tells you when the baby's 'leaps' are) about the fact that this was the worst possible time for separation anxiety, and here it was: ten months.

The problem was that we were supposed to be leaving her with my stepmum for the day, on the Thursday of that week, so we could go to a wedding. Uh-oh. Yes, we were a little nervous and apprehensive about this, but we had been planning for it for a while. Elfie had been looked after for an hour, here and there, a few times in the last month and had been absolutely fine. But these first signs were worrying: she *knew she was in a strange environment.*

For the next few days, she had to follow us everywhere we went. Even if we walked to the other side of the room, she crawled after either one of us. Worse still, she couldn't even be left just with me. Nadine *had to be there at all times* or she would freak out and not stop until her dear mother returned. So there was only one thing for it. We tried, on the Wednesday, to leave her with my stepmum Sonia for an hour without either of us, and we both went upstairs after waving her goodbye.

It went terribly. She didn't calm down *at all* after a full (very painful) hour, even though she had all of her favourite toys, singing and dancing and a very lovely lady looking after her. We had assumed it would only last 15 minutes at most. We also already knew that she loved Sonia because she had met her before in Dubai and they had bonded really well straight away.

It's difficult to describe the pang of hearing that shrieking wail – knowing it means the thing you love more than anything else in the world just wants you to come back and hold her – while you're already conflicted about whether or not you're even supposed to be leaving her, if that's how it makes her feel.

Perhaps we could have pushed through this and it would have changed quickly, but we felt like we had to message the friends who were hosting the wedding and explain the situation. It just didn't feel right to leave her without us for an entire day. In the end, she was able to come along (there were a few other children of close family there as well) and she ended up having a wild old time, dancing with us on the dance floor late into the evening, charming everyone and grinning wildly the whole time. She was silent throughout all of the speeches, except for the tiny clanking together of a small pair of castanets. She was the model guest! Far better-behaved than me, I think.

A friend of mine said, "Weddings are for babies. They bless them, as all fairy godmothers know." That really made me wish that I knew more fairy godmothers. They seem to be in short supply these days.

The rest of the holiday went well, with lots of socialising and late evenings without any trouble from the little one at all. There is a great picture of her in an Italian restaurant, wearing nothing but a nappy, *absolutely covered in tomato sauce*, with a long piece of pasta hanging out of her mouth. Tagliatelle, in case you were wondering. I know you were. How many different types of pasta can you name? These things matter.

We developed a fantastic game to play with her when socialising, perfect for every time she starts getting fed up. Randomly, I will give people the sign, and we will *all just start clapping and cheering and staring at her*. I know, I used to moan about parents overpraising their kids too, but I have a long time to save for her therapy bills and this is just gold. She suddenly lights up and starts clapping as well, absolutely ecstatic.

The highlight of the trip for me was the late-night karaoke in the pub. Elfie was enchanted by my quite average performance, and we have a video of her loving the vibes. She's a party girl, for sure.

By the end of the holiday, we were socially satiated and very much ready to get home, back to some semblance of orderly chaos, rather than the wild chaos of carting our little family from house to house, day after day.

Wednesday 27th April

As I arrived at work this morning, post-holiday, I received a call from Nadine. Immediately, I imagined the worst, and this time I wasn't far off. Nadine had bent down to clean up under the high chair whilst Elfie was sitting in it, and she climbed out within five seconds and it collapsed underneath her. She fell directly downwards onto her head onto the marble floor with a colossal, Earth-shaking thud and screamed like mad. She wouldn't calm down for a long time, and she had some blood coming out of one nostril and an enormous bruise appearing. This made me, with my zero medical knowledge, assume brain damage.

After calming down, she wasn't herself. She wasn't babbling and acting as she normally does, so Nadine went straight to A&E after the phone call. I was in shock and just wanted to cry. I had to go into my client's house and explain the situation and why I was a little off. I decided to stay and continue my lessons, but I felt terrible. It was almost impossible to focus properly, but I just about managed it, waiting for Nadine's message to update me. Thankfully, the doctor said she was fine and the blood from the nose was just a surface tissue wound. She was behaving normally after Nadine returned from the hospital.

Good lord, it was one of the most terrifying phone calls of my life. It is unbelievable how quickly something horrendous can happen. Luckily, the good ol' mind has given me the perfect solution: just lock her in a small box forever so that *nothing* can happen to her. Phew! What a relief.

Yeah, that's not quite right, is it? A bit more balance says we need to re-examine her environment and make sure no other imminent dangers are lurking, which she has suddenly become able to unlock. Who would have children?!

I am reminded to have faith. I am an ardent fatalist and believe we are looked after. I am also reminded to do the unthinkable – to *accept the possibility of tragedy*. Terrible things can happen sometimes, to people of any age. Accepting this is probably not a popular move here, but it has done something quite strange and interesting to the fear of it, and made me wake up again to how grateful we ought to be for everything.

Sunday 1st May

Elfie has been charming people constantly at the local pool. She waves enthusiastically and relentlessly until someone responds, and the other day she made a group of middle-aged ladies go completely wild because of how cute her frolics were. You could see the nurturing essence of the sacred feminine bursting from all of their faces.

I told my brother yesterday that I missed her terribly, after one day of work, and he couldn't understand it at all.

"You saw her this morning!"

Exactly. That was *ages ago*! That's how it feels. That's how much I enjoy her company.

Having said that, leaving her for five seconds also means something has been peed or pooed on, so leaving for hours means I can skip that part. Swings and roundabouts! Just another parenting paradox.

I also had my first-ever phone call with her this week, which was shocking and delightful. She suddenly jumped into the conversation I was having with Nadine and babbled away to me for a while. It was so surreal; it felt like the world of the phone had been its own independent realm up to this point, where only adult conversations were allowed. Nope. Not so. She just waltzed in, straight past the bouncers, presumably flashing some sort of VIP badge on her way in.

Monday 2nd May

"Ooh, you're a bit dirty considering you've just had a bath!" Nadine says to Elfie.

"Oh! I literally never make any attempt to clean her when we have a bath," I reply, amazed at my own sentence and laughing out loud.

"What do you mean?! Why not?"

Well, the answer is because I just see it as our bonding time and forget. I don't clean myself either, but that's because I shower in the morning. Anyway, there we are. Lesson learned. *When in the bath, clean baby.*

We have been trying to sell our car over the last few weeks and, unfortunately for Nadine, she had to do most of the jobs because the car was registered under her name. Because I'm working a full schedule, this meant she had to do it with Delphine, and she was dreading it. This turned out to be rather prophetic.

She spent three hours in the bank trying to close the loan, because she had to try to count all the money with Delphine on her lap, and nobody was allowed to help her because of some bank rule straight out of Terry Gilliam's *Brazil*. Elfie was constantly grabbing the notes, obviously, and apparently it was so comedic that Nadine was genuinely laughed at by the cashier. She really enjoyed that.

The following day brought another such adventure: four hours, this time, to take the car to do an inspection. That was also great fun. Babies LOVE sitting on chairs for hours, in quiet rooms, waiting for their turn to be seen by the bureaucrats. LOVE it.

Then we had to do further testing yesterday and, just on the way home, we received a call from the bank (ten days after paying off the loan) to say that there was an outstanding balance. So in the three hours of Nadine counting out money at the bank, *they* ended up getting the amount we owed wrong. This meant we couldn't sell the car, so we had to go to an ATM (after getting home, all with the little one) to pay off the rest. I asked the bank, with a hint of desperation, "Please make sure that you give me the correct details on the nearest ATM to my house."

Alas, no. We made the trip and it was the wrong ATM, which didn't provide the only service we needed. Such is life, right? The customer service agent kindly and surprisingly paid off the remainder of our loan from his own account and then sent us his details to repay him. Does that make him qualify as a 'legend'? I can't trust myself anymore about where that line is, but my gut says yes. I'd better do that, come to think of it. Thanks for reminding me, future reader.

Tuesday 10th May

Elfie has been standing now for a couple of weeks, and today it happened: her *first steps*. I'm so happy to say that I saw it live. It was awesome…and terrifying. The whole world is now accessible! Oh dear!

Nadine's mum said we should put reins on her immediately – so she thinks it's normal – and my mum chimed in that it would be like breaking in a wild pony. We will just skirt right past all of that.

Her first foray as a biped led her a few precarious steps across the kitchen to our rabbit, Bilbo, to feed him a carrot. Not the worst thing to do with her new-found powers!

Diary of a Mindful Dad

Saturday 21st May

We took her to soft play for the first time in Dubai today, and it's something of a tragedy that it has taken us so long to go. It was incredible. She was ludicrously excited and went around like a total nutter the entire time. Climbing everything, crawling at the speed of light and walking more steps than ever, over and over again. Yet any time another child was near her, she stopped whatever she was doing and began interacting with them with 100% of her energy. She was so wonderful with them that it was really quite heart-melting. All she ever wanted to do was offer them things to hold, like she does with us. Each offer was a pure and spontaneous act of kindness and connection, each so beautiful to behold.

Watching the simplicity of this made me reflect on how much of a mess we have made of this in the adult world. We are so lost that apparently we need online articles to tell us that kindness and giving are 'good for our health' to motivate us to be 'kind' once in a while, or we need to be cajoled by someone else into 'random' acts of kindness. Not really random, are they? It's a contrived decision to do one 'kind' thing. If only they were truly 'random' in the carefree sense Elfie gave me a glimpse of today; she just loves to share her things. I'm hoping some of her natural, simple selflessness will rub off on me.

Later in the day, another lovely thing happened. We are back into the routine of Nadine always putting Elfie to bed; I do all of the routine with her, but when it comes to rocking and putting her to sleep, it's always Nadine. I think this is just a consequence of us not needing anyone to look after her any time soon.

Because of this, I've fallen into the trap again of thinking that I don't 'need' to put her to bed, so I shouldn't. I should go and do something else.

Tonight, for some reason, I remembered what had happened before, when I overcame resistance to doing this. I stayed for much more of the process, on purpose, and Elfie came over to me on the bed, consciously desperate for an *actual cuddle*. There was something different about it, as if she really *knew* what cuddling was and had learned how to 'do it properly'. Now that's a 'leap' I can get on board with! It lasted a few minutes, and she was affectionately squeezing my face and my arms and smiling at me. A truly touching experience, filled with love. Yet again, I was rewarded by life for going against the momentum of the past, for trying something different.

Sunday 22nd May

I amused myself today by imagining Elfie writing one of these entries, so here is her update:

Diary of a Mindful Dad

As an 11-month-old, it's still clear that the universe revolves around me, but it appears to be defective. Sometimes I want something and – even if I scream for it – it doesn't materialise. The pretty one keeps trying to make me say 'Dada' all the time and pointing at the silly one. It's very boring and odd. I try to call him 'Nana' instead because I know that really winds them both up. I am guessing 'Nana' must be some sort of insult. I'm still enjoying making a mockery of their idea that they have free will. My favourite thing is to act all independent so they leave me alone, and then almost die straight afterwards. They absolutely hate it! Ah, good times. I hope I remember all this.

Tuesday 24th May

Nadine and I had a wonderful anniversary yesterday of the first time we met each other properly – 15 years ago. During dinner, we came to a discussion about sex, and I opened up about how my relationship with it has evolved throughout pregnancy and since Elfie's arrival, and the challenges it has brought.

Nadine was open to hearing about it and very supportive, and it blossomed into a fruitful discussion about all sorts of things. For one thing, she opened up to me about the fact that she had found it difficult to spend time alone since having Elfie. Every time she drives to her one client, she said that her mind inevitably spins towards questions of ageing and mortality. This is something which I have also considered even more than usual since becoming a dad, because creating the next generation naturally confronts you with it. Nadine has never liked thinking about such things, and she said that she just tries to ignore it immediately every time. I said all sorts of things that any self-respecting husband who is also massively into existential questions would.

My opinion is that when such deep, profound and difficult questions come to us, it's an opportunity for us to learn and grow by facing them. I think they are the source of our deepest lessons and such lessons transform our lives. If we always run away from these things until the end of our lives, are we really living?

Another significant topic which we touched on is the issue of self-esteem and body image. Nadine's body has changed, as with anyone who gives birth, and it brings with it very difficult lessons. It was hard to hear how this feels, and we moved together to a nicer way of viewing it all. Can it be seen as yet another big lesson she is getting from having children – the opportunity to go beyond the way she previously saw and defined herself? Can it be seen as a gift and a source of strength? Imagine if our self-esteem can remain intact despite our bodies going through changes which we really don't like: wouldn't that bring us more security and strength? This doesn't mean ignoring feelings of disliking ourselves. No. Honour them, accept them, feel them. But use this as a springboard to seeing ourselves anew, like a butterfly emerging from a chrysalis. Oh, we aren't defined by our body looking a certain way; we are way more than that? Good news, right? Maybe, but of course it's also easier said than done. Again, like all the other lessons offered by this adventure, it's not a problem to be solved, but something deeper to be attended to consciously and with care.

It was lovely to bring all of these questions and difficulties out into the open; it felt tremendously healing, and it made me wonder how this can ever happen if we are always eating dinner in front of the TV. When is there space to speak about the things which really matter?

Wednesday 25th May

Just commit totally, that's it. Give everything to being with them in that moment. Then the magic opens up. Put the bloody phone away and dive in.

The first thing on the menu today is 'hiding in the tent'. Just what it says on the tin. She hides in the tent and is very cute, I pretend not to know where she is, then appear like a madman and make the perennially scary noise, "BOO!"

Repeat.

When Nadine returned home from work, she described her extreme sense of separation from Elfie – how hard it was, and how it made her reflect on the fact that primate babies normally don't leave their mother's side until age two. If only we were those sorts of primates. Do we really have to separate so early? Says who? Do we have the courage to go against the powerful and all-knowing voice of 'the crowd'?

Thursday 26th May

Can healing yourself heal your child?

Yesterday, I was seeing my client whose mother practises the extraordinary form of therapy I mentioned earlier – the one that involves directly and purposefully feeling the emotions of others – when something amazing happened as I was leaving.

Very uncharacteristically and suddenly, as I was walking out, my client said, "Mr Watts?"

"Yes."

"I think I was bullied and that's why I am shy."

It blew me away. He never speaks about his personal experiences or his past. We spoke about it for a while, and I had goosebumps at the power of his insight.

Then, as I walked out, I noticed his parents in the room where they do their therapy work. They had just finished.

"Were you just working?"

"Yes, why?"

"What were you doing? Your son just suddenly opened up about his past."

They were really pleased and visibly unsurprised. They told me they had been working together on some of their own 'baggage' relating to this. That's exactly how they were hoping this would work. *Heal yourself, heal the world.* Clear the energetic field, and it will ripple out. I was also unsurprised, but very much amazed, and felt a bit like Alice taking another step into a post-materialist wonderland. We all laughed together at the illusion of space and separation and went our 'separate' ways.

Friday 27th May

We are now at the stage where we need to confront the terrifying fact that she has her *own will*. Up until now, she has had to do pretty much whatever we want her to do all the time, within reason, and there is no fighting back on her part.

Now, it's a different world. Food time goes like this:

We prepare her food and give it to her with an attitude of love and care.

She chucks it on the floor.

We pick it up.

She picks up one piece, chucks it on the floor again, then looks at us as if to say, *"What you gonna do about it?"*

We freeze, inwardly acknowledging that we have *lost*.

She refuses to eat anything she doesn't *love* the look of.

We start to try and make it fun by offering her the good old timeless classic: *food pretending to be a train*.

No dice.

She pushes our hands away repeatedly.

Then she only wants *our* food.

What the hell should we do about all this? Nadine points out that this is probably why millions of parents feel they need to give up and just give the child the foods they like, but we want to try hard not to fall into that cycle as well (as I'm sure they all did). This means that a very powerful word has been thrown around a hell of a lot in this house:

"No!"

What is that?

It is a magical *boundary*, a *forcefield*, an enforcing of your own will over theirs to *change their world*. I've noticed that we have been instinctively, and somewhat inevitably, using this 'magic word' when Elfie is causing chaos, now that she can understand us a lot more. But I hate the *feeling* of it, I hate *closing her down*. I hate the idea of being an authority over anyone, and I've hated authority for as long as I can remember. Obviously, this is going to be a very difficult parenting challenge for me going forward.

I think we're getting a bit tired of being talked down to and told what to do as a society, too. Maybe this is why there seems to be a fascination at the moment for books with 'Fuck' in the title. This means *I'm your friend. I'm real. I'm like you.* I'm sure that if this had been called *Diary of a Fucking Mindful Dad*, it would reach a much wider audience. What do you reckon?

Six to Twelve Months

Saturday 28th May

Does it matter how we react when Elfie experiences a very heavy, supposedly 'negative' emotion? Surely it does, and more than we could possibly imagine. The famous line from *Hamlet*, "Nothing is either good or bad but thinking makes it so" resounds in me as I consider this topic. Labelling certain experiences as 'bad' or 'negative' causes so much trouble.

This afternoon, during a walk around the local lake, Elfie didn't get something that she had suddenly wanted, and a huge eruption of frustration appeared in her and made an explosion of noise.

This time I didn't react. I was quiet. The question dawned on me with full force: how on Earth should we respond? It's not like I haven't thought about it before, but this was different. This was an insight into *how important that question is*: inwardly, I was totally stopped by the question and could not move anywhere.

This stopping gave way to something new, and revealed that *this stopping itself is the key*. The most important thing possible is surely to be silent, inwardly and outwardly? Not necessarily for long, but for enough time for all parties involved to *notice the opening*. That's what it is: an opening.

Remember, waves of emotion being experienced by someone else are teaching *us* as well as them, so we should *pay attention*. What is happening? If we don't create this space, there can be no noticing. That mysterious, silent space can work wonders if only we *let it*.

Yet in our modern world, we have no time for that. Poisoned by short-term focus, the mind jumps in and wants to solve whatever is happening immediately, preventing this deeper, quieter form of intelligence from arising and operating. As a society, we haven't stopped to notice that the way we live *this moment* is the way we live *all moments*. This sort of 'child's emotion and parental reaction' situation happens 100 times a day, and will remain the same in kind, though different in its expressions, as she grows up. How important is it to get this right? Could anything be more important in parenting?

If we can create the opening, the intelligent energy which takes form in that space acts of its own accord, in that moment, and produces something unexpected and alive. In this case, it gave me one cryptic word: *Listen*.

She was in the midst of such a powerful storm, and making such dramatic noises, and then I used this magic word. I whispered it, really close to her, and held my ear at the same time, following the word 'listen' with a lovely, enticing shh, like something interesting was happening (which *was* the case). It did something mysterious to the momentum of the emotional outburst and redirected all of her energy exactly where I wanted it: the present. Inner *and* outer, because there is no difference! It's just *the moment itself, and everything in it*. Something subtle shifted, in a palpable way, and nothing was shut down.

Does that mean this can be used as some sort of technique? Ha! I wish. If I try that again, without making the opening, I assume it will fail miserably. So we can't rely on the ideas which come from that space, and fix them into solid 'techniques', because that's missing the point! But what we can do, instead, is *try to keep opening it*.

In mindfulness courses, people learn about being 'unreactive'; this means, first, to watch their reactions *as they happen*. And it is *hard*. It takes enormous effort, hundreds and hundreds of times, to go beyond any of it. So much momentum goes against the possibility of that observation – it's all so fast.

And this is why! All of your life, ever since you were a baby, everyone around you has reacted *immediately* to your so-called 'negative' emotions: an emotional response, expressed in words; a tone of voice; a physical movement, towards or away from you; a facial expression. It all tells us that what is happening is *bad* and we need to *act on it straight away. Do something! Anything! It's not welcome.*

So when you experience fear now, as an adult, all of these systems kick into gear with such speed that we are *almost* powerless to change anything. Almost.

We try to solve them, hide from them, push them away or squash them in less than the blink of an eye. Then we are lost, and we don't even know it.

If we can create this space for our children, right from this young age, we can give them the capacity to understand themselves, without being *told how* they should experience something. If we are doing it all wrong, which we generally are in this field, why would we want them to copy us?

If we want our children to understand themselves, which brings long-term psychological health, we *can't assume that we understand them*. The 'I'm the adult, I already know what's going on' act just won't cut it here. Uh-oh. Believing that is the *most powerful way to stop paying attention*.

We don't already know what this is.

The waves of emotion which rise up within Elfie are *unknown to me*. As her parent, then, surely the best thing I can do is create a big, quiet, loving, wide open space *within me* for whatever arises *within her*?

Sunday 29th May

Nadine has finally managed to get Elfie to say "Dada", and it was beautiful to behold: music to my ears. Some defective, reptilian software in me is really pleased that this was her first word instead of anything else, and my selfless wife deserves the credit for trying to encourage her for a long while to bust out this particular trick. The world of words has opened!

Diary of a Mindful Dad

<u>Monday 30th May</u>

Why shouldn't I eat the last baby yoghurt? If they didn't want me to eat it, they shouldn't have made it so nice. Apparently, it's just 'cooked apples', but I smell witchcraft.

<u>Tuesday 31st May</u>

I discovered today that everything is a hazard! Yep, everything.

What's the harm of her sitting in the sink? Except the obvious – climbing out and falling onto the hard floor – it's fine, right? "My nan used to do it all the time with me!" someone says.

"Surely it's not a hazard if she can't fall out and it doesn't even have any manky old food in it?!" some other rhetorical being chimes in.

Well, she used her 11-month-old baby superpowers to make it a hazard. Just take a moment to imagine that thing in your sink which collects all the crap. You know the one.

How can that thing be dangerous? Well, she decided to take it apart. Yep, it comes apart. Into four pieces, our one. One of them is just perfect to choke on, somehow. Ridiculous.

This is the main theme of this age, for us. So much is easier now than before, partly because she is much more independent. But her mobility brings so much danger into the picture which didn't previously exist. She needs *constant monitoring*. You follow her around the house while she does her thing, just making sure *she doesn't die* (the current house motto, probably a little distastefully), and it's so easy to take your eye off her. Nadine is doing this pretty much all day and she says, unsurprisingly, that it gets incredibly boring. The mind inevitably wanders off, and when we are together now, something very stressful occurs as a result of this:

We kind of feel like we are both looking after her, both

monitoring her. We have an often unspoken awareness of when the other one is looking after her and when it is our turn. If Nadine suddenly goes into the other room, it's obviously my 'turn'. The issue with this is that, of course, often *we don't realise* that the other has subconsciously given us custody. Often I just say, very unhelpfully (but not quite as unhelpfully as saying nothing): *"I haven't got her!"*

This translates as: "I was looking after her because you can't but now I'm suddenly not anymore for a reason which I don't have time to share and she's doing something which could seriously injure her and so you have to immediately stop what you're doing and look after her."

Nadine inevitably huffs and puffs and stops her from falling off the bed. This is a *good* example. A few times recently, though, something bad (but not *really* bad) has happened, because we haven't realised the other one 'hasn't got her'. *It's bloody exhausting!*

Wednesday 1st June

There's something you've always known, but you've never believed it to be knowledge. Just a whisper, perhaps. Some insight so wonderful, but just out of reach. Nobody talks about it, but you feel it deep in the recesses of your soul. You've always felt it.

Well, you'll be pleased to know, folks, that the definitive proof is finally here:

Farts *are* funny.

Elfie farted at the table and burst out laughing loudly as a result. It was a true 'Eureka' moment! So put your feet up and enjoy it. The next time anyone audibly farts, ever, in any situation, you can laugh without any guilt at all. It *is funny*. Isn't that a relief?

On a somewhat similar note, lately I've been really enjoying how *matter-of-fact* she is – as if everything she does is eminently *reasonable*. Many of us could do with a bit more of this sort of attitude. Every morning she offers her bread to Nadine, and then to me, and then to Nadine again, an unspecified number of times, before deciding – with a very satisfied look – that it is ready to be eaten by her, and then she nods approvingly before finally eating it. It's great.

Or the way she forces me to drink, which is one of her new favourite things: Nadine will be holding her whilst she gets herself a glass of water, and then I come over. Elfie pushes the glass aggressively away from Nadine, forces it into my face, and nods repeatedly as I drink.

"Yep, that's it. Good boy."

As soon as I'm done, and enough nods have been completed, she forces it into my face again, and again, and again, until the whole glass is gone. It's just such a funny evolution she has gone through; now she can make what she *wants to happen* a reality, and each time, it creates a little opening into her inner world as it shines out.

Friday 3rd June

Isn't it adorable that children split their age into smaller chunks of time than a year? I asked a client how old she was today, and she replied very proudly: "Seven and three-quarters."

So matter-of-fact again. It was beautiful. Why is this, and when do we stop doing it? A relatively boring and probably true thought is that the younger you are, the less time you've been alive for, and so each chunk of time feels longer to you. So, as we age, time seems to speed up, because we can conceptualise huge chunks of time – even decades.

Yet there is something so nice about it, as if it allows children or is a consequence of them valuing and making more out of their time. Perhaps this is another lesson from these wonderful miniature beings.

Six to Twelve Months

Nadine hit the nail on the head yesterday.* She explained why this age is so difficult, and why I had experienced a frustrating and quite boring time with Elfie yesterday when I was looking after her on my own. She is old enough to move around, but not old enough to control her movements safely. She can get up on things like the sofa, but can't get down. She wants and doesn't want things with equal intensity and can't understand why these desires don't always fit with reality. She's tantalisingly close to having the world the way she wants it11111111111111111111111111111111111111111111111111111111111111111111111111

Annoying? You're telling me. That was me having to rush upstairs to make sure she didn't wake up after half an hour. I put her dummy back in her mouth with one hand and held a cat's annoyingly loud bell on her collar with the other, the cat then proceeding to lie down on my chest so I couldn't move (presumably, I now see, after pirouetting nonchalantly across the keyboard). That was the next 45 minutes for me, half sleeping, half meditating, half hoping I would remember all the things I was going to write. Yep, three halves. Deal with it.

Thankfully, it allowed me to realise this would be a good thing to write, because it sums up a lot of this journey: *interruptions*. Not being able to do things. Having your laptop smacked really hard (she just did that upon returning to this plane, after making a huge gremlin sound).

Did I even get time to write about when she broke my laptop and Nadine's phone the other week? I have no idea.

All of this makes me reflect on the writing of this book and how I will feel about it when it is finished. Of course, I will be

---

* Poor nail, really doesn't seem to catch a break, does it? That, my friends, is a dad joke…I think. I'm assuming that a dad joke is just a joke that isn't very funny, which is exactly my wheelhouse.

pleased at the ironic accomplishment, finally managing to write a book only when I had *no time* to do it. I will also feel relieved to not 'have to do it' anymore, forcing myself to write when I have so little free time and would love to do all sorts of other things. I want whatever is currently masquerading as a weekend to do a much, much better job of it. I want exchanges like—

"Can I go and put some pants on?"

"Only after I've cleaned this piss off my foot!"

—to be a thing of the past. Amusing memories, rather than things happening right now. That literally just happened.

Yet, despite all this, I *will miss it*, because I know that things we 'have to do' are often the sweetest soul food and the most meaningful aspects of life. I would also be lying if I said I haven't hugely enjoyed writing this a lot of the time. I will miss keeping a record and suspect that I will continue to do so. Don't worry, I'll try not to make it into another book.

Saturday 4th June

In every school worth its salt, there will be at least one primary teacher asking their class to play the old classic game 'Sleeping Lions'. For those of you who are unfamiliar with this, it's very simple. The teacher has had enough. The adult translation of the title is: "Lie down and shut up for as long as you possibly can."

I've developed a similar one with Elfie for when times are tough. It's called 'I bet you can't find me'. Here's how to play:

1. Take a duvet
2. Throw the duvet on the floor
3. Lie down under the duvet
4. Try to go to sleep
5. When the baby approaches, confidently declare, "I bet you can't find me!"

6. Hold the sides of the duvet down so that said baby cannot lift it up for as long as your heart can bear
7. Once you give in and let them see you, make an excellent face and then go back to step 4

Unfortunately, this won't get you peace for very long. Still, it's worth a try.

Speaking of peace, I have been making more of an effort to spend time in silence with Elfie in the last few days, and it's been really nice. It allows us to connect on a different level from normal.

Something which we are lacking, though, is playtime with her *together*. It's always either Nadine or me being with her; it's rare for both of us to be giving her full attention at the same time, and doing something enjoyable. Isn't that a shame? I wonder how common that is, and if it might be a natural blind spot in parenting, because we all sorely need time to ourselves. Noticing this, we made a conscious effort to play with her *together* today, and it was different in a special way. It felt like something we need to remember.

Sunday 5th June

Do you know what my favourite thing about babies' toys is? It's the small, circular batteries inside which, if ingested, *will kill them*. Don't worry, though, no baby would be crazy enough to *eat* them, because they look just like lovely little treats. Oh, wait. *What?*

I came home this evening to a very tense mood. Nadine was on edge:

"I don't know if she's been *button-batteried* or not," she said. *Oh dear – it's a verb.*

Nadine had found a small packet of 'button-batteries' in one of the kitchen drawers, which had somehow eluded us (as we had already tried to find and chuck them all out), and she quickly put them in a temporary bin bag which was hanging on the kitchen door. Elfie has never touched one of those bags. What more invitation does a baby need than this wonderful lack of precedent?

Thirty seconds with her eyes off her, and Elfie had the bag down and the pack of batteries was on the floor. "*Shit!*" Nadine almost certainly thought – repeated a few times, I suspect. An hour of catastrophising and checking in with Dr Google later, and I returned home from work. Feeling very much like a poor man's Sherlock Holmes, I was able to retrieve the packet from the outside bin and check carefully how it seemed that the three missing batteries had been removed.

What struck me was fascinating. I noticed, in the top right corner, a minuscule brown cat hair, with a microscopic filament of dust from the kitchen curtain stuck to the top of it. I deduced, from its particular shade of brown, that the hair could only have come from our latest addition to the zoo: Squish. Now, I know, from my past dealings with Squish, that she is prone to bouts of sleeping on the floor outside the utility room where the washing machine is. But our washing machine is quite aggressive, you see – likely due to its traumatic childhood – and it often forces into the air, and subsequently onto the ground, anything which we are foolish enough to rest on top of it temporarily. I also know, from memory, that the curtains in the kitchen were washed approximately 35 hours ago, and left on top of the washing machine accidentally. But that's not all: the real nail in the coffin was the trail of slightly moist pawprints on the floor, which revealed the unmistakable journey of an animal with only *three legs*. She had a leg amputated when she was just one year old: *it had to be Squish*. I looked again at the battery packet and saw, just as I had expected, extremely faint claw marks in the empty battery spaces in question.

Once I applied the ever-cited Occam's razor to these seemingly unrelated facts, the conclusion was inescapable: *somehow* Squish, sleeping soundly by the washing machine, had been startled by the clean, yet damp curtains falling on her, and fled to the kitchen for safe harbour, only to *slip on the packet of button-batteries on the floor*, which had already been emptied by an adult, and flick them perfectly into the air and into one of the open kitchen drawers, leaving one solitary hair on the top of the packet.

Not really, of course. There was no such hair, and that was all utter nonsense. I just got a bit carried away ever since mentioning Mr Holmes; I've always wanted to make one of those deduction trails myself – haven't you? They usually make just as little sense as that one. Just enjoy it. It took me ages to invent that ludicrous chain of events, and it was just for you!

What *actually* happened is that I surveyed the packet with my perfectly ordinary powers of observation, and it seemed 95% clear that it was an adult that had purposefully removed each of them. So I calmly showed my lovely wife the packet again, which she had previously only been able to survey with fear-drenched eyes. The fear subsided after a while. Not fun. (Except pretending to be the omniscient detective, of course.) Let's hope I was right.

Monday 6th June

We went to the park again this morning, as we've been doing every day. I've only managed to join in for a week or so, and it's been beyond marvellous. The weather is just on the edge of too hot in the shade (38°C or so!), and the Elf explores to her heart's content. Her natural free intelligence shines as she discovers everything around her without restrictions or boundaries. It's truly beautiful to behold her seamlessly blending in with the rest of the natural world.

How close can you get to a crow? She was genuinely playing with one earlier, and Nadine was amazed by how close to her it wanted to be. It remained within one metre, completely unafraid. It must have sensed her innocence and realised she wasn't a threat. There was a clear sense of natural kinship there, and their brief playdate reminded me that *we are nature*, not something outside of it, as it often seems.

Monday 7th June

I just noticed a bit of inner baggage that I have taken on from someone else, and I've had to dissolve and discard it by recognising it as such. I've had many parents of clients over the years who have tried to change the way I work or change the way I behave according to what they think is right, and it is so easy to subconsciously take this on and move to the beat of someone else's drum, if we aren't careful. We come to subconsciously *believe* the viewpoint they have offered to us and *live through it*, for a while. I was feeling pressured with a client, and it turned out to be because his mum's anxiety had been transmitted to me and I had not been sufficiently aware of this taking place. I had carried it along and allowed it to shift my thinking about his situation.

This sort of thing is happening to us all the time, and it's one reason why it's so vital for us to have a clear awareness and understanding of our inner world. If we never have space and clarity, how can we identify what's what? What are you carrying? Where did it come from?

As usual, it's just mindfulness 101: *notice what's happening*. In the noticing, something different comes into being. Suddenly factors which were 'distorting' our consciousness don't need to be seen like that. They are only doing so when we bend according to their will and live through them as if they were true. If we are aware and mindful of what we are taking on, then everything which comes to us and feels like *dissonance* is simply helpful in the end: new information, new energy, which can be integrated for growth.

When life gives you lemons, who cares? We love lemons.

That sort of thing.

Wednesday 8th June

I used to think I wanted to be a stay-at-home dad. Really, all I was thinking is that I would love to not have a job.

However, this really isn't the case, because I love my job, and this little girl doesn't want a stay-at-home *anything*, because she gets way too bored being stuck in this house for so long. She needs nursery.

In honour of this, Nadine and I went to visit two this morning. This was quite a fascinating experience for us both, considering that we have spent most of our careers in schools, on the other side of the fence, putting on our best smiles and hoping the children would behave themselves when the visitors came to look around. Add to this my revulsion at most of the education system, and it was always going to be an enlightening morning.

So this is where it all begins, I realised. I had imagined that nursery would be very free-form and not in any way structured like school, but I was wrong: it felt exactly like school had already begun. The assembly line! Get them trained to stand in a line, listen and copy everyone else...already. Shame. Another brick in the wall, aged one?

But hanging onto such negativity only prolongs the inevitable. Unless we want to go and live on a desert island (which we have obviously considered), I have to confront the reality that my little baby daughter is going to become part of society...*this society*, with all its various sicknesses. And she can't delay it beyond this September, because Nadine is going back to work part-time. So here we are! I remind myself that it could definitely be worse, and society brings with it many blessings as well, despite all the crap.

Naturally, one of the biggest anxieties about nursery is how she will cope without us. She is extraordinarily attached, partly because none of her other family lives here. This means that she has had less exposure to being looked after by others (remember the wedding fiasco?) than many other babies might have. How difficult is the separation going to be? When I brought the topic up with Nadine recently, lots of anxiety came up for both of us, and it wasn't the right time to discuss it properly. So I decided to do something different. To specifically set aside a time for both of us to bring this conversation into being and witness, explore and, if necessary, release and transform our feelings about it.

We did this later on, and it actually made me feel far *more* sad than I did before, as the feelings came to the surface, because I was *truly allowing it to show itself*, feeling it *on purpose*. We discussed the fact that 'naturally' children would not leave their mothers so early. We hated to consider that we were forcing her away from us at an unnatural point, just because of the society we have no choice but to exist in. So did Nadine. That's not very nice, is it?

But there are shades of grey to be considered, as different cultures around the world have different approaches to raising their children, with some being more community-based than others. Yes, it makes sense that Elfie should not be separated from Nadine, and that is a vital, unfortunate and far-reaching fact. But at the same time, for humans, isn't it also unnatural to live in a house just with your parents, not knowing anyone who lives on your street?

Neighbourly relationships always go the same way with me, I've noticed. After the pleasant waving and small talk when we move in, full of positivity, I make the strange decision to *actually try to get to know them a bit*. Only the ones on either side, of course; anything beyond that would be *weird*.

Invariably, when I cross the threshold into the dwelling place of that enigmatic creature – *the neighbour* – I have a marvellous time.

Wow! I think. *These people are great! They have thoughts, feelings, gripes and chuckles just like me! And they live just next door?! Amazing. Maybe we're going to have parties together and stuff and be best friends the whole* time we live here?! We might even have to move to the same place after this! Could we share the removal costs?

Then, of course, we *never speak again.*

Both parties are relieved. Phew! Now we can get back to the safe, comfortable, neighbourly wave once a week or so, the occasional and cosmically-written passive-aggressive reactions of the mind to any slight encroachment on any aspect of our life from any aspect of theirs, and for the rest of the time pretend nobody else lives anywhere near us.

We are a world away from natural, in this day and age, whichever way you look at it. Thankfully, at nursery, Elfie will be loved by other adults in the community and interacting with other children, two factors which are surely natural and healthy for her development. Our focus needs to be on the challenge in front of us, and this one is unavoidable, whether we like it or not.

Thursday 9th June

I'm so sorry, every child in the universe, including Delphine, if you are unfortunate enough to read this one day, but no: we don't want to watch you on the monkey bars more than twice.

"Watch me! Watch me!" has been a catchphrase in our house for years. Unfortunately, the reason is that I sometimes want Nadine to watch *me* do something, exactly like an annoying little kid. I never say it, of course, but she knows. She knows. Then the mockery begins.

This evening she summed it up perfectly: "Nobody wants to watch anyone do anything, unless it's amazing. And even then, only once." Isn't she lovely? So cynical! I love it. Did you know that 'Diogenes the Cynic' (where the word comes from) apparently did an actual turd – yes, *turd* – on the floor at a Plato talk, in protest? What a legend. No sly, passive-aggressive tweets – just a real, proper statement. He was the original troll.

Diary of a Mindful Dad

<u>Friday 10th June</u>

Nadine looks at me, disappointed, after rolling her eyes for the 10,000,000th time. "I'm going to come back and she's going to be all messy with a shitty nappy and no clothes on, and she won't have been fed!"

She's leaving the house for an hour, and this is a beautiful expression of how much faith she has in me. She sees my feigned offence and changes her tactics, looking me strongly in the eye, speaking very slowly and clearly for my benefit, to ensure she successfully tears me away from writing this book:

"You're going to feed her and change her nappy. Then you're going to put her in these clothes, put your clothes on and be ready to leave when I get back."

If only she always did that, life would be so simple. A proper instruction manual for everything. *IKEA life*. That's the kind of life I need, I think.

"What on Earth would you do without me?" she said yesterday, after the edamame fiasco. Edamamegate. I'm still feeling the effects of it now.

I love Edamame beans (did you know that every single soy product is just edamame beans, because they are soy beans? Mind blown). So I looked up a recipe for really garlicky, really spicy ones a year or so back, and had it as a regular snack. Soy sauce (read: edamame-bean sauce), white wine vinegar, sriracha sauce, garlic, salt. Something like that.

Well, yesterday it was the end of my working week and I couldn't be bothered to look up the recipe. Overconfident is probably the right word here; I suddenly reckoned myself a pretty good chef, despite all available evidence only being to the contrary. It all seemed to be going well until I saw Nadine burst out laughing at my facial expression as I was eating the third or fourth bite. I looked exactly like Elfie when she eats a lemon or drinks tonic water, before astonishingly going back for more. Confused and revolted sums it up, I think.

I couldn't work out if it was nice or not. It just had a ridiculously strong flavour, and I guess that's generally what I'm going for, with my primitive culinary inclinations. However, her reaction made me wonder: *Is this awful? Why am I continuing to eat it?*

"What did you do to it?" she asked, hoping for exactly the kind of conversation which ensued to ensue.

I faithfully recounted the details, my pride in my favourite dish dwindling by the millisecond.

"Raw garlic? You didn't cook the garlic?"

Ahhhh, that's what that is. Suddenly, it all fell into place. I don't think the random chucking of oil and vinegar without measuring helped, but it was the garlic which had really done a job on me. It just wasn't nice at all.

Nisargadatta Maharaj has taught me that we should be beyond the need of help, spiritually speaking. I think I'm pretty much there with that. But 'beyond help' is probably a bit more apt when it comes to everything else. A dear friend once remarked that, without Nadine, I would be walking around Egham with a tin pot on my head trying to contact aliens. He's probably right. I do genuinely reckon I would have found some, though.

Little did I know, I was due to walk headfirst into another clanger later that evening. I put Elfie into the bath, turned the tap on and began to brush my teeth and other things of that nature. She picked up the plug and started trying to put it into the plug hole. *Bless her heart!* I thought. *She's so sweet. Look at her trying to put that thing into that hole. Awwww!*

Carried on with what I was doing. I genuinely left it for three minutes or so before realising that my baby of 11 months is better at practical, mechanical tasks than I am, and was trying to run her own bath because I couldn't.

Nobody who knows me is surprised.

Nadine never lets me forget the time that I told a class of

five-year-olds that the continents were floating on water. Look, I panicked, OK – I don't know what happened. What made me feel better, though, was going around and asking other members of staff (remember: these people *teach your children*) to instinctively say what was underneath England at that moment, and at least 30% of people said 'water'. It was great.

One person – I kid you not – genuinely paused to consider whether we might actually be *underwater* while searching for a response. God's honest truth. A great advert for homeschooling right there, eh?

Or how about this one, my personal favourite. When the pandemic began, a fantastic prank WhatsApp voice note went around featuring someone speaking about how his 'cousin was in the Ministry of Defence' and detailing the government's plans to help the citizens during lockdown. He said that the plan was to take all of Wembley Stadium and turn it into a giant oven, using the underfloor heaters to heat a lasagne the size of the football pitch, and then to airlift portions by drone and drop them into people's houses. It was excellent.

The best bit, though, was when Nadine showed me a message from her group of teachers at her school.

"Oh my God! This is just such a crazy time."

Imagine believing that? That is *way* worse than my continents gaffe.

Saturday 11th June

I just love the way Elfie manages her affairs with such conviction. We went out to a friend's house yesterday, a gathering of ten or so people, many of whom didn't know each other very well. So we had this sort of energetic jostling and meandering going on, with everyone trying to feel comfortable enough in their own skin to just happily 'be something like themselves'. You know what I mean.

Then she strolled in, casually, my little Elf. Boy, did she stroll in. It was more of a stomp, actually. Her entrance said:

I AM HERE.

She stood bang in the middle of the circle of seats, looked one of the group straight in the eye and simply started yelling:

"Aaaaaaaaahhh!!!!"

Not in a scary way, as that reads – just a non-specific, extremely loud noise. It was a lightning bolt, a jolt. A call to freedom!

Wow, did that shake things up. Everybody was laughing their heads off, in the subconscious realisation that this little 11-month-old was far more comfortable in her own skin than all of us were. She transformed the vibration. I raised the point that it would be so nice if we could all be that carefree, and one person said adults only generally are when it's an extremely close group, or when alcohol is involved. I think he's probably right, but isn't it a shame? Can't we love ourselves like she does?

It would be nice to think we can, and while we're at it, we could do with loving *everything else* like she does too.

Listen to how she woke up yesterday: I believe it is the cutest thing she has done since she was born (I think she's trying to help me end the book on a high):

I was there when she first opened her eyes. Within one second, she had flipped herself around and waved – *to her cuddly toys*.

I was melting.

Then she looked up at the wall, where there were six framed pictures of colourful woodland animals. She waved eagerly and matter-of-factly at all of them as well, blinking and nodding all the while. I couldn't believe it.

Then, last of all, she turned and waved again, this time to the cuddly elephant and dog sitting high up on a shelf on the other side of the room.

Honestly, my heart was blown to bits. I couldn't handle it. Seriously, how adorable is that?!

She accepts their existence, and their *need to be loved*, implicitly.

Yet it was the way she did it that I loved so much. It wasn't an eagerness to be friends, it was just such an *obviously reasonable thing to be doing*. No question of it whatsoever. She is their friend, and it is imperative for them to know that she is awake now and for her to greet them. She does what she does, it's perfect, and that's that.

So, I ask you, dear reader, why should we walk into a group of people, heads down, hiding ourselves to any degree at all? Why aren't we proud and happy with our presence, eager to participate in whatever comes our way? That sounds like freedom, and fun, to me.

Sunday 12th June

Now that Elfie is walking, she lulls us into a false sense of security and makes us think that we don't need to watch her so much. She went up the stairs independently today, in ten seconds, when she was out of sight. It's a real wake-up call and a reminder to be vigilant, but this is so demanding on a continuous basis. Nevertheless, it's very nice that she's so independent now, and it's so funny and cute to watch her walking around on her own.

I taught a lesson today on the theme of 'parents', in which I tried to create an opportunity for a group of teenage students to go a little beyond the surface and be open and honest with one another. One boy became overcome with emotion towards the end because the discussions had made him realise just how appreciative he is of his parents, and everything they have done for him. It was incredibly touching to witness him being truly vulnerable in front of a group of other teenagers; that is no easy feat!

This lesson was online, and I've been the victim of the Zoom revolution just as much as many others all over the world: in the beginning, I *couldn't stand* seeing myself talking on the screen. 'Zoom surgery' is the name given to people seeking cosmetic surgery after watching themselves speaking on Zoom calls, and I get how it can go that way.

But do you know why we usually dislike ourselves in photographs or on video? It's because we usually see our *mirror image*. So when we see a photo, it *doesn't look like us*. The brain thinks the image doesn't fit, and it interprets this as the image *looking bad. Bad, not different.* This is so strange, but it reveals a lot about our psychology. It means, for example, that every viewpoint which we hear which *isn't our own* is received on some level as *bad*. I think we can all see how this distortion manifests itself in exchanges of views.

I ask people to 'unmirror' their screen on Zoom calls to see how they actually look. It's very uncomfortable, every time, but over time we get used to it and the brain adjusts its image of what 'we' look like. Exposure therapy for our own face. I found it so jarring at first, just like when you hear your voice on a recording and think you must have been body-swapped with some sort of deranged mouse.*

I can only imagine what little Elfie, blessed with her unconscious and infinite self-esteem, would think of all this anxious self-consciousness. She really has taught me a deep lesson there, as babies are doing unconsciously all over the world every day.

<u>Monday 13th June</u>

Unfortunately, in our house, bedtime is called 'the shutdown' because it takes so long to sort out the zoo. Oh, to be able to just go to bed, even just on the sofa! That would be almost unbearably hassle-free. In another life maybe. I hope these cats are grateful for all of our efforts, but I'm not convinced.

---

* To help with this one, just listen to one of your own WhatsApp voice notes on double speed; that will sound *so bad* you'll be relieved to return to the sweet comfort of your 'normal' weird voice.

Diary of a Mindful Dad

A wise person said, of the difference between cats and dogs: "Dogs think: 'These people feed me, they give me shelter; *they must be God.*' Cats think: 'These people feed me, they give me shelter; *I must be God.*'" That feels like my cats' vibe, for sure.

On 90% of nights, I bring myself to sleep purposefully through meditation. I've been doing this for about two years now; it just started suddenly one day, when I felt the desire to meditate in bed.

I sit with my back against the headboard, and I imagine counting sheep, but with a twist. According to a research paper published in Australia in 2019, the brain relaxes better if the sheep each have different-coloured wool, and if you tap your teeth together to the rhythm of your favourite song as you count them.*

Did you believe that? Admit it! You did! You'd already planned to do it tonight! One cheeky little 'scientific study' and everyone is all in. Do you know they did a study on how easily people believe things when they are told they did a study about it? That one *is* true. Don't trust me anymore, do you?

Anyway, *actually* meditating in bed just feels right, like this is exactly what my energy wants to do. To completely settle, bringing everything to rest. Every time, I know when it's done and lie down to sleep and drop off quite quickly. I can't imagine what it does to the mind to binge-scroll TikTok videos instead, at this time, which is what many of the teenagers in one of my classes are doing.

Our state of consciousness determines so much about what is possible for us. TikTok speeds us up and meditation slows us down; would you rather live in the TikTok Time Zone or the Treebeard Time Zone? Treebeard may not seem like he's having that much fun but, to be fair, nor does someone who's been scrolling for two hours.

---

* More details here: www.stercustauri.com

Six to Twelve Months

As we meditate, our state of consciousness becomes more powerful, until it catches up to the speed of thought and beyond. At that threshold, it seems to 'swallow up' the thinking energy and drop into a deeper, more magical realm.

Tuesday 14th June

Anyone might be forgiven for thinking a sex offender was living with us:

"You'll get boobie in a minute – stop pulling at my top!"

That's what she's been saying all year; I still haven't seen any evidence. Kidding. Nadine's outburst was, of course, directed at our little treasure.

After being rebuffed, Elfie toddles – *the perfect verb* – over to her bookshelves and chooses a book by herself. This has been going on for just a few days and we find it adorable; it has also shown us we need to buy a new batch of books for her now, as we are all a bit bored of the current selection and know them almost by heart.

A nice new part of the bedtime routine after this is that we give Elfie a little massage with proper massage cream. She *loves* it! Cannot get enough. It's truly lovely to interact with her little body in this way, and I've noticed a definite change in the atmosphere when we do it. 'Positive touch', as they call it in some schools when teachers ask the children to give their partner a little back rub, really does seem to have some mysterious and wonderful power. I guess we shouldn't be surprised?

Wednesday 15th June

This morning, Elfie was stung by a wasp, just after she had started her time in the park. She was buzzing with happiness (ironically) and then BANG! That was it. I've been stung by a wasp once, and so has Nadine, and we know how painful it is. She went berserk, and it was the most loudly she has ever cried, except when she banged her head so badly that time.

It went on for about ten minutes or so, and then that was it. I was quite impressed by this. The sting was right under her foot, but she was happy to walk so shortly after it had happened. It reminded me of something I have taught children so many times, which is the power we have to reduce or enhance pain using attention and the energy of the mind. In school, you see hundreds of incidents where a minor fall which draws a minuscule amount of blood can send a child off kilter for the entire day; they have a sour face on and look for sympathy for hours on end for it. I was quite ruthless on this at school, but tried to do it nicely, showing the power we have to just forget about it and 'look the other way' after a time. Attention is like a magnifying glass, and whatever we focus on becomes our reality; why make pain your only reality for hours?

Elfie doesn't yet have the 'software' which creates a story around it, attaches it to an idea of 'me' and plays it over and over. She really had forgotten within 15 minutes max, but we hadn't, and here I sit, hours later, still banging on about it.

Friday 17th June

Daddy Daughter Day again today, or hour and a half, rather. But it can sometimes *feel like* a day without my lovely wife's help. She gave me very solid instructions, yet again – *delivered slowly so that I could understand.*

Again, I have no idea how she does it (I don't mean delivering the instructions); looking after the little one all the time and doing the food and everything. I was in the kitchen trying to prepare the food, with Elfie, and she was literally grabbing hold of my pants so I couldn't even walk around the kitchen. It would have been hilarious for an onlooker to observe. So that's how I prepared food: waddling around backwards as she held on for dear life and followed everywhere. If I tried to push her away, she went nuts, so I stopped bothering.

Then, halfway through the meal, I stopped holding the plate down with my fingers for one innocent, naive, solitary second… and she chucked the entirety of it on the floor.

Done. Fail. Vintage dadding. Mindful dad my arse.

Sunday 19th June

Happy Father's Day!

I delivered an assembly today on the topic of Father's Day and parenting, and my brief was simple: I wanted to make the children feel *terrible for being born.*

Not really, but kind of. I wanted to show, after my year, how much they should appreciate their parents, so I guilt-tripped them for about five minutes about all the things their parents could no longer do *because they were born.* And I tried to remind them, in a variety of ways, about how much fun their parents' lives *used to be.*

It was great. It was a tribute, an ode, to all parents.

But I'm not horrible. So I ended it by telling them all the things their parents could now do *because* they existed, and reminded them that they are a blessing.

My dad used to annoy me in millions of different ways. Here's one:

"You're overtired!"

I can't wait to use that on Elfie; it's so gloriously dismissive, dismissing not only what you have just said or done but *everything else you say or do until you become unconscious.* That's the sly bit which I really like. You are worthless from now on, nothing useful to contribute at all, and you will not be acknowledged. It used to piss me off beyond belief, and that's why I can't wait to use it myself!

This evening, after work, Elfie presented me with a beautiful card to mark the occasion, complete with adorable little coloured handprints and a couple of pictures of us together. Taking it from her tiny little hands and seeing her innocent little smile made it a special moment, and it stopped time in the way all special moments do. I have a history of getting into grumpy-old-man mode about people having to get each other cards for things, but I must admit that this one shut me right up. It really is a delight.

Monday 20th June

Today was Delphine's first birthday, and I always knew it would be where this book ends.

The living room was a scandalous nest of treats. Every crack and crevice contained some sort of strange gift, wrapped by one person or another in our family, or too big and amazing to be wrapped. Far too much. Nadine had bought things here and there over the last few months, when she saw and liked them, and she didn't realise how much she had bought.

"Oops!"

She was the perfect recipient, totally joyful and suitably rapt in wonder. She ravaged the wrapping paper and explored every new toy with the absolute vigour that we expected, nay, *required* of her.

I remember one Christmas, when my brother received *The Big Book of Trains* (designed for kids up to five, when he was about 13) from a distant relative, and he slowly pushed it under an armchair, looked at me and whispered, "And we'll *never speak of it again.*" Imagine the exact opposite of that.

About ten times during the day, she looked at me from afar, clearly said, "Dada!!!" and walked eagerly towards me, hugging my legs tightly, asking to be picked up, held, cuddled and loved. It brings me a feeling beyond description.

We had a beautiful day and went to the local soft play again, and she was on terrific form, smiling and exploring constantly. That was when it happened.

I had been curious about what the universe would bring us on this day, knowing it was the last entry for the book; it didn't disappoint.

A much older baby steamed into the play area, the only other child there, and *boy, did he mean it*. He was huge, twice her size, and he was strutting around as if he owned the place. In fact, all the staff knew his name, so maybe he did? But he was cool; he had a great way about him. I admired his gumption, let's say. What a word that is, eh? Let's bring it back.

Anyway, Elfie inevitably went over to try to make friends, and they had a bit of back and forth, as they do at this age; never properly interacting, kind of 'half in, half out'. Then it came to the point when they both wanted to play with toys next to each other, on a play table which had lots of different things on it. Nadine, a few onlookers and I watched with mounting curiosity. *Uh-oh. How's this going to play out?*

He made the wrong move. He went into the no-fly zone, the invisible line they had drawn between the two of them, and tried to do something with one of her toys. Then he bumped her backwards with his backside. That was it. With a frighteningly efficient swipe of her arm, she grabbed him by the T-shirt and pulled him backwards. I'm not kidding, as a result of this single-armed throw, this poor boy tumbled backwards by about two feet onto the floor, landing in a sorry heap as if it were the end of a boxing match.

She didn't bat an eyelid.

We were as stunned as the boy on the floor. I still have no idea how she managed to make such an impact with such an apparently casual gesture, but the message was clear: she doesn't like to be messed with. We are going to have our work cut out for us with her, and so are her future playmates.

When we got home, we did a 'cake smash'. *What's that?* you may ask. Or not. It's where you give the baby a cake and let them have their way with it. The whole scene was set, Nadine ready to take photographs, expecting her to destroy it in seconds, like she has with every single meal up until this point. But we forgot – *she's a baby*.

Her job is to never give you what you expect.

So, instead, she very carefully and gently ate some of the little sprinkles, one by one, off the top. After a while (and a bit of encouragement), she did start hitting it with her hands a bit, but there was no smashing going on at all.

Ironically, at bedtime, she had such a sugar high that she was making the 'Hulk smash' movement over and over again, just without any cake there! Weird kid, huh?

Then we slowly but surely started the bedtime routine, for the last time of the year. I had been looking forward to this like a sacred moment, but then, right on cue, life happened.

An unexpected Zoom call with a grandparent to say hello to her on her birthday. I took my eye off her for *literally one second*, and a cat scratched her on the face, *just above* her eye.

Ah, yes, *life*. I forgot. *It must never go as planned.*

It was a bad one. There was a lot of crying and a big old searing scratch on her face. Nadine and I were both devastated that it had 'ruined her special evening'. My mind (and perhaps Nadine's too) jumped around at the speed of light, wondering about what would happen in the next house, with her being so mobile, the space being smaller, and all of the cats having to stay inside for three weeks to adjust to the new surroundings. This is literally next week. Oh God! Cat-astrophising aplenty, of course.

Then, as I was watching this mind-dance, *I saw my Elfie*.

She had stopped caring completely.

Ahhh, yes. Ahhhhhhhhh, yes. That's it.

All of a sudden, she was *so happy*.

She started playing like mad, laughing and asking us to read her favourite book.

One last lesson in this first year from my own personal mindfulness coach. One last jolt out of the frantic adult mind. Don't get me wrong; lots of those thoughts concern real questions we should consider. We don't want our baby being scratched by cats. But now? No. Not now.

After a book or two, we rocked her to sleep, slowly but surely. Her favourite night-time song vibrated through the room, from our hearts to hers, as the big, bright moon watched on. I kissed her three times on the head, transmitting as much love as I could possibly muster. I watched her close her magical little eyes for the last time in her first year.

There she was. A little package of wonder, wrapped up so snugly in her light green sugar-glider costume, sucking unconsciously on a pink and white dummy, placed gently into her bed, drifting off into dream.

I stayed and looked at her, just for a while – my beautiful baby bear. And I knew that she was *perfect*, cat scratch and all.

Later that evening, 9pm

I wrote the last entry just after putting Elfie to bed. Now, a little later, I feel incredibly emotional, far more than I thought I would, and so much of it seems to be related to this book. It has been such a large part of my life this past year, causing so many challenges, highs, lows and in-betweens, and now that's it. But it's not really about the book.

The book has changed my perception of this day: this first birthday of a wonderful new human being on this marvellous Earth. Ordinarily, I'm not sentimental about birthdays, but of course this one was always going to be different. Still, without the book, I don't think it would feel quite so momentous. It feels like the end of something significant – a kind of death. The close of the first long, wild stage of the parenting journey.

Something about constantly reflecting on what has been happening and how interesting, difficult and mad it's all been has transformed this moment totally. The most important thing I feel is a profound sense of how meaningful it has all been, and that it is over now. There are no takebacks. I can't change what I did during this year, and every moment gone really is gone. I feel this is a microcosm of the whole journey of life, and a smaller version of how people must feel at the end of it.

My cat is staring at me, with her piercing eyes *fully locked into the moment.*

I can see now why I have felt such a strange, deep sadness (and it's not because of the cat).

It is because I am being shown the terrible beauty and profundity of the passage of time. Nadine and I look at the pictures of Delphine in front of her birthday banner, not smashing the cake, looking perfectly angelic, and they are all just desperate, beautiful attempts to stop.

To stop time. To hold life in our hands, just for a moment. To keep her like this, to keep *it all just like this.*

Yet even in the pictures, we are caught between movements. There is no real stopping. We can't hold onto it and it doesn't stop.

Time, that trickster. Blink and you'll miss it. What? Everything.

She will grow up and out of Eden. The mind crystallises what it sees and tries to make it live forever, yet it moves on. We trick ourselves into thinking that all of this is ours: this life, these loves – but they are only given to us, for a while. We are lucky, deeply lucky, to witness any of it at all.

The Buddha knew, of course. Impermanence is King in this realm. When this is borne in mind, the mind goes into the heart. There and then Love reigns supreme, and that Queen knows what the mind cannot.

That every moment matters. That *this is the only moment, and it matters.*

She whispers to me that I mustn't miss even a single chance to be there for the people close to me and to 'show up' in my life. To be present. Knowing it was Delphine's birthday, and that everything which happened today was the *last opportunity* I had to reflect on this amazing journey for this book, sanctified so many moments and actions.

It showed me how each event carries within it little glimmers of the archetypal story of life, and that if we are *truly* looking, we might just catch a glimpse of that and be offered a chance to participate.

It changed the way I approached so much of this magical day; I had extra energy and motivation to *be there*, *to engage* and to drink deeply from whatever was offered to me. This made me a much better dad, husband, teacher and friend, and infused everything with meaning.

Upon reflection, I realise that this 'Birthday Mindset' is the best way to capture my attitude and what 'mindfulness' has done for me in my life. This is the microcosm of that macrocosm; extra attention, extra desire to engage and participate, extra accountability for my actions, extra love.

So much more love.

I feel extraordinarily sad that the year is over, and it has completely caught me by surprise. I didn't feel anything like this until after she went to bed, closing her glorious little eyes.

Time moves us all so mysteriously, and so fast. Blink and you'll miss it.

The feeling I am left with is simple but special. I just want to be here for whatever life has for me, *all of it* – good, bad or ugly.

I just don't want to blink. I just don't want to miss it.

The little girl upstairs has been sitting, sleeping, crawling, walking, and maybe just about running on an enormous, luminous marble spinning boldly in the vast, infinite, apparent emptiness. She's been doing this for 365 spins of the marble. Before that, she was somehow inside my wife. Before that, I really don't know, and neither does anyone else.

All that matters to me is that she is here now, sleeping soundly.

My beautiful daughter, and the star of this particular show, Delphine Eva Watts.

I love you, Elfie. You are magnificent beyond compare. Thank you for bringing your light into our lives.

May it shine on, and on, and on…beyond even time itself.

Afterword

<u>Monday 27th June</u>

One week after Elfie's birthday, I finally have a chance to reflect properly on the journey so far as a whole. Writing this book was, in many ways, deeply ironic and contradictory. I have sought to be an excellent husband, and yet, on many occasions, I have not been able to be there for my wife fully for writing it. I seek to fully attend to the world, and yet part of my energy is dedicated to *reflecting on* what is happening, so that I can relay it to and explore it with an imaginary audience. In short, I seek *presence*, but this book has *tangled me up in time*. There is no doubt that this effort has distorted my actions in myriad ways, some for better and some for worse. Doesn't this sound exactly like the perfect, confusing sort of mess of life to you?

In case you haven't gathered by now, parenting is totally exhausting and relentless. I realised, just now, that I haven't felt like work has actually finished for the entire year of her life. Driving home, after x number of hours, I know there is so much energy still to expend every…single…day. No day off. No lie-ins. Ever. That is easily the toughest aspect of this journey, overall, I would say; except, perhaps, for the fears concerning her health in the first few months, and the miscarriage. Those experiences are tough in a different way.

Afterword

I always used to say that babies were the 'ultimate mindfulness teachers'. Yet the truth is I had only spent time with about two or three, that I could remember, and that time was very short. I meant it in the sense that their attention is so free, so open and so powerful. They *are where they are*, and they open something in us when we bear witness to them.

I think I was right about this. When I spend time with Elfie, I am brought out of the adult morass and back into contact with my true self, my essence – that part of me which never changes. I return to this and I see that it is true, good, simple and free; this is infinitely healing.

What I had not understood, though, was just how true this comment was about all of the other, more challenging aspects of mindfulness. Throughout the first stage of this incredible journey, my wife and I have been tested to what we (probably falsely) hope is the limit. I have had to call upon my training in matters of the mind and heart more than I had expected to, and I am extremely grateful to my past selves for spending so much energy and time trying to understand the 'inner world' and the mysteries of life. Without this, I believe I would have been 'just getting through' so much of this first year, rather than being present and appreciating events as they unfolded.

I expected this journey to bring with it a lot of love and a lot of stress – both of which it brought in spades – but I did not anticipate how much it would *change me*. Parenting has had a seismic effect on *every aspect of my life*, and people seem to respond to this fact in different ways. You can try your best to avoid this, to keep your previous life *undisturbed*, but avoidance is avoidance; it is a poisoned seed and it will show its fruit, somehow, sometime.

Becoming a parent changes your relationship with your partner; stretching it, bending it, and calling for an equivalent *increase* in compassion, attention, listening and affection. This is incredibly demanding when you are already tired and overloaded. The difficulty of making these extra efforts, and the failure to do so, can surely cause long-term damage to this sacred bond. Yet it is also only by making these extra efforts that we can move into a deeper layer of our relationship, and allow it to transform as it is meant to. This isn't something I *have learned*, because it is ongoing. A constant challenge, like all the others – demanding presence, intention and the best of me day after day.

Parenting changes the way you view your career, your childhood, your parents, your personality, your foibles, your habits, your desires and ambitions – *everything*.

And we are supposed to change, aren't we? Elfie has changed the way I see all of life, and these changes are *real* and they are *natural*. In the background of every challenge, and every difficulty, Nadine giving birth to this little girl has also given birth to a love in me which is *indescribable*.

At the beginning of this journey, I wondered how mindfulness would affect it. Have any of these things I've been trying to understand and live actually '*worked*'? Well, what does that mean? If we mean eradicating messiness and difficulty from life, then the answer is an emphatic "No!" and thank God for it. There is such a strong narrative in the 'wellness industry' – a truly odious oxymoron – that we need to know how to *deal with* or *manage* things to somehow avoid difficulty in life. But that's the bloody trap! Life isn't to be avoided! We aren't supposed to 'deal with' having a baby in a really relaxed way or anything like that – why does that matter? We're supposed to live it!

Comfort is, in some sense, a disease of the psyche – like a slow, dull rot. If what you want is your life to be perfectly neat and tidy, wrapped up tight so that no light can get in, I hope I haven't helped with that at all. I don't want to help you find some rigid control over your inner world and your life, which is what much of the wellness industry seems to promise. I'd prefer this book to do the opposite – to encourage *surrender*. Surrender to the *adventure*, surrender to the *unknown*.

Afterword

Where are these words coming from now? The mind foolishly, mistakenly attributes these thoughts to its own understanding. Yet six hours ago, I had never heard these words, I had never thought these words. I was not privy to what is happening right now. Suddenly, the desire comes to write the end of my book: "That must be my doing!" we think, and then off we go. Energy comes, the push, the urge to create words *appears* and the words *appear with it*.

Who is controlling this? Who is making this happen? Am I? It feels, when I really look, that I am just participating in it. This book has its own story to tell.

How about you? Where did the desire to read this book come from? Did you 'create it' yourself? If you really go into that, I think you will be surprised. At the beginning of the book, I suggested that the control we believe we have in our lives might be an illusion. Seeing the truth of this, now, in this moment, returns me to the humility of *not knowing*, and the magic of adventure.

With those eyes, I see that everything around me is a miracle. I can press a button on my device, and a recording of my baby making sounds will appear in my consciousness, invisible. I can't see it, but *there it is*, in my world. It is pure magic.

Delphine's existence is pure magic.

Just as I wrote that sentence, Nadine said, *"Look! She's looking at you!"*

That event, just that 'little' look, is a miracle. It is a gift, a blessing. Did you feel it? That *spark*?

She is sitting right next to me, at the piano with Nadine. Normally, she sits on me and we play together; this is the first time Nadine has done it with her. She associates me with the piano, so she is mashing the keys and looking straight over at me for approval. It's adorable beyond belief to me, her father; her little face and deep, wide eyes are so incredibly precious. This is the first time she has ever looked for my approval in something.

Diary of a Mindful Dad

Her birth was a miracle. Her first year has been a miracle.

Many people all over the world believe that 'death' is the end. The main reason for this, I think, is that for there to be another world *after this*, which is equally or even more amazing to live in and behold, seems so 'far-fetched'. How could that be possible? How could it even happen? It seems, to many, so much more 'logical' that what seems to be the 'end' is exactly that: the end of everything. I realised recently that there is a simple reason why I do not agree with this viewpoint, and it has already been stated.

This existence, this life, is a miracle. Biologists may have been able to understand a huge amount of the reproductive process and the growth of a human being, the evolution of our species, and physicists have seen a lot of how the 'physical' universe 'works', but there is still an impenetrable mystery at the centre of it all. As Terence McKenna famously put it, science says: "Give us *one free miracle* and we'll explain the rest."[52] That miracle is *everything suddenly appearing from nothing for no reason.* No matter how far back we go in time, the question of the *origin, the essence* – the greatest riddle of all – is still shrouded in mystery. Yet here we are.

Consciousness, or whatever we mean by that, is here. Life is happening, and human beings are somehow able to reflect on this, and on their own existence. As Einstein said, "The most incomprehensible thing about the universe is that it is comprehensible."[53] He knew how mysterious the mind is. If Delphine's wondrous life started with something the size of a poppy seed *inside my wife's body*, then why should another world be so hard to believe in? That seems no more miraculous than this one to me.

I don't know how I came to be here, and I don't know what I am. All I have been given is here and now and it is always mystery: ineffable, unknowable.

This means that everything of value which I have learned, seen or done during this book is a *reality*, not a concept or a bunch of words, despite my attempts to encode and communicate them in that form.

Afterword

I have spoken about 'attention', 'meditation', 'mindfulness' and other such cryptic and mysterious things throughout the book. But there is no such thing as attention, there is no such thing as meditation and there is *no such thing as mindfulness*! These are *words*. At best, these words are signposts – they are 'almost things'. They are shifty, squishy, melty terms which dart around here and there, and any meaning they might seem to have completely disappears when the reality of what they are trying to describe is actually present.

Even words like 'thoughts' and 'feelings', which seem so *normal* to us, are infinitely mysterious and unknown.

Once, when I was working on another book on the nature of mind, I was sitting up in bed with my pillow against the headboard, in meditation, and I suddenly saw mind as it actually is, for the first time. I saw that mind is a total miracle and it is absolutely nothing like what we think it is. After my body found its place in that bed and became still, something appeared. Dancing, darting, flashing into and out of my experience. It was what we call 'thought', but it wasn't thought. It was pure, incomprehensible mystery. Where had it come from? I had absolutely no choice but to watch, open-mouthed in wonder, the activity of 'mind' from a totally new perspective. It seemed unbelievable that I had never seen it like this before, and it's another example – like pregnancy and birth – of something which is too 'mind-blowing' (please excuse this very last pun) for us to be conscious of on an ordinary basis.

'Emotions' – waves of energy which engulf our being, unbidden, uninvited, unseen, are like fairy dust, orchestrating the drama of our lives; yet they too are total mystery. It doesn't matter how many minds or techniques have been used over the ages to come to a real understanding of what emotions are, it is only the raw presence of them which is real, or which can show what they actually are, and this cannot be truly touched by concepts or theories about them. They are just an abstraction.

This also points to the somewhat horrifying realisation that we cannot control *any of this*, and we will never 'understand' parenting. We can't find a formula which will 'work' for parenting, or for life, because there is no such thing! It's like trying to close a circle with infinitely short lines; you can never quite get there. And if we miss just a little, the circle is not closed.

On my wedding night, I was fortunate enough to be shown, in a strange sort of vision, that the energy of mind can never close the circle, but the intelligence of love can. Love does not separate and it does not cling. It does not need to bind or to hold because it is ever ready for new wonders, looking as it does with the eyes of a child, at this moment only, and whatever it contains. But love is destructive and devastating, easily capable of clearing all in its path. It is so totally *now* that we are barely able to meet it when it shows itself. Love says: *surrender.*

If there is no formula, everybody has to find their *own* way and everybody's way is *different*, and this goes for both the spiritual search and the journey of parenting. Who decides what's a good way to do things? Do you really want a set of guidelines on how to live? If we live like that, before we know it our lives will be over, and it will all have taken place in the most narrow and restricted of corridors. Death to that sort of life, because we are *wild creatures,* and we need more than that to really satiate us.

So many times when I mentioned this book to people (because that's what you do when you are writing a book – and people don't get bored of it *at all*), they raised an eyebrow as if to say, "How can you write a book about parenting? Are you an expert?" Of course not, I hadn't even had a baby yet! But are there any parenting experts? What would that even mean? I can't tell you how to be a parent! Obviously. I haven't got a bloody clue.

My potpourri of parenting mistakes and wonders is *mine*, not yours. Your mistakes in your journey are utterly, wonderfully yours and none of us can walk the journey for another. The number of factors which create the crazy situations we find ourselves in, and the responses we end up making, are infinite, and they coalesce to offer a journey which is perfectly *yours*, which can *never* be held and enclosed by the mind. We cannot protect ourselves against difficulty in advance, nor prepare for the all-encompassing profundity of love when it hits us unexpectedly.

We've all been lied to on so many different counts. We've been told that being rich and famous matters, that having other people admire you is a great thing, and that having a perfectly neat and tidy life is ideal. I think it's all bollocks.

We've been told that there are people whose lives are perfect, and if they aren't Instagram 'influencers' – God save us from them – then it's wellness gurus and religious leaders. We try to fit our lives into theirs somehow, but always find our wild selves bursting out of the sides. Our *wild selves*. Because we are wild! Don't let your square little house or the straight lines of the TV screen fool you.

Having a baby, in many ways, is one of the *wildest things we can do*. It totally destroys all comfort. The comfort zone no longer exists, and we struggle to try to find just a square of it. Naturally, in that situation, the temptation is to *turn away*. To run for the hills.

Yet I have found that when I turn away from the parenting adventure, to try to cling to the past or an idea of some other, easier way, like a shrivelled shrub, I shrink.

When I turn towards my child, and *everything* she brings, I see that she is an awakening spark. At this moment, her existence brings me everything I *need* in life: a constant challenge to selfishness, a look at myself from another point of view, an invitation to kindness, to open the heart, a reminder to face the riddle of time and mortality.

On so many occasions, during this journey, when I have followed her spark and 'fully faced' a significant challenge, I have been given some sort of gift in return.

These 'little' moments seem to stop time and open up the

eternal, when we stand in the gateway of what we truly care about and stop the momentum of the past in order to look in that direction, to bring that to life. Suddenly, then, we seem to come into contact with the transcendent. Suddenly, I see the wonder, the joy, the realness of the rollercoaster, which the deepest part of me seems to be yearning for.

I have spoken and written so much about 'conscious living' in my life, but I think that none of it points to the reality more than this book. For me, this book has opened up a view of the 'other universe'. The 'other universe' is the one we never see, the one in which we *didn't make that choice*. For me, this book – a moment in time, in my life, crystallised – offers a glimpse of this, by contrast: how things might have been if I had *turned away* from the adventure, if I had lived it *asleep*. If I had lived it without noticing, without caring, without loving.

This book reminds me of why I rescued all these animals, why I want to look properly at my wife, and why I want to *do the right thing*. As Maya Angelou's grandmother told her: "You know what right is! Just do right."[54]

What you have witnessed in this book are the fumblings and ramblings of a man genuinely trying to find and understand what matters most, at the same time as trying to raise a child. I have failed for much of the time and also failed to convey the real flavour of whatever has been experienced, but I know I cannot and do not need to do any better than this. I'm glad that it took me one instead of 20 years of parenting to realise that I can't '*do parenting right*'. Even if you could theoretically raise the 'perfect child' (which is obviously impossible), you would be burdening them with an ideal of perfection! So there is no glitch or shortcut.

Although I explore the miracles of mindful awareness for a living, in this book you have witnessed *me being taught* a *perfectly customised mindfulness course*. Unsurprisingly, because it is about *life*, this book has ended up covering most of the classic topics. And funnily enough, despite my choosing not to use chapters, life

Afterword

ended up presenting these lessons pretty much sequentially. My baby, my wife and the journey itself have taught me about fear, resilience, gratitude, wonder, health, stress, resistance, wellbeing, kindness, time, mortality and more.

Yet nothing can show the fruits of mindfulness better, from my point of view, than the previous, very emotional, chapter. The outpouring of emotion I experienced on Delphine's birthday shows that mindfulness can 'work' in the most important way: to open the heart, waking us up to how important this moment is.

In a memorable episode of *Modern Family*, Jay said: "90% of being a good dad is just showing up."[55] The more I unravel the meaning of 'showing up', the more that number edges towards 100 for me.

The realness at the end of the book was hard-earned. Not through achievements, not through becoming rich or famous or doing something fantastic and glamorous. Just by showing up.

Publishing a diary is a strange and vulnerable act – to invite 'strangers' into the inner workings of my life. You may have noticed, by now, that I am overly sentimental and often quite annoying. You might have heard that 'real men' aren't supposed to *feel things*, and wonder if I should tone that all down just a notch. You may feel a bit sorry for my lovely wife, living with me, because I'm too 'intense', I look 'too deeply' into things, or because my incompetence in practical areas is so genuinely extreme that it borders on the theatrical. Or you might, on the other hand, actually quite like me, and miss my strange musings once you close this unusual book. But the one thing I doubt anyone would accuse me of is *not showing up*.

I doubt the heart would have opened its sacred chamber as it did, gracing me with that transcendent glimpse of love, time and mortality after I'd put Elfie to sleep, if I hadn't truly shown up. Is that transcendence not proportionally related to how much *we try? How much we care? How much we bring?*

The central theme of this book is the miracle of birth and all that it brings with it. Birth is so precious because *life* is so precious, and that means we are supposed to do anything we can to *live it fully*. No matter which regrets any of us may have in our final days, they will all come down to this: *Did I live fully?*

Mindfulness isn't about being calm, not really; it's just relaxing to stop living in an unhealthy and unnatural way. Peace of mind and heart is a byproduct of a step towards sanity. Mindfulness has everything to do with *being here now*, with dissolving the mind's misguided movements away from this moment. It's just asking us to *live*.

Often it seems like everything in the world we have made is trying to *pull me away from this moment*. Yet Delphine has reminded me, over and over again, that *this is where I belong*.

The final words of this book, then, are her sacred gift to me, and they offer me a light in the darkness, in a world which so easily puts us to sleep. They are a gift of love, encoded into words and now, thanks to her, engraved into my heart:

I just don't want to blink. I just don't want to miss it.

Notes

1. Roger Dobson, 'Trying for a Baby Can Make Men Impotent', *Independent*, May 19, 2012, https://www.independent.co.uk/news/science/trying-for-a-baby-can-make-men-impotent-7768832.html.
2. Rupert Spira, *The Nature of Consciousness: Essays on the Unity of Mind and Matter* (Oxford: Sahaja Publications, 2017).
3. Rumi, *The Essential Rumi*, trans. Coleman Barks (San Francisco: HarperSanFrancisco, 1995).
4. David R Hamilton, *Why Woo-Woo Works: The Surprising Science Behind Meditation, Reiki, Crystals, and Other Alternative Practices* (London: Hay House, 2021).
5. Jon Kabat-Zinn, 'Some Reflections on the Origins of MBSR, Skillful Means, and the Trouble with Maps', *Contemporary Buddhism* 12, no. 1 (2011): 281–306, https://doi.org/10.1080/14639947.2011.564844.
6. Zindel V Segal, J Mark G Williams, and John D Teasdale, *Mindfulness-Based Cognitive Therapy for Depression: A New Approach to Preventing Relapse* (New York: Guilford Press, 2002).
7. Mark McCartney et al., 'Mindfulness-Based Cognitive Therapy for Prevention and Time to Depressive Relapse: Systematic Review and Network Meta-Analysis', *Acta Psychiatrica Scandinavica* 143, no. 1 (January 2021): 6–21, https://doi.org/10.1111/acps.13242.
8. Drew Berry, 'Animations of Unseeable Biology', TEDxSydney, May 2011, video, 12:55, https://www.ted.com/talks/drew_berry_animations_of_unseeable_biology.

Notes

9. Jaron Lanier, *Ten Arguments for Deleting Your Social Media Accounts Right Now* (New York: Henry Holt and Company, 2018).
10. Betty Hart and Todd R Risley, *Meaningful Differences in the Everyday Experience of Young American Children* (Baltimore: Paul H Brookes Publishing, 1995).
11. Shantanand Saraswati, *Good Company: An Anthology of Sayings, Stories and Answers to Questions by His Holiness Sri Shantanand Saraswati the Shankaracharya of Jyotir Math* (London: Element Books, 1992), 97.
12. Harvey Karp, *Baby Bliss: The Expert's Guide to a Contented Child* (London: Vermilion, 2003).
13. Tiny Happy People, 'How Men's Bodies Change When They Become Fathers', *BBC*, June 6, 2022, https://www.bbc.co.uk/tiny-happy-people/articles/zvnhjsg.
14. Amanda Ruggeri, 'Male Postnatal Depression: Why Men Struggle in Silence', *BBC Worklife*, June 6, 2022, https://www.bbc.com/worklife/article/20220601-male-postnatal-depression-why-men-struggle-in-silence.
15. P D Ouspensky, *A New Model of the Universe* (New York: Vintage Books, 1997).
16. Jessica Pasley, 'Study Finds Acid Reducers May Pose Risk for Children', *VUMC News*, November 6, 2019, https://news.vumc.org/2019/11/06/study-finds-acid-reducers-may-pose-risk-for-children/.
17. Centers for Disease Control and Prevention, 'Therapeutic Drug Use', *National Center for Health Statistics*, 2022, https://www.cdc.gov/nchs/fastats/drug-use-therapeutic.htm.
18. Richard P Bentall, *Doctoring the Mind: Why Psychiatric Treatments Fail* (London: Penguin Books, 2009).
19. Jiddu Krishnamurti, *The Collected Works of J Krishnamurti* (Ojai, CA: Krishnamurti Foundation of America, various years).
20. Bruce H Lipton, *The Biology of Belief: Unleashing the Power of Consciousness, Matter & Miracles* (Carlsbad, CA: Hay House, 2005).
21. George I Gurdjieff, *Beelzebub's Tales to His Grandson* (New York: E P Dutton, 1950).
22. John Koenig, 'Midding', *The Dictionary of Obscure Sorrows*, accessed August 3, 2021, https://www.dictionaryofobscuresorrows.com/define/midding.

23. Jiddu Krishnamurti, *Dialogue 6 with Allan W Anderson*, San Diego, February 20, 1974, published by the Krishnamurti Foundation Trust, video, https://www.youtube.com/watch?v=G2GvJ6N4aXg.
24. Samuel Gibbs, 'AlphaZero AI Beats Champion Chess Program after Teaching Itself in Four Hours', *Guardian*, December 7, 2017, https://www.theguardian.com/technology/2017/dec/07/alphazero-google-deepmind-ai-beats-champion-program-teaching-itself-to-play-four-hours.
25. Healthline, '2-Month Vaccinations: What to Expect', accessed May 20, 2025, https://www.healthline.com/health/baby/2-month-vaccinations.
26. Seattle Children's 'Immunization Reactions', accessed May 20, 2025, https://www.seattlechildrens.org/conditions/a-z/immunization-reactions/.
27. NCT, 'Fever: Treatment at Home', accessed May 20, 2025, https://www.nct.org.uk/baby-toddler/your-babys-health/common-illnesses/fever-treatment-home.
28. Central Intelligence Agency, *Stargate Collection*, CIA Reading Room, accessed June 6, 2020, https://www.cia.gov/readingroom/collection/stargate.
29. Timothy G Dinan and John F Cryan, 'Gut Instincts: Microbiota as a Key Regulator of Brain Development, Ageing and Neurodegeneration', *The Journal of Physiology* 595, no. 2 (2017): 489–503, https://doi.org/10.1113/JP273106.
30. Stanislav Grof, *The Adventure of Self-Discovery* (Albany: SUNY Press, 1988).
31. Rupert Sheldrake, *The Science Delusion: Freeing the Spirit of Enquiry* (London: Coronet, 2012).
32. Bernardo Kastrup, 'The Magical Trick of Disappearing Consciousness', *Metaphysical Speculations* (blog), September 2, 2014, https://www.bernardokastrup.com/2014/09/the-magical-trick-of-disappearing.html.
33. Bernardo Kastrup, The Idea of the World: A Multi-Disciplinary Argument for the Mental Nature of Reality (London: Iff Books, 2019).
34. Jiddu Krishnamurti, *The Urgency of Change* (San Francisco: Harper & Row, 1970).

Notes

35. Bernardo Kastrup, *Science Ideated: The Fall of Matter and the Contours of the Next Mainstream Scientific Worldview* (Winchester, UK: Iff Books, 2021).
36. Eckhart Tolle, interview by Russell Brand, *Under the Skin*, podcast, Luminary, 2019.
37. Nisargadatta Maharaj, *I Am That: Talks with Sri Nisargadatta Maharaj*, trans. Maurice Frydman (Durham, NC: Acorn Press, 1973), 228, 298.
38. Georg Feuerstein, *The Yoga Tradition: Its History, Literature, Philosophy and Practice* (Prescott, AZ: Hohm Press, 2001).
39. Ray Cummings, *The Girl in the Golden Atom* (New York: Grosset & Dunlap, 1922), chap. 5.
40. Peter Russell, 'The Quantum Eraser: Persistence of Information and the Delayed-Choice Experiments', *Science and Nonduality*, https://scienceandnonduality.com/article/the-quantum-eraser-persistence-of-information-and-the-delayed-choice-experiments/
41. Rob Bryanton, *Imagining the Tenth Dimension*, YouTube video, 10:11, posted by '10thdim', July 2, 2007, https://www.youtube.com/watch?v=JkxieS-6WuA.
42. Jesse Armstrong and Sam Bain, *Peep Show*, season 2, episode 2, aired November 19, 2004, on Channel 4.
43. Damian Carrington, 'Three-Quarters of UK Children Spend Less Time Outdoors Than Prison Inmates—Survey', *Guardian*, March 25, 2016, accessed February 6, 2021, https://www.theguardian.com/environment/2016/mar/25/three-quarters-uk-children-spend-less-time-outdoors-than-prison-inmates-survey.
44. George Gurdjieff, *Views from the Real World: Early Talks of Gurdjieff* (New York: E P Dutton, 1975).
45. Jiddu Krishnamurti, 'Why Can't Man Live Peacefully on the Earth?' public talk, United Nations, New York, April 11, 1985, accessed May 20, 2020, https://jkrishnamurti.org/content/why-cant-man-live-peacefully-earth.
46. Tommy Edison, *The Tommy Edison Experience*, YouTube channel, accessed March 10, 2022, https://www.youtube.com/channel/UCld5SlwHrXgAYRE83WJOPCw.

47. Mary D S Ainsworth et al., *Patterns of Attachment: A Psychological Study of the Strange Situation* (Hillsdale, NJ: Lawrence Erlbaum Associates, 1978).
48. John Bowlby, *Attachment and Loss: Volume 1, Attachment* (New York: Basic Books, 1969).
49. Ronald E Purser, *McMindfulness: How Mindfulness Became the New Capitalist Spirituality* (London: Repeater Books, 2019).
50. Nisargadatta Maharaj, *I Am That: Talks with Sri Nisargadatta Maharaj*.
51. David Cayley, *Enlightened by Love: The Thought of Simone Weil*, April 2002, podcast, 54:38, CBC Radio One, transcript available at https://www.davidcayley.com/podcast-transcripts/2020/6/25/enlightened-by-love-the-thought-of-simone-weil.
52. Terence McKenna, Appreciating Imagination (Esalen Institute, 1997), transcript, The Library of Consciousness, Organism.earth.
53. Albert Einstein, *Ideas and Opinions* (New York: Crown Publishers, 1954).
54. Maya Angelou, *Mom & Me & Mom* (New York: Random House, 2013).
55. Bill Wrubel, writer; Jason Winer, director. 'The Bicycle Thief', *Modern Family*, Season 1, Episode 2, aired September 30, 2009, on ABC.

Acknowledgements

The creation of this unusual book has been a truly wild ride, and so many key people have given their time, energy and expertise to bring it to life. I'm just the kind of person who is inclined to thank literally everyone I've ever met, but apparently I need to *not do that*. Here goes.

Firstly, I want to thank my wonderful mum, who brought me into this world – in a birth even more dramatic than Elfie's – and patiently pored over this manuscript with me to catch my many blunders.

Nadine, in addition to everything else, you deserve enormous thanks for giving me the space to write this, even when it was hard, and for allowing me to share our mad life with the outside world.

I'm grateful to you, Briar, for passing on the nudge for me to write this book in the first place, and for having faith in me to do the work I do.

Patrick, you believed in this book enough to make it a reality, and I will always be so thankful for that. You gave me the vital inspiration and support I needed to make it what it has become.

Richard, you showed me what this book was truly meant to be. Guy and Freya, you brought it to life with your artistic gifts. And Stella, you helped me get everything together and over the finish line. Thank you all.

Acknowledgements

Beyond the book itself, there are many others who deserve warm thanks for their profound influence on my life – without whom I would not have lived this adventure in a way that justified writing anything about it.

David, thank you so much for waking me up, *and keeping me awake.*

Valentin, thank you for never allowing me to put life into a box. It really doesn't like that.

And Sam – thank you for showing me the importance of doing the right thing, no matter what.

To the mystics, thank you for shining your light in my direction and blessing my life.

To my amazing brothers and the rest of my family, thank you for supporting us through this journey in so many ways.

Finally, to Delphine, my tiniest ever teacher, thank you so much for calling forth this adventure.

This book would not exist without each of you, and for that, I am deeply grateful.

www.ingramcontent.com/pod-product-compliance
Lightning Source LLC
Chambersburg PA
CBHW020516080526
44583CB00013B/614